Manifesting the Spirit

Manifesting the Spirit

Believers as Sacraments

Mbanyane Mhango

RESOURCE *Publications* · Eugene, Oregon

MANIFESTING THE SPIRIT
Believers as Sacraments

Copyright © 2021 Mbanyane Mhango. All rights reserved. Except for brief quotations in critical publications or reviews, no part of this book may be reproduced in any manner without prior written permission from the publisher. Write: Permissions, Wipf and Stock Publishers, 199 W. 8th Ave., Suite 3, Eugene, OR 97401.

Resource Publications
An Imprint of Wipf and Stock Publishers
199 W. 8th Ave., Suite 3
Eugene, OR 97401

www.wipfandstock.com

PAPERBACK ISBN: 978-1-6667-0628-4
HARDCOVER ISBN: 978-1-6667-0629-1
EBOOK ISBN: 978-1-6667-0630-7

09/29/21

Scripture quotations marked (NKJV) are taken from the Holy Bible, New King James Version®. Copyright © 1982 by Thomas Nelson. Used by permission. All rights reserved.

Scripture quotations marked (NRSV) are from the New Revised Standard Version Bible, copyright © 1989 the Division of Christian Education of the National Council of the Churches of Christ in the United States of America. Used by permission. All rights reserved.

Contents

Preface | vii
Introduction: The Believers as Sacraments of the Spirit | ix

Chapter 1: Manifesting the Lord's Spirit: Christ-like Believers | 1
Chapter 2: Manifesting the Regenerating Spirit: Baptized Believers | 27
Chapter 3: Manifesting the Empowering Spirit: Charismatic Believers | 60
Chapter 4: Manifesting the Relational Spirit: Fruit-Bearing Believers | 93
Chapter 5: Manifesting the Communing Spirit: Communicant Believers | 114
Chapter 6: Manifesting the Comforting Spirit: Suffering Believers | 144
Chapter 7: Manifesting the Eschatological Spirit: Hopeful Believers | 167

Conclusion: The Spirit and Sacramentality of All Believers | 180
Bibliography | 187
Subject Index | 193
Author Index | 217
Scripture Index | 219

Preface

THE TRIUNE GOD'S ESCHATOLOGICAL mission is to dwell with believers forever (Rev 21:1–4). Believers' present encounter with the Spirit of God's presence in Christ is only a foretaste. They look forward to encountering God's presence fully in the eschatological kingdom. Meanwhile, believers show concrete signs of a personal encounter with the Spirit via Christ. Drawing from the sacramental principle that the natural manifests the spiritual, the corporeal manifests the incorporeal, creation manifests the Creator, the finite manifests the infinite, etc., this book claims that believers manifest God's Spirit in Christ. Jesus is the Spirit-manifesting Man *par excellence*.

Jesus Christ stands at the heart of all sacramental thinking, since he fully revealed God's presence. As the primordial sacrament of the encounter with God, Christ shapes and informs the claim that believers are sacraments of God's presence. These are believers who reflect Christ in word and deed through the Spirit's assistance. The theological view that believers are sacraments links to several theological trajectories including but not limited to Christology and pneumatology.

The sacramentality of believers demands that they reflect Christ in word and deed through the Spirit. The term "sacrament" brings together orthodoxy (right belief or doctrine), orthopraxy (right practice or action), and orthopathy (right affection or passion). It is my conviction that one way someone can be known, even God, is by knowing what that person has said, says, or is saying, or what the person has done or is doing. In other words, what people say or do reveals who they are (Prov 23:7; Matt 12:34; Luke 6:45).

Biblical narratives provide a hermeneutical lens for conceiving the believers as sacraments. The term "sacrament" has ontological (metaphysical), epistemological, and ethical implications. In addition, sacramentality intersects with anthropology, Christology, soteriology, pneumatology, ecclesiology, and eschatology, among other disciplines. Significantly, the claim that believers are sacraments has an ecumenical import because God pours out the Spirit upon all flesh (believers).

The Spirit poured out at Pentecost is egalitarian and demonstrates God's desire to break human-engendered barriers. This Spirit encounters and manifests in and through all believers. Thus, each contributes to making Jesus visible by the Spirit. It flows from this that all believers are sacraments of God's Spirit in Christ. As sacraments, the believers reflect Christ in word and deed. In this way, they fulfill Christ's call as ambassadors and carry out the Great Commission.

I am deeply grateful to those who helped me along the journey of my doctoral studies, including the writing of this book; they are too numerous to mention. However, a few are in order, and they include: Phyllis Nyame-yie Agyin Mhango (my wife); Alicia, Charissa, and Yawaka (my children); Mr. William Bill and Mrs. Julie Arthur; Dr. Cornelius Bekker; Dr. Amos Yong, Dr. Clifton Clarke, Dr. Opoku Onyinah, Mr. Omari and Mrs. Doreen Boateng. I also thank Sandress, Jonathan, Ntchindi, Tawonga, Nellie, Tamala, and Nkhondo (my siblings), for their encouragement.

I dedicate this book to the late Mr. Lyson Manombo Manoah Yawaka (my father), the late Mrs. Alice Mutyioka Mhango (my mother), and the late Lizzie Mhango (my sister). Lastly, I thank the Lord for the grace to serve him in both the academy and ecclesia. I invite you to join me in exploring in this book our calling to be sacraments of a personal encounter with God's presence.

Introduction

The Believers as Sacraments of the Spirit

> And they went out and proclaimed the good news everywhere, while the Lord worked with them and confirmed the message by the signs that accompanied it.
>
> (MARK 16:20)[1]

EVEN A CURSORY READING of the biblical text suggests that God encounters and manifests his presence in and through human beings. Both people who approach the Bible with a hermeneutic of suspicion and a hermeneutic of trust would admit a level of fascination with biblical stories of divine-human encounters. To be sure, the most fascinating biblical stories of encounters between divinity and humanity pertain to Jesus Christ, the prophet from Nazareth of Galilee (Matt 21:11). As the God-Man (John 1:14), he shapes and informs all encounters between God and humans. In this sense, we should read biblical stories of divine-human encounters through the lens of Christ.

The incarnation of Christ demonstrates God's desire to encounter and reveal his presence in and through human flesh. Put in another way, Jesus shows that the immortal being encounters and reveals his presence in and through mortal beings; the infinite being in and through finite beings, the incorporeal being in and through corporeal beings; the infinite

---

1. Unless otherwise stated, all Scripture quotations are from the New Revised Standard Version (NRSV).

being in and through finite beings, the spiritual being in and through natural beings, etc. Spirit manifestations suggest that the heavenly realm and the earthly realm come together in and through believers in Christ.

For example, in the Old Testament, Moses stretches his rod over the Red Sea and stops the waters from flowing, which allows the Israelites to cross over as the Egyptians pursue them (Exod 14:21). Samson uproots the Gaza city doors and doorposts and carries them on his shoulders to a mountain top (Judg 16:3). To the amazement of the Israelites and Philistines, the youthful David kills Goliath, the giant and renowned warrior, with a slingshot (1 Sam 17:50). Elijah and Elisha use a mantle to strike and split the Jordan River and cross over (2 Kgs 2:7, 8, 14). How did Moses, Samson, David, Elijah, and Elisha do these things? God acted in and through them. In other words, Moses, Samson, David, Elijah, and Elisha rendered God's presence visible.

For example, in the New Testament, afflicted individuals come into contact with Peter's shadow and are set free (Acts 5:15). Similarly, those who make contact with Paul through handkerchiefs and aprons are delivered from sickness and demonic powers (Acts 19:12). Amazingly, Stephen is killed as he confesses Christ (Acts 7:59). Peter, Paul, and Stephen make God's presence visible to others.

The above stories demonstrate the mystery of God's action in and through human flesh. A sacramental imagination elucidates the nature of divine-human encounters. Precisely, God's action in and through believers creates moments of sacramentality. Put another way, those that encounter and reveal God's presence are sacramental. Thus, biblical and post-biblical believers in and through whom the Spirit of God's presence is tangibly expressed are sacraments. Though the word "sacrament" itself is not in the Bible, the sacramental motif is implicit in biblical texts.

A sacramental imagination is implicit in Paul's writings because he holds a believer's ontology (nature of being) as spiritual and natural (1 Cor 3:1; Gal 6:1). Sacramentality privileges the non-dualistic or non-dichotomist view of believers. Following this theological trajectory, this book posits that the believers are concomitantly spiritual and natural, thus basically sacramental.

Few subjects have generated more intense debate in Christian thought than sacraments. Some church traditions conceive the Water baptism and the Lord's Supper as ordinances, while others hold them as sacraments. The term "sacrament" has a broader meaning than how scholars often use it. A reductionist view of sacraments polarizes and engenders a false dichotomy between the so-called sacramental churches or theological traditions on the one side and the non-sacramental churches or theological traditions on the other side of the spectrum.

The notion that Jesus Christ is the primordial sacrament offers a theological remedy to the otherwise regrettably minimalist conception of a sacrament. Driven by the incarnation of Christ, a sacramental imagination brings together Christology, ecclesiology, pneumatology, anthropology, and eschatology. A sacramental imagination takes seriously manifestations of the eschatological Spirit of God's presence in and through believers from Pentecost to the *eschaton*.

The Gospels discuss Jesus' Pentecost, which is a historical and radical event. This is because the descent of the Spirit upon Jesus at the Jordan river (Matt 3:16; Mark 1:10; Luke 3:22; John 1:32) paved the way for the descent of the Spirit upon the disciples (Acts 2:1–4) and all subsequent believers (Acts 2:39). This is in many ways what Saint Irenaeus implies when he says, "So when the Son of God became the Son of Man, the Spirit also descended upon him, becoming accustomed in this way to dwelling with the human race, to living in men and to inhabiting God's creation."[2] In other words, Jesus' Pentecost foretells the disciples' Pentecost.

Although the Spirit of God manifested in and through select Old Testament believers, the Pentecost event in the New Testament democratizes this pneumatic experience. This is not to suggest that believers operate as silos that are standalone containers of the Third Article. Pentecost accents that no believers are spectators but participants in the drama of redemption. It is upon this theological conviction that all believers contribute to manifesting the Spirit of Christ. These Spirit manifestations occur in and through the believers both individually and collectively.

Notably, Christ is the Spirit-manifesting Man *par excellence*. In other words, it is in and through Christ that one finds full manifestation of God's presence. It flows from this that Christ is the standard for evaluating believers' manifestations of the Spirit. This assertion is in keeping with the theological conviction that Christ is the primordial, primary, great, root, foundational, fundamental, or basic sacrament of the personal encounter with God's presence. Seen in this light, Christ justifies the view that believers are sacraments of personal encounter with the Spirit. All believers manifest the Spirit of God's presence in Christ whether ordained/clergy or laity.

2. Irenaeus, "Against Heresies."

Introduction: The Believers as Sacraments of the Spirit

Pentecostals and Charismatics emphasize palpable or visible encounters with the Spirit. Precisely, they abhor esoteric, cerebral, abstract, or disembodied spirituality. Church traditions that have a penchant for concrete, tangible, visible, or perceptible manifestation of the Spirit will find the discussions that run through the tapestry of this book both theologically stimulating and spiritually enriching. In fact, even believers who identify with sacramental churches like Roman Catholic, Anglican, Lutheran will discover fresh ways of conceiving the idea of sacramentality.

Unlike the platonic view that dichotomizes or bifurcates between the natural and the supernatural realms, sacramentality brings together the creation and the Creator. Sacramentality is neither naturalistic nor spiritualistic, as it allows for the possibility of matter to be bearers of the supernatural or spiritual. The Pentecost event demonstrates this sacramental worldview since the Spirit (the Creator/supernatural) manifested in and through the disciples (natural/matter).

At Pentecost, the Spirit is manifested in and through a rushing wind which symbolizes the breath of resurrection life (Ezek 37; cf. 2:7; John 20:22), a fire which symbolizes the eschatological time of judgment (Acts 2:3), and tongues, or glossolalia, symbolic of the power of the eschatological kingdom (Acts 2:1–4).[3] Because Pentecost is a continuing event, the Spirit continues to manifest in and through believers. All the believers who show signs of a personal encounter with the Spirit of Christ serve as microcosmic and macrocosmic sites of God's grace.

More importantly, believers manifest the Spirit's presence in and through their words and deeds. This is what Jesus seems to imply when he tells his disciples, "You are the salt of the earth" (Matt 5:13) and "You are the light of the world" (Matt 5:14). Jesus uses the terms "salt" and "light" metaphorically to highlight that believers are bearers of the Spirit. This suggests that the believers are means of grace for the sake of fellow believers and unbelievers. Put differently, believers' bodies function as location, sites, or signs of the grace of the Spirit of God's presence.

The Spirit of God's indwelling presence enables believers to reflect Christ, the true light (John 8:12; 9:5). The believers cannot be the salt of the earth or the light of the world apart from the Spirit of Christ (John 5:15; Luke 24:49; Acts 1:8). The salt and light symbolize the visibility, palpability, perceptibility, tangibility, or audibility of the Spirit in and through believers. Salt and light have physical or material properties, and

---

3. Keener, *Spirit in the Gospels and Acts*, 193.

Introduction: The Believers as Sacraments of the Spirit

thus resonate with sacramental characterization of believers. Believers are both salt and light because of the Spirit's indwelling presence (Rom 8:9, 11; 1 Cor 3:16; 6:19).

In keeping with this, Paul relates God's indwelling presence to believers as temples of the Spirit when he writes, "do you not know that your body is a temple of the Holy Spirit within you, which you have from God, and that you are not your own?" (1 Cor 6:19). That finite beings (believers) host the infinite Spirit of God's presence is, in and of itself, a *mystērion*, or mystery. This is also reminiscent of what Jesus means when he says, "Out of the believer's heart shall flow rivers of living water" (John 7:38). Believers' visible-making nature stems from the Spirit.

Although Pentecostals have historically distanced themselves from sacramental thinking, the claim that believers are sacraments resonates with Pentecostal thought and praxis. This is so because Pentecostalism accents Spirit encounters[4] or experiences.[5] Pentecostal encounters with the Spirit are palpable or concrete; hence, they shape and inform the sacramentality of believers. This is why *the sacramentality of all believers* I postulate takes Spirit manifestations seriously.

In Christ one finds the full manifestation of God's Spirit (Luke 4:18–19; Acts 10:38). The Pentecost event inaugurates the 120 disciples as sacraments of God's presence. This does not mean that believers should expect to experience the Spirit accompanied by phenomena like wind and fire as at Pentecost. Instead, it is to stress that the Spirit poured out upon all flesh[6] engenders all believers as "human channels of God's grace which followers seek after."[7] To the extent that believers render God's Spirit visible, they are sacraments. The Pentecostal experience of Spirit baptism empowers the believers to witness effectively to God's salvific mission in Christ.[8] This suggests that the Great Commission and the sacramental being of the believers belong together.

This book seeks to inspire believers to embrace this sacramental reality consciously. The believers' sacramentality accents their being and their actions, or who they are and what they do. Bolstered by this thinking, believers should subject themselves to spiritual disciplines to enhance

4. Warrington, *Pentecostal Theology*.
5. Neumann, *Pentecostal Experience*.
6. Yong, *Spirit*.
7. Asamoah-Gyadu, *Sighs and Signs of the Spirit*, 66.
8. Menzies and Menzies, *Spirit and Power*.

their sacramentality. This is in keeping with the Pentecostal non-dualistic worldview. To be sure, Pentecostals expect the Spirit of God in Christ to intervene in the believers' real life situations.

Walter J. Hollenweger challenges Pentecostals to embrace the breath of the Spirit, who uses physical realities to speak of God's grace.[9] Hollenweger notes an embedded sacramental worldview in Pentecostalism. In keeping with this, I suggest that Pentecostals and Charismatics should not domesticate their view of sacraments to rites such as Water Baptism and the Lord's Supper, as crucial as these are. Instead, they should conceive sacrament to speak of their way of being. Precisely, I posit that Pentecostals envision themselves as partakers of the divine nature, participating in transferring divine grace (2 Pet 1:4).[10] This promise relates to all believers.

Pentecostals use their physical bodies to provide concrete expression to the Spirit. Further, Pentecostals insist that the Spirit manifests in and through their anointed bodies primarily, while they also use materials such as anointing oil for therapeutic purposes,[11] albeit only secondarily. For example, God's healing grace flows in and through the believers when the Spirit leads them to lay hands upon the sick. This is a common rite among Pentecostal believers.

Pentecostals find inspiration in Jesus, who manifested the grace of the Spirit so much that multitudes sought to touch him mostly for therapeutic purpose (Matt 8:3; 14:36; Mark 1:41; 3:10; 5:27, 30–31; 6:56; 7:33; 8:22; 10:13; Luke 5:13; 6:19; 7:14; 8:45, 47; 18:15; 22:51). The Spirit also manifested palpably in and through individuals in the Old and New Testaments (Judg 14; 1 Kgs 17; 2 Kgs 6; Acts 3: 6; 6:8; 15:5; 19:12). There are several examples of believers that can be held as sacraments of the Spirit of God's presence in the Old and New Testaments.

While the Spirit manifests in and through select individuals in the Old Testament, he manifests in and through all believers in the New Testament. This means that all believers are temples of the Spirit of God's presence in Christ both individually and communally (John 14:17; Rom 8:9–11; 1 Cor 3:16; 6:19; 12: 7; 2 Cor 13:3, 5; Gal 1:15–16; 2:20; 4:19; Eph 3:17; Col 1:27; 2 Tim 1:14; Jas 4:5). Put differently, all believers are signs of the grace of the Spirit.

9. Hollenweger, *Pentecostals*, 14.
10. Tomberlin, *Pentecostal Sacraments*, 113.
11. Clarke, *Pentecostalism*, 101–2.

Introduction: The Believers as Sacraments of the Spirit

Seen in this light, Christ merits as the perfect sign of grace. Put differently, Christ is the Spirit-bearer *par excellence*. The scale of Spirit manifestation in and through Christ surpasses any human being in history. In his famous sermon, Jesus quotes the prophet Isaiah in a way that others before him ever did, "The Spirit of the Lord is upon me, because he has anointed me . . . He has sent me" (Luke 4:18–19). Jesus clearly understands that his mission to set captives free would issue in and require the Spirit's manifestation. The Spirit manifests in and through Jesus so tangibly that people desire to touch his body or his clothes for therapeutic reasons. Multitudes that touch him are delivered and testify about their encounters with God's presence (Acts 10:38).

At Pentecost, the Spirit rests upon the 120 disciples and manifests his presence tangibly. This enables them to draw the attention of many Jewish visitors from the diaspora (Acts 2:1–4, 5–12). The Spirit enables them to speak in tongues that the visitors are able to hear in their own native tongue. The disciples become human sites or signs of grace of the Spirit of God's presence.

Notably, the outpoured Spirit fulfills Jesus' promise to the disciples that "you will receive power when the Holy Spirit has come upon you; and you will be my witnesses" (Acts 1:8). This Pentecostal experience is not meant to be limited to the early disciples but extends to all believers (John 21:23; Acts 1:11; 1 Cor 1:7; Phil 3:20). To the extent that believers manifest concrete signs of grace of the Spirit, they fit as sacraments of an encounter with God's presence.

Believers are temples of the Spirit (1 Cor 3:16; 6:19; 2 Cor 6:16). In ancient times, the temples were places where human beings encountered the supernatural. In ancient Israel, the temple served as a place to encounter the God of Abraham, Isaac, and Jacob. Put differently, the temple was a place where heaven and earth came together. A cloud over the tabernacle signified the descent of heaven on the earth (Exod 40:34–38; Num 9:15–22). At Pentecost, wind, sound, fire, and tongues symbolize the coming together of heaven and earth in and through the disciples' bodies. Pentecost engenders them as both microcosmic and macrocosmic temples of the Spirit.

The most significant theological conviction in contemporary sacramental theology is the view that Christ is the primordial sacrament of the personal encounter with God's presence through the Spirit. During his earthly life, Christ manifested the Spirit of God's presence in unsurpassable ways. In the Old Testament, select individuals such as the judges, prophets, kings, priests, etc., provided tangible manifestation to the Spirit of God. These made God visible to all.

Pentecost democratized the Spirit and inaugurated sacramentality of all believers in New Testament in contrast with the sacramentality of select believers in the Old Testament. Because Pentecost transcends denominational, ecclesial, or church boundaries, believers' sacramentality has ecumenical implications. This is because the same Spirit of Christ indwells all the believers.

However, in the Old Testament, the Spirit does not indwell the believers. In the New Testament, he does. Throughout his earthly ministry, Jesus taught that the Spirit would indwell his disciples (John 14:17)[12] both as individuals and as a communal body (1 Cor 3:16–17; 6:19; 2 Cor 6:16).

The thesis that all believers are sacraments of the Spirit in Christ opens space for a fresh theological trajectory. The thesis insists that Christ-like individuals render God's presence visible in words and deeds. It is in Christ that one finds full manifestation of God's presence (Col 1:15; Heb 1:3). Thus, Christ merits as the human site or sign of the Spirit of God's presence *par excellence.*

Jews expected the Spirit of God's return in the last days to usher in the messianic age or of the eschatological kingdom. A common belief among Jews was that the Spirit of God neither rested upon nor manifested through prophets after the deaths of Haggai, Malachi, and Zechariah. This expectation was fulfilled through the advent of Christ upon whom rests the Spirit in such manner that surpasses all Old Testament prophets and all persons in history (Luke 4:18–21). Christ is the Spirit-manifesting Man *par excellence* and shapes and informs all the divine-human encounters.

Some scholars conceive the moment Jesus breathed upon the disciples as the Johannine Pentecost (John 20:21–23). Other scholars conceive the Johannine instance as a *proleptic* act that anticipated the Lukan Pentecost where the Spirit is poured out on all the 120 disciples (Acts 2:1–4). The Spirit poured out manifests tangibly in and through the disciples that even unbelievers recognize them as true followers of Christ the Spirit-bearing Man *par excellence* (Acts 4:13).

Pentecost is a gateway to manifestations of God's presence. It democratized pneumatic experiences in and through all the believers. I unpack the thesis that believers are sacraments through experiences of

---

12. Other early manuscripts read "is in you" not "will be in you," which conveys the same meaning of "indwelling."

Introduction: The Believers as Sacraments of the Spirit xvii

conversion, the Water Baptism, the Lord's Supper, Spirit baptism, the gifts and fruit of the Spirit, corporate worship, unjust suffering, and eschatological hope. These experiences are helpful for clarifying the thesis due to the multifaceted nature of sacramentality.

More significantly, sacrament integrates the theological triad of orthodoxy (right belief), orthopraxy (right practice), and orthopathy (right affection). Granted that the theological view of believers as sacraments is rooted in Christ the primordial sacrament,[13] I follow a broad definition of sacrament that is not limited to the ecclesial rites like Water Baptism and the Lord's Supper. I now invite you to join me in the theological exploration of *the sacramentality of all believers.*

---

13. Osborne, *Sacramental Theology*, 89.

CHAPTER 1

Manifesting the Lord's Spirit
Christ-Like Believers

> To each is given the manifestation of the Spirit.
>
> (1 COR:12:7)

PAUL INSIGHTFULLY NOTES THAT believers manifest God's presence (1 Cor 12:7). Elsewhere, he accents that God indwells believers (Rom 8:9, 11; 1 Cor 3:16; 6:19; cf. John 14:17). This is unique to New Testament believers. Nonetheless, Old Testament believers also manifest God's presence. This implies that believers are sites, locations, signs, symbols, and means of grace. The Spirit-manifesting believers point others to God's reality and draw or inspire them to encounter Christ. "Sacrament" is a fitting theological term that aptly captures the believers' ontology or the character of rendering God's presence tangible in words and deeds. To clarify this theological conviction, let us first reflect albeit briefly upon the early and the salient history of sacraments.

Early History of Sacraments

From apostolic times until the twelfth century, there was a relatively broad view of the sacraments. While Water Baptism and the Lord's Supper were accepted as the most important rites, gestures, festivals, fasting, preaching, almsgiving, foot-washing, vows, or promises were understood as sacraments. By the twelfth century, the broad view of sacraments narrowed down to seven to include the Water Baptism, confirmation, Eucharist, penance, anointing of the sick, ordination or orders, and matrimony or marriage, especially within the Roman Catholic Church.

The English term "sacrament" historically links to *mystērion*. The term "sacrament" derives from the Latin word for "sign," *sacramentum*, and the Greek word for "mystery," *mystērion*. In secular contexts, *mystērion* referred to a religious rite or an oath and was used in military contexts when an individual was inducted into the army. The word "mystery" has three meanings in Pauline thought. Firstly, *mystērion* refers to the divine plan of salvation (1 Cor 2:7), which is now fully disclosed in and through Jesus Christ (Rom 16:25–26) by the Spirit (Eph 3:3–5). Secondly, it refers to Jesus Christ as the incarnation of God's mystery (Col 1:27). Thirdly, *mystērion* refers to liturgical celebration (*leitourgia*).

Paul uses "mystery" in reference to those baptized into the death and resurrection of Jesus (Rom 6:1–11) and to the celebration of the Lord's Supper (1 Cor 11:26). Although there was no transparent sacramental system in the initial stages of Christianity, central to a community's life was the rite of initiation (Water Baptism) and the rite of sharing a meal (the Lord's Supper). The *anamnēsis* of the Lord's actions was a constitutive element of Christian gatherings, as was the proclamation of the Word or sermons.

The Latin writer Tertullian was the first to use the term *sacramentum* in *De spectaculis*, where he calls the Eucharist a sacrament.[1] He also employs *sacramentum* in his *Five Books against Marcion*, where he calls Water Baptism a sacrament as in his other work, entitled *On Water Baptism*. To be sure, he held a broad view of *sacrament* beyond initiation acts of Water Baptism and the Lord's Supper. For example, Tertullian refers to charity as "the highest sacrament of the faith"[2] and relates sacrament to martyrdom.[3]

This broad view of sacrament continued until the twelfth century. More precisely, Peter Lombard systematized sacraments and set them as seven external signs of invisible grace.[4] This became the official view of the Roman Catholic Church. At the council of Trent, the number of

---

1. Tertullian, *De spectaculis*, 3.10.
2. Tertullian, *Writings*, 12.133–34.
3. Tertullian, *Writings*, ch. 9.
4 Lombard, *Petri Lombardi Libri*.

sacraments was officially set at seven. From the sixteenth century to the time of Vatican II, Protestant reformers decided to return to the sources, especially Scripture (*sola Scriptura*) and the patristic fathers.

Protestant reformers insisted that Scripture identifies the Water Baptism and the Lord's Supper as sacraments. They also emphasized the significance of proclaiming the Word and the centrality of faith for Christian life. Moreover, they did not accept the idea that the sacraments confer grace in and of themselves. This was in contrast to the Roman Catholic Church's position, but reformers were in agreement that sacraments are promises of grace to come in eternal life.

At the Second Vatican Council, the view that the church is a basic sacrament gained steam. In fact, the Vatican II documents suggest that the Roman Catholic Church holds this theological view. A problem with this theological conviction is that it leaves out non-Roman Catholic churches. The Roman Catholic Church's official position is that all churches subsist within it. This implies that the church as a sacrament refers to the Roman Catholic primarily and others secondarily.

The thesis that believers are sacraments does not depend upon the sacramentality of the church. Instead, it draws from the sacramentality of Jesus. Roman Catholic scholars postulate the view that Christ is the primordial, foundational, root, basic, or fundamental sacrament. The views that the church and Christ are sacraments are against the council of Trent and Lombard's seven sacraments. Osborne, a Roman Catholic scholar, rightly claims that if Jesus is the primordial sacrament, then it is in and through him that the definition of a sacrament is determined and not through the rituals.[5] The manifestation of the Spirit is critical for conceiving Christ and his followers as sacraments. Spirit manifestations in and through Christ offer a hermeneutical lens for interpreting Spirit manifestations in and through believers.

Sacramentality of Christ and of believers intersects partly on pneumatological ground. This is so because the Spirit who manifested in and through Christ manifests in and through the believers. Moreover, the efficacy of the rites of Water Baptism and the Lord's Supper depends on the Spirit. Precisely, the Spirit mediates Christ's presence as believers undertake ecclesial rites. A definition of a sacrament should take seriously the Spirit's manifestations. The sacramentality of believers holds that a church institution cannot domesticate God's Spirit in Christ (John 3:8).

---

5. Osborne, *Sacramental Theology*, 62.

Defining Sacrament

Several factors determine what constitutes a sacrament. They include but are not limited to the following: firstly, they are instituted by Christ, hence all Christians are expected to observe or practice; secondly, they are concrete or material in nature like water used in baptism or bread and wine used in the Lord's Supper; thirdly, they are signs or symbols of grace and facilitate or inspire an encounter with God's presence and thus are means of grace; fourthly, they participate in the reality of God they signify or symbolize; and fifth, they make or render visible or tangible God's invisible grace or presence.

The Gospels confirm that Jesus Christ instituted Water Baptism (Matt 28:19; Mark 16:16; cf. Luke 20:4; John 4:2) and was himself baptized (Matt 3:16; Mark 1:10; Luke 3:21; John 1:33). Christ also established the Lord's Supper (Matt 26:26, 28; Mark 14: 22, 24; Luke 22:19; 1 Cor 11:25, 26; cf. John 6:54) that he himself also observed or practiced. The sacraments share their origin in Christ. Significantly, within Jesus dwells the Godhead bodily (Col 2:9). Hence, he is the visible sign of God's invisible presence *par excellence*. Moreover, Christ ordained his disciples to be visible signs of God's presence by the Holy Spirit (Acts 1:8). This book explores the role of believers in making visible God's invisible presence. This promise traces back to the Old Testament.

In the Old Testament, God promised the Israelites that he would manifest his presence in certain places. For example, God assured the Israelites he would answer their prayers in the tabernacle Solomon built and dedicated (2 Chr 7:15). In fact, God said that he had chosen and sanctified the temple (2 Chr 7:16). Thus, the temple itself inspired the Israelites to pray and expect God to answer their prayers favorably (2 Chr 7:14).

This implies that the temple functioned as the Israelites' normative place to encounter God's presence. Heaven and earth came together in the temple because of God's promise to encounter the Israelites visibly and tangibly. This promise fostered the expectation among the Israelites to encounter God's tangible presence. Through this encounter, the Israelites made God's presence visible especially to other nations.

Drawing from this, we can infer that Israel's temple and the Israelites served as visible signs of encounter with God's presence to other nations. In this sense, Israel's temple and the Israelites were means of grace. More adequately, they were sacraments of encounters with God. His presence manifested tangibly or visibly, for example, like fire (2 Chr 7:1–3) and cloud (2 Chr 5:14; cf. Exod 40:34). God did not manifest his presence without appropriate Israelites' dispositions. In fact, they could not coerce God's presence without regard to the status of their relation to him.

The temple reflected God's relationship with his people. God promised to attend to their prayers from the dedicated temple. In this way, the temple reflected God's grace and mercy, and, thus, the Israelites could boldly approach his presence. This is reminiscent of the New Testament motif that believers are encouraged to boldly approach the throne of grace and mercy (Heb 4:16).

The fact that God promised or ordained the temple as a place for the Israelites to have an encounter with him along with clear instructions to facilitate such encounters satisfies the basic conditions of a sacrament. More relevantly, in the New Testament, God not only visits but dwells in temples of human flesh, not temples of stone (Acts 7:48). Jesus Christ referred to his body as a temple in contrast to the temple in Jerusalem, which took forty-six years to build (John 2:21).

God spoke by Joel the prophet that he would pour out his Spirit upon all flesh (Joel 2:28–29) which implies temples of human flesh. As the Old Testament temple functioned as a place to encounter God's presence, the New Testament believers encounter him from any geographical location. That is to say, the believers' encounters with God are not geographically conditioned. Christ (Eph 3:12) enables the believers to encounter God by the Spirit's indwelling presence.

Seen in this light, God who encountered the Israelites and manifested his presence in and through Solomon's temple now encounters and manifests his presence in and through believers. As the Old Testament believers (the Israelites) were signs and means of God's grace to other nations, the New Testament believers (Jews and Gentiles) are signs and means of God's grace to other nations. Accordingly, they are sacraments of a personal encounter with God's presence. The indwelling Spirit is key to understanding the sacramentality of all believers. God the Father promised the Spirit (Isa 66:1–2; Joel 2:28–29; John 14:16–17, 20, 21; Acts 1:4; 7:48; 17:24); God the Son asked the Father to send the Spirit (Acts 2:16, 33), and God the Spirit was poured out (Acts 2:4; 8:17; 10:44; 19:6). God encounters and manifests his presence in and through the believers. The view of the sacramentality of believers resonates with the broader meaning of sacrament.

Broad Meaning of Sacrament

The term sacrament has a broader meaning than is often used in theological debates. For example, Larson-Miller defines a sacrament as "any action, or thing, or person that reveals and mediates God's presence and draws people into an encounter with the divine."[6] In keeping with this, some scholars conceive Scripture,[7] the church,[8] the assembly,[9] and Christ[10] as sacraments.

An ecclesiological framework has mostly shaped the theological debate on rites or rituals often referred to as sacraments or ordinances. This is a point of departure for the central thesis of this book which uses a pneumatological framework or approach. This is largely so because the Spirit's manifestation is not determined by church tradition or denominations. In fact, the Spirit encounters and manifests in and through believers irrespective of ecclesial or denominational affiliation or ordained (clergy) or non-ordained (laity). Thus, a pneumatological approach is apt for clarifying sacramentality of believers.

Drawing from this understanding, believers are sacraments of God's presence. This claim takes the biblical motif seriously that the believers are individually and communally temples of the Spirit or indwelled by the Spirit (John 14:17; Rom 8:9, 11; 1 Cor 3:16–17; 6:19; 2 Cor 6:16; 2 Tim 1:14; Jas 4:5). However, scholars have fleshed out the sacramentality of the church and the assembly; yet few, if any, have explored the theological conviction that individual believers are sacraments. As I establish in this book, the believer's sacramentality does not suggest a sense of individualism or isolationism. One's faith is nurtured within a community of fellow believers.

Instead, it is to accent that God's presence with the believers communally is the same as God's presence with individual believers. The indwelling Spirit enables the believers to manifest and to mediate spiritual presence.[11] Believers render the Spirit or spiritual presence tangible both

---

6. Larson-Miller, *Sacramentality Renewed*, 20.

7. Boersma, *Scripture as Real Presence*.

8. de Lubac, *Catholicism*, 76; Moltmann, *Church in the Power*, 199–203; Rahner, *Church and the Sacraments*, 18; Semmelroth, *Church and Sacrament*, 81.Vorgrimler, *Sacramental Theology*, 32–42.

9. Hicks et al., *Gathered People*.

10. Schillebeeckx, *Christ, the Sacrament of the Encounter with God*.

11. Tillich, *Systematic Theology*, 120–22.

within and outside ecclesial worship contexts such as the marketplace or public sphere. Thus, the believers are sacraments of the Spirit for both sacred (church) and secular spaces (market space).

Through Spirit manifestations, believers enable others to see, discern, perceive, and inspire encounters to God's presence. As Spirit-indwelled, the believers are mobile temples of the Spirit. Even better, they are versatile means of grace of the indwelling Spirit of Christ. This is why Christ tasked his disciples to be his witnesses from Jerusalem, Judea, Samaria, and to the ends of the world by the Spirit (Acts 1:8). The disciples were to witness individually and communally.

Moreover, the disciples were to carry out this witnessing task in and through their bodies. The materiality of the disciples' human bodies or the believers' is the same as that of Jesus. But Christ's body differs from the believers since he is without sin. The concrete being of the believers enables them to play host and to reveal God's presence. Believers' bodily experiences contribute to their witnessing task. This is particularly the case with sufferings they experience by virtue of professing faith in Christ, similar to how he suffered by virtue of the redemptive mission. Therefore, the believers manifest God's presence in humanly relatable ways as Christ.

The human body is the normative mode for concrete expression of the Spirit of God's presence. This contrasts with Spirit manifestations in and through non-humans, such as the burning bush (Exod 3). The human body is God's primary mode for providing concrete expression to his presence. That is to say, the body allows the believers to manifest God's presence to others in humanly relatable ways that reflect Christ. For instance, believers' Christ-like character and charismata engender them as signs or means of God's grace and as sacraments of the Spirit.

To tease out the sacramentality of believers, let's consider the ontology of symbols or symbolic ontology. Symbols or signs reflect the relationship between the manifested and the signifier. More adequately, symbols or signs are characterized by the play between presence and absence, appearing and disappearing. Moreover, a "visible *significant* renders present an invisible *signifié*."[12] It flows from this that a believer who manifests signs of the Spirit is a visible *significant*. The *significant-signifier* relation thus clarifies the believers' sacramentality as those who

---

12. See Depoortere, "From Sacramentality," 56.

express God's presence tangibly.[13] It is the Third Person of the Trinity that believers reveal.

In this sense, I maintain that the believer who manifests the Spirit is sacrament of God's presence. The Spirit upon Christ engendered him as the primordial sacrament of God's presence just as he indwells the believer and engenders him or her as sacrament of God's presence. To be sure, this theological conviction relates to the believer who reflects Christ in word and deed. The tangibility, visibility, palpability, or concreteness of the Spirit via the believers establishes them as human locations, sites, signs, symbols, means of grace, and sacraments of God's presence.

St. Augustine held a sacrament as a visible sign of God's invisible grace. A sacrament is not static but dynamic as it refers to a moment of divine self-disclosure and human response. A believer moved by the Spirit fits this characterization. In sacramental events, God discloses his presence in and through believers in word and deed. God's actions are primary, while believers' actions are secondary. For example, God acted primarily and Peter acted secondarily when he instructed him in a vision to go and minister to Cornelius and his household (Acts 10:15; 11:19).

As Peter spoke, the Spirit fell upon Cornelius and his household because the Spirit himself spoke in and through Peter (Acts 10:44). Thus, there was a dynamic relation between Peter and the Spirit so that the latter found concrete expression in and through the former. It is in this sense that Peter functioned as a means of grace of the Spirit. In fact, Peter inspired both Cornelius and his household to encounter the Spirit of God's presence in Christ.

Specifically, Peter's bodily activities became channels of grace for manifesting the Spirit. It is in this sense that Peter fits as a sacrament of the Spirit, as he pointed to the reality of God. The sacrament-reality dynamic in Peter is discernible when he rightly concludes that "I truly understand that God shows no partiality" (Acts 10:44). His words pointed others to God's reality.

Believers exhibit sacramental characteristics when the Spirit discloses his presence in and through them (Acts 3:16; Gal 2:8; Phil 2:13). This does not suggest that believers are passive. In fact, the Spirit's actions are seen in and through believers' actions. In reality, believers respond to the Spirit's actions. This makes sense when we conceive grace as the gift of the Spirit himself.

---

13. Gause, *Living in the Spirit*.

Grace is not a gift that the Holy Spirit bestows on believers but the Holy Spirit itself.[14] This means that grace is an encounter with God's personal presence. Christ epitomizes this grace motif as the primordial sacrament of the encounter with God's personal presence.[15] The Spirit is the point of immediate contact between the Godhead and humankind, especially the believers.

Believers do not cause Spirit manifestations directly, but indirectly, much like the relationship between the moon and the sun. The Moon reflects light the Sun produces. Without the Sun, the Moon is useless, as it depends on the Sun. Similarly, believers manifest the Spirit only as they are enabled by the latter. After all, believers do not merit the Spirit of God's indwelling presence. It is by grace through Christ's work that the Spirit indwells believers (Acts 2:38).

Believers signify and point to the Spirit's reality just as the Moon signifies and points to the reality of the Sun's presence. Spirit-manifesting believers remind others that Christ continues to work on the earth. The Spirit manifests in and through believers to point others to Christ, not the believers themselves. In other words, the Spirit manifestations are meant to inspire others to an encounter with God. It is noteworthy that just as the Sun is superior to the Moon, the Spirit is superior to believers. Moreover, as the Moon relies on the Sun, the believers rely on the Spirit.

Another important sacramental principle advances that the sacraments are inferior to the reality they represent. To see how the principle applies to believers' sacramentality, let us first see how this principle relates to Christ's sacramentality. To begin, the human actions of Christ reflect divine actions. More adequately, it is in his humanity that Christ is the sacrament of God's presence. It is when the Spirit manifests in and through his humanity that Christ is the primordial sacrament of God's presence. Christ's divinity is not the sacrament of God's presence. This is so because Christ's divinity is of the same nature as the Father and the Spirit.

When he assumed the human body, Christ's humanity was subordinated to God or the divine (Phil 2:8). Therefore, it is in his humanity that Christ is the sacrament of the personal encounter with God's presence. To claim otherwise is to subordinate the divinity of the Son to the Father and the Spirit. This is not theologically sound and heretical. Believers are

---

14. Coffey, *Grace*, 79.
15. Schillebeeckx, *Christ, the Sacrament of the Encounter with God*, 5.

sacraments of the Spirit of God in Christ because their nature is inferior to God (Ps 8:4, 144:3; John 8:58; Acts 17:28; Heb 2:9).

Seen in this light, sacraments are rooted in the gracious act of God who chooses to manifest his presence in and through natural beings like the human body, which is relatively inferior. Put in another way, sacraments engender in grace because the infinite God chooses to manifest concretely in and through actions of the finite beings (believers). It is thus a privilege for believers to function as signs and means of grace of the Spirit of Christ's presence.

Jonah as Sacrament of the Spirit

This book understands grace as God's personal presence in believers through the Spirit of Christ. In addition, the Bible conceives a sign as something impersonal or a person. Persons who manifest the Spirit can be held as signs and means of grace. For instance, Jesus describes Jonah as a sign (Matt 16:4; Luke 11:29). Jonah's actions pointed others to the reality of God at work in and through him. Jonah did not just point to but participated in the reality of God by the Spirit.

Significantly, Jonah could not function as a sign of God's presence without the Spirit's sovereign presence. God wanted to manifest his presence to the people of Nineveh in and through Jonah. Precisely, God wanted to manifest his presence through the prophet Jonah. It is in this sense that Jonah's actions reveal his encounter with God. The Holy Spirit constituted Jonah as a sign and means of God's redemptive grace to the Ninevites albeit not for his personal gain.

Next, Christ calls Jonah a sign because he manifested God's presence to the lost people of Nineveh. Jonah spent three days in the belly of a great fish before he preached God's Word that resulted in the Ninevites' conversion. Thus, Jonah served as a sign of God's grace of forgiveness.

Notably, he is a sacrament of an encounter with the Spirit (Jonah 1:2; 3:10). The sacramentality of Jonah intersects with that of Christ because the former spent three days in the belly of a fish, while the latter spent three days in the belly of the earth (Matt 12:40). Also, Jonah is a sacrament of the Spirit for the Ninevites, whereas Christ is the sacrament of the Spirit for all humankind.

The Spirit constitutes believers as concrete signs and means of God's grace but not for personal aggrandizement (Matt 10:8). Thus, believers are channels of grace for others' benefit. Moreover, sacraments are not for self-serving purposes. This is why sacraments are signs of grace. As signs of grace, believers will draw others to God not away from God. This is why the sacramentality of believers emphasizes the sacramental principle of *ex opere operantis*. This principle postulates that sacraments do not function as a magic wand or a vending machine at one's disposal. Instead, sacraments require appropriate spiritual disposition for their efficacy.

As such, the sacramentality of believers requires that they cooperate with God through appropriate spiritual disposition. For example, in the Old Testament, Samson and Jonah show that manifestation of God's presence demands the discipline of partnering and cooperating with God. Jonah attempted to run away from God (Jonah 1:3) while Samson revealed the secret of his strength to Delilah against God's instruction (Judg 16:17). Both rendered God's presence visible.

As sacraments, believers do not only manifest God's presence through charisma but also character. Sacramentality of believers demands that charisma and character be held in tension. In particular, baptism with the Spirit, the gifts and the fruit of the Spirit enhance the sacramentality of believers. The believers who show concrete signs of the Spirit participate in God's presence.

This reflects the sacramental principle that sacraments render visible the reality they symbolize or signify.[16] When the believers reflect Christ's charisma and character (1 John 4:17), they inspire others to encounter God's presence. As acts of the human body render the soul visible,[17] believers' acts render the Spirit tangible[18] similar to Christ as the primordial sacrament.

Christ the Primordial Sacrament of the Spirit

Although Jesus was born without a sexual union between Mary and Joseph, (Luke 1:35) he was like any other human in his physical being. Jesus' physical appearance was not different from humans born of a union between a man and a woman. Nonetheless, Jesus also maintained his

---

16. Rahner, *Theological Investigations*, 252.

17. Rahner, *Church and the Sacraments*, 38; Rahner, *Theological Investigations*, 247; Osborne, *Christian Sacraments in a Postmodern World*, 86.

18. Vorgrimler, *Sacramental Theology*, 30–31; Schillebeeckx, *Christ, the Sacrament of the Encounter with God*, 13–17.

divinity. The church fathers like Augustine and Aquinas, conceived Christ as the *mysterium Dei* or the mystery of God, the *sacramentum Dei* or the sacrament of God, and the means of salvation, respectively. Theologians describe Jesus as fully God and fully human. The people who met Jesus in person could not see any difference in his physical appearance from others (Mark 6:3; John 18:4–8). The palpable or tangible manifestations of the Spirit in and through Jesus set him apart from others (Matt 9:33; John 7:46). The scale of manifestation of the Spirit in and through Jesus' life surpasses that of any human being to have ever lived or will ever live.

Notable Roman Catholic scholars like de Lubac[19] and Schillebeeckx[20] held Jesus as the sacrament of God's presence. His life, death, and resurrection revealed concretely the Spirit of God's presence in an unprecedented manner (1 Cor 3:16, 6:19; 2 Cor 6:16–7:1; Eph 2:21–22). Christ's whole life manifested the Spirit of God.[21] For example, Jesus manifested God's presence when he spoke with Moses and Elijah at the mountain of the Transfiguration (Matt 17:1–5; Mark 9:2–7; cf. Exod 34:35), and as John baptized him (Matt 3:16; Mark 1:10; Luke 3:22; John 1:32).

As the Father sent the Son to manifest his presence by the Spirit, the Son sends believers to manifest his presence by the Spirit (John 3:16; 20:21). According to the New Testament, Jesus is the full bearer of the Spirit (Luke 1:35; 4:18–21; Acts 4:27). This is why Christ baptizes with the Spirit (Mark 1:8; Acts 1:5). The Spirit's power flowed in and through his human body (Matt 12:23; 13:54–55; Luke 4:32; 9:42–43; Acts 10:38). Christ is the sign of the Spirit *par excellence*.

Paul says that the Godhead's fullness dwells in Christ through the Spirit (Col 2:9). Christ promised that God's presence would indwell believers both communally and individually (John 14:17, 23; Rom 8:9–11; 1 Cor. 3:16–17; 6:19; 2 Cor 6:16, 13:5). God's indwelling presence is the exclusive privilege of believers. Precisely, believers are given the Spirit as a guarantee (2 Cor 1:22; 5:5). The believers who show signs of the Spirit are sacraments of God's presence.

At Pentecost, the Spirit engendered the disciples as signs of grace. Like Christ, believers render the Spirit as tangibly present to other believers as well as to unbelievers. For the purpose of this book, believers reflect Christ in experiences of conversion, empowerment, fellowship,

---

19. De Lubac, *Catholicism*, 76.
20. Schillebeeckx, *Christ, the Sacrament of the Encounter with God*.
21. Vorgrimler, *Sacramental Theology*, 30.

fruit-bearing, suffering, and eschatological hope. The Spirit is linked to all these experiences. It is for this reason that the converted, the empowered, the fellowshipping, the fruit-bearing, the suffering, and the hopeful, are sacraments of a personal encounter with the Spirit of Christ. To be sure, it is in the course of manifesting the Spirit that believers are sacraments of God's presence.

The Nature of Spirit Manifestation

The Holy Spirit is God's personal presence in believers. As Jesus is God with us (Matt 1:23; 18:20) the Spirit is God in us (Rom 8:9; 1 Cor 6:19). The Father and the Son indwell believers by the Spirit (John 14:19–31; Rom 8:10; Gal 2:20; Eph 3:17–19; Col 1:27; 1 John 3:24; 4:16; Rev 3:20). This is the same Spirit who hovers over the waters of creation (Gen 1:2) and overshadows Mary's bringing about Jesus Christ's incarnation (Luke 1:35). The Bible also refers to the Spirit as the Spirit of Jesus (Acts 16:7; Phil 1:19), the Spirit of God (Gen 1:2; Matt 3:16, 12:28; Rom 8:9, 14, 15:19; 1 Cor 2:11; 7:40; 12:3; Eph 4:30; Phil 3:3; 1 Pet 4:14; 1 John 4:2), and the Spirit of Christ (Rom 8:9; 1 Pet 1:11).

This does not mean Paul and Peter subordinate the Spirit to Christ or pit the Second and the Third Persons of the Trinity against one another. Instead, Paul and Peter stress the joint work of the Spirit and the Son. The church fathers held the Spirit and the Son as the two hands of God. Moreover, the mutual work of the Spirit and the Son is evident from Christ's conception, virgin birth, vicarious death, bodily resurrection, and ascension. At Pentecost, Jesus sends the Spirit to indwell all the disciples and subsequent believers (Acts 2; Rom 8:9, 11; 1 Cor 3:16, 6:19). The Spirit does not draw attention to himself but to Christ (John 16:14). As the Spirit is incorporeal by nature, he finds concrete manifestation or expression in and through believers. In particular, the believers' actions in word and deed engender them as signs of grace that point others to the Spirit of God's indwelling presence.

In addition, the Greek word *phaneroō*, or *phanerosis,* means to manifest or reveal. Spirit manifestations relate to the broad view of sacrament as "any action, or thing, or person that reveals and mediates God's presence and draws people into an encounter with the divine."[22] Most theological discourses on sacraments focus on the rites of the Water

---

22. Larson-Miller, *Sacramentality Renewed*, 20.

Baptism and the Lord's Supper. This book asserts that believers who manifest God's presence are sacraments. By manifesting God's presence, believers draw or inspire others to encounter the Spirit of Christ. At Pentecost, for example, the disciples manifested and inspired others to encounter the Spirit of Christ (Acts 2:37). This shows that the 120 disciples functioned as means of grace of the Spirit.

Beside the sound, wind (Acts 2:2), and fire (Acts 2:3) that characterized God's presence in the Upper Room, the 120 disciples spoke in tongues as the Spirit enabled them (Acts 2:4). Thus, the 120 disciples manifested the Spirit and drew the three thousand others to a salvific encounter with Christ (Acts 2:38). Thus, the 120 disciples rendered God's presence tangible. Through the Pentecost event, Christ instituted the 120 disciples as sacraments of the Spirit (Acts 1:4, 5, 8).

Next, it is a sacramental principle that Christ instituted sacraments. However, sacraments point to the reality of the Trinity. The disciples' actions at Pentecost point others to the reality of God's presence through the Spirit of Christ. More adequately, the Father sends the Spirit upon the disciples in response to the Son's request (John 14:16, 15:26). In this sense, the actions of the Father are simultaneously actions of the Son and the Spirit. Peter rightly captures this Trinitarian motif when he tells the Pentecost crowd that something divine is happening in and through them,

> Indeed, these are not drunk, as you suppose, for it is only nine o'clock in the morning. No, this is what was spoken through the prophet Joel: In the last days it will be, God declares, that I will pour out my Spirit upon all flesh, and your sons and your daughters shall prophesy, and your young men shall see visions, and your old men shall dream dreams. (Acts 2:15–17)

Here, Peter interprets the event of Pentecost as the reality of God's presence manifesting in and through the actions of the 120 disciples. It seems reasonable to suggest that the climax of this manifestation of the reality of God's presence is the tongues-speaking disciples (Acts 2:4). This tongues-speech demonstrates that the disciples encountered the eschatological reality of God's presence, albeit not yet fully. Thus, these tongues-speaking disciples fit the hermeneutical rubric of the "already" and the "not yet" or "this is that" and "this is not that."[23] In other words, the disciples experience the powers of the coming age, but only in part.

---

23. Wolfgang and Green, "Between This and That."

The Pentecost event allows the disciples to participate in and to manifest the reality of God's presence. The descent of the Spirit upon the disciples suggests that Christ has instituted them as sacraments of the Spirit. As such, they are sacraments without borders. The disciples are to manifest the Spirit of Christ in Jerusalem, in Judea, in Samaria, and the uttermost parts of the earth (Acts 1:8). Sacramentality of all believers resonates with the democratization of the Spirit, in direct contrast to the Old Testament believers.

Since all believers are Spirit-indwelled (John 14:17; Rom 8:9, 11; 1 Cor 3:16, 17, 6:19; 2 Cor 6:16; 2 Tim 1:14; Jas 4:5), they can manifest God's presence. Though invisible in nature, the Spirit manifests tangibly or perceptibly in space and time and in and through the human agency of the believers. The incorporeal nature of the Spirit necessitates the sacramentality of believers. But Spirit manifestations also link to the First Person and the Second Person of the Triune God.

The Spirit Manifestation and the Trinity

It is worth pointing out that the Spirit manifests in and through believers to glorify Christ (John 16:14). Since the Father sent the Spirit upon the Son, it implies that Spirit manifestations also honor the Father (Matt 3:16; Mark 1:10; Luke 3:22; John 1:32). Turner rightly says that "the Spirit is the self-manifesting and empowering presence of both the Father and the Son."[24] By manifestations of the Spirit, believers point others to the reality of the Father and the Son. But Spirit manifestations occur in between the "already" and the "not yet" eschatological tension.

Upon Christ's return, he will present the believers to his Father (John 14:3; Jude 1:24). In the meantime, the believers proleptically encounter with the Father and the Son. That is to say, they foretaste the eschatological encounter with the Father and the Son by the Spirit.[25] In Spirit manifestations, the believers point to their eschatological encounter with the Father and the Son.

Believers neither encounter nor manifest the full breadth of the Triune God in this age. Peter holds the outpouring of the Spirit at Pentecost as the beginning of the last days (Joel 2:28–29; Acts 2:16–18). Believers

---

24. Turner, *Holy Spirit and Spiritual Gifts*, 170.
25. Saliers, *Worship as Theology*.

manifest the Spirit in triumph[26] and lament.[27] In personal triumph, believers point to and render tangible the Spirit of Christ, the triumphant Man *par excellence*. In personal lament, believers point to and render tangible the Spirit of Christ, the lamenting Man *par excellence*. God's indwelling presence justifies the view of believers as temples of the Spirit.

The Believer as Temple of the Spirit

In religious traditions, physical temples point others to the god(s) they represent. In other words, temples are held as physical expressions of metaphysical realities. In the Old Testament, the Israelites conceive the temple or tabernacle as the place to encounter God's presence. This conviction continues in the New Testament where the Israelites associate synagogues as special places to encounter God's presence (Acts 7:48; 17:24). Jesus countered this belief and insisted that there would come a time when people would not need to go to a particular location to worship God. Precisely, Samaritans would not have to go to Jerusalem to worship God (John 4:21). Samaritans could in fact encounter God's presence from any location since God is Spirit/spirit (John 4:24).

For Jesus, what counts is to encounter and to worship God in spirit and in truth (John 4:23). The human heart is the privileged place for personal encounter with the Spirit of God's presence. God's indwelling presence yields believers as temples of the Spirit. Thus, believers can point others to the reality of God's presence within. By manifesting signs of the Spirit, believers make or render visible or tangible the reality of God's presence similar to the temples of stone.

In his humanity, Christ is the temple of the Spirit *par excellence* (Isaiah 61:1–2; Luke 4:1; 18–19; Mark 1:8; Acts 1:5; 11:16). The Spirit's presence upon Jesus engendered him as such. He enabled others to encounter the Spirit of God's presence. Similarly, believers are temples of the Spirit, both individually and communally (1 Cor 3:16–17; 6:19; 2 Cor 6:16). As temples of the Spirit, believers manifest God's presence when praying (Ps 143:6), praising, worshiping (Ps 147:7), fellowshipping (Matt 18:20; 1 Cor 1:9; 2 Pet 1:4), etc.

By engaging in these activities, the believers demonstrate communion with the Spirit of God. Although the Spirit always indwells the

---

26. Courey, *What has Wittenberg to Do with Azusa?*
27. Torr, *Dramatic Pentecostal/Charismatic Anti-Theodicy.*

believers, he finds concrete manifestation in and through their physical activities within and outside ecclesial contexts. Within ecclesial contexts, God's presence manifests in and through the individual believers' bodies and the corporate body. The experience of God in the corporate body allows the believers to foretaste the eschatological communion, especially in multi-racial, multi-ethnic, multi-cultural, or multi-national churches.

Consequently, believers are conduits or channels for the tangible expression of grace held as God's personal presence by the Spirit. Believers' inspiring words and deeds render the Spirit concrete. This character of believers is reminiscent of Jesus as the prophet mighty in word and deed (Luke 24:19) who expressed the Spirit palpably. As words and deeds are not disembodied, the believers who speak inspired words and undertake inspired activities are means of the Spirit. For example, Paul, who miraculously heals a man who has never walked since his birth (Acts 14:8–20), is a means of grace, as he provides concrete expression to the Spirit. The words and deeds he uses to minister to the disabled are not means of grace in and of themselves but Paul.

This is not to suggest that Paul is a cause of the Spirit's healing grace. Instead, the Spirit uses him to manifest his therapeutic presence. In such sacramental events, believers always retain their natural ontology when they manifest the Spirit. Thus, the sacramentality of Spirit-manifesting believers upholds the creator-creature distinction.

The Spirit's Manifestation and Heidegger's Phenomenology

To clarify how the believers concretely manifest the Spirit, let us consider how Heidegger distinguishes between a phenomenon and an appearance within a phenomenon. For Heidegger, a phenomenon shows itself from itself. In contrast, an appearance announces the reality beneath a phenomenon. The reality beneath a phenomenon cannot reveal itself without a corporeal other.[28] This is so because the nature of the reality in a phenomenon is such that it cannot be manifested fully or directly without the means of a corporeal other. It means that the corporeal other enables the incorporeal reality to manifest its presence concretely. Drawing from this, God's presence is the reality beneath a phenomenon of Spirit manifestation in and through believers. A believer's inspired word or deed is an appearance that manifests God's reality underneath a phenomenon.

28. Heidegger, *Being and Time*, 52.

To illustrate Heidegger's reality-sign dynamic, Moses' face shines when he descends Mt. Sinai with two stone tablets, manifesting the reality of the Spirit (Exod 34: 29–30, 35) manifests the reality of the Spirit. Although the Spirit is invisible, he appears tangible to the Israelites in and through Moses' shining face. In other words, Moses is an appearance that gives concrete expression to the Spirit's reality beneath the phenomenon of his shining face. As the Israelites discern the Spirit's presence in and through Moses, he (Moses) is a site of grace. Significantly, Moses is a sacrament of the reality of God.

Moses manifests the Spirit and thereby facilitates the Israelites' encounter with God. In this sense, Moses is a means of grace to the Israelites. The finite or created, reveals the infinite or the creator. Although it is Moses' face that shines, his soul, body, and spirit encountered God. In other words, Moses' face only provides physical expression to the reality of God's presence.

On their part, Macquarie and Robinson, the English translators of Heidegger's book *Being and Time*, employ the symptom-disease analogy to clarify the sign-reality dynamic. This is important for explaining the sacrament-reality relationship. Precisely, an appearance functions like a disease's symptom, which only announces the disease's presence. One only sees the symptoms and not the disease itself because the former is essentially a manifestation or revealed event. A symptom is thus quintessential to a sign or an appearance that announces, informs, or manifests the reality's presence beneath a given phenomenon, i.e., the disease. This is because the disease itself is incapable of revealing itself directly without the disease's symptoms.

Therefore, the disease is the hidden reality beneath a phenomenon that only announces its presence in and through tangible symptoms of a disease (an appearance). The fact that a disease cannot directly and concretely show itself from itself or without the other (symptoms) suggests that the two are interdependent. The symptom is an appearance that reveals the underlying disease similar to a sign or sacrament that reveals the Spirit's reality beneath the phenomenon of divine manifestation in and through the believers. In other words, symptoms render tangible the existence of a disease. More preferably, the symptom renders palpable the disease's existence.

We can infer from this that the sacraments make the reality of God tangible by the Spirit. More adequately, sacraments render God as visibly, tangibly, or perceptibly present by the Spirit. Framing this theological conviction about this book's claim, believers are sacraments who render God's reality as tangibly present by the Spirit. Notably, the believers are sacraments only as they render God's presence tangible by the Spirit. This presence of God is not a proxy but is real.

The Spirit of God's indwelling presence in and through believers is as real as that in and through Jesus. As the symptom of a disease announces the latter's presence, a believer's Christ-like words and deeds reveal God's real presence by the indwelling Spirit. Even so, this presence is hidden to some extent, so much so that what is tangible is only in part (1 Cor 13:12).

As one does not see the fullness of a disease but only its symptoms, one cannot see God's full presence in and through believers. Believers look forward to the day in the *eschaton* when they will see the fullness of God's presence (1 Cor 13:12). This shows that a sacrament differs from the reality signified. Notably, the reality determines the extent to which the sacrament discloses that reality (John 5:19; 8:28). On this side of life, God's fullness is revealed in and through Christ (Col 2:9).

Thus, Jesus says whoever sees him sees the Father (John 14:9). Christ fully manifests and draws people to encounter God's presence by the Spirit. However, it is not adequate to say that Christ's inspired words and deeds are sacraments of the personal encounter with the Spirit. This is because Christ is inseparably linked to his words and deeds. Instead, it is in the speaking and in the doing that Christ serves as the sacrament of the personal encounter with the Spirit of God.

Similarly, believers who reflect Christ in words and deeds are sacraments of God's presence. Believers cannot reflect the life of Christ apart from the Spirit. Nonetheless, it is not the believers' Christ-like words and deeds by themselves that are sacraments of God's presence. Instead, the believers who speak inspiring words and undertake inspiring deeds are sacraments. This is because inspiring words and deeds flow from the Spirit within the believers. Even so, the words that one speaks and the deeds that one does are inseparably linked to the person's soul, body, and spirit. God's indwelling presence permeates the totality of believers by the Spirit. After his ascension, God's presence manifests in and through the believers who reflect Christ in words and in deeds.

To clarify, let us again consider the relation of symptoms and diseases; symptoms may manifest a disorder in one or more parts of the human body. It is the total person in and through whom the symptoms show to be considered sick or ill. This is why people typically say "I'm not feeling well," or "I'm sick or ill," or "I'm under the weather," though the symptoms may physically appear in one or any select parts of their bodies.

This is what I mean when I say that even though a part or parts of someone's body may show symptoms of an illness, sickness, or a disease, it is the person that is considered ill or sick. For example, one does not say "my head is sick" or "my body has a fever" but rather "I have a headache" or "I have a fever." Paul alludes to this thinking when he speaks of believers as members of the body of Christ (Rom 12:5; 1 Cor 6:15; 12:12, 22–23; Eph 4:25; 5:30). Moses' total being (body, soul, and spirit) encounters God.

Moses' shining face is reminiscent of symptoms that announce a disease as it manifests to the Israelites of his encounter with the God of Abraham, Isaac, and Jacob. The symptoms of a disease not only announce the disease's presence but also participate in that very disease. Thus, we cannot compartmentalize Moses's shining face as separate from the rest of his being (body, soul, and spirit). Likewise, the believers who show signs of grace via inspiring words and deeds are sacraments of encountering the Spirit of God's presence in Christ. Pentecost is a classic event where the 120 disciples encounter and manifest God's presence and thus are sacraments of the Spirit.

Pentecost fulfilled Joel's prophecy about the eschatological Spirit (Joel 2:28; Acts 2:16–17). Christ's promise to his disciples about the eschatological Spirit echoed Joel's prophecy (Luke 24:49; Acts 1:8; 2). The disciples had a proleptic experience of the Spirit as Christ gave them the power to heal the sick, raise the dead, cleanse the lepers, etc. (Matt 10:8; Mark 3:15; 6:13; 16:17). In this way, the disciples showed signs of an encounter with God's presence by the Spirit. The same Spirit is poured upon believers today. The Lukan Pentecost event was characterized by tangible signs of the Spirit's presence (Acts 2). The egalitarian nature of the Pentecost event broke down barriers that stood between people groups or individuals. This can be deduced from the fact that the Spirit came upon all 120 disciples simultaneously with no marked distinction.

Pentecost demonstrates God's desire to disclose his presence in and through male and female believers, individually and communally, clergy and laity, rich and poor, etc. Each of the 120 disciples did contribute to rendering God's presence tangible or visible. Before he ascended, Jesus instructed the disciples to wait in Jerusalem for the Spirit (Luke 24:49). Pentecost is thus inauguration of the sacramentality of all believers as they undertake God's redemptive mission.

The Believer as Sacrament

This book advances that believers are sacraments of a personal encounter with God's presence. These are Christ-like believers who signify, reveal, or manifest God's presence in word and deed. Spirit manifestations are God's actions in and through believers. By manifesting the Spirit, the believers inspire or deepen other believers' faith, hope, and love (1 Cor 13:13). Seen in this light, the Spirit-manifesting believers function as means of God's presence. This is because such believers draw others into a personal encounter with God by providing concrete expression to the Spirit. In this sense, Spirit-manifesting believers are characteristically human sites or signs of God's grace.

The sacramentality of believers differs from the sacramentality of Water Baptism and the Lord's Supper as believers encounter and manifest God's presence through the indwelling Spirit. As such, believers are sacraments of direct encounter with God's presence. In contrast, believers encounter God's presence indirectly via elements of the Water Baptism and the Lord's Supper. It is noteworthy that some deem the waters of baptism and the bread and wine of the Lord's Supper as spiritually charged by the Holy Spirit invoked through *epiclesis* to mediate God's presence.

The ways in which human beings encounter God's presence are more direct than indirect. Put another way, human beings only respond to what the Spirit initiates. Though believers work in partnership with God, this is always at the initiative of the latter. For example, Luke shows us this picture when God encounters Cornelius (Acts 10:4). The Spirit prompts Peter to meet with the Gentile guests via a vision (Acts 10:20). More relevantly, the Spirit encounters Cornelius and his household as Peter preaches (Acts 10:44). Peter and his colleagues are caught off-guard and express wonder at the Spirit's mode of encounter and manifestation in and through the Gentiles (Acts 10:46). This happens before Peter administers Water Baptism (Acts 10:48). This shows that we need a different approach to tease out the sacramentality of believers and Christ from rites.

Theology of sacraments or ordinances focuses on Water Baptism and the Lord's Supper. The debate centers on the manner in which one can or cannot encounter God's presence through participation in these rites. Typically, if you say that one can encounter God's presence through participation in these rites, you are sacramental. In contrast, if you say that one cannot encounter God's presence through participation in these rites, you are non-sacramental.

It seems to me that debates predicated on rites to determine what is sacramental or not, or what is sacrament or not, is reductionist or minimalist. Such debates overshadow the fundamental meaning of sacrament in its relation to Jesus in whom dwells the Godhead bodily (Col 2:9). It is Christ who fully reveals the Triune God's presence. Although all creation reveals God's glory or presence, human beings especially the believers, play a vital role (Ps 8:5; Rom 1:20; Heb 2:9).

This book explores the sacramentality of believers shaped and informed by Christ as the primordial sacrament of the encounter with God's presence. Among the several events that Jesus encounters and manifests God's presence are when he submits to John's baptism and celebrates the Last Supper (Matt 26:26–28; Mark 14:22–25; Luke 22:19; John 4:1–2; 1 Cor 11:24). But one cannot adequately understand Christ as the primordial sacrament through his experiences of the Water Baptism and the Last Supper only. His whole life or ministry confirms his sacramentality.

Experiences of Water Baptism and the Last Supper only reveal God's presence upon him. The Spirit already worked in Christ (Luke 2:40, 46, 47, 52) but descended upon him bodily at his Water Baptism (Luke 3:21, 22). This way, he manifests God's cleansing presence (John 1:29). At the Last Supper, he manifests God's redeeming presence to the twelve disciples. It flows from this view that Jesus is the water-baptized Man and the Last Supper-participant *par excellence*. It is Jesus who provides the meaning of Water Baptism and the Lord's Supper and not vice versa.

As the one who instituted or ordained Water Baptism and the Lord's Supper, it seems reasonable to interpret these rites through the lens of the baptized and the communicant Christ. The sacramentality of Jesus is apart from yet can be clarified through Water Baptism and the Lord's Supper as the sacramentality of the Israelites in Egypt is apart from but can be clarified through the Passover (Exod 12) and the Red Sea crossing (Exod 14). Similarly, the sacramentality of believers is apart from but can be fleshed out through the Water Baptism and the Last Supper.

Drawing from this, believers who submit to Water Baptism and partake in the Lord's Supper (communicants) are sacramental in their character. This is so because the Spirit drives the believer towards baptismal waters and the Lord's Table. In other words, submission to the Water Baptism and participation in the Lord's Supper enables the believers to disclose their encounter with the Spirit. Of course, there are other ways that believers reveal the Spirit of God's presence. This book's thesis takes seriously the biblical motif that God's presence indwells the believers.

Precisely, God indwells believers by the Holy Spirit. Both the Father and the Son indwell believers through the Spirit (John 7:37–39; 14:20; 17:23; Rom 8:10; Gal 2:20; Eph 3:17–19; Col 1:27; 1 John 3:24). Christ asked the Father to fulfill his promise to send the Spirit (Joel 2:28–29; Luke 24:49; John 14:16; Acts 1:5, 8; 2:1–4). Significantly, he is the Spirit-bearer *par excellence* and the Spirit baptizer (Matt 3:11; Mark 1:8; Luke 3:16; Acts 1:5; 11:16). Seen in this light, the believers can also be understood as sacraments of a personal encounter with the Spirit of Christ.

To discuss the Spirit of Christ is not to pit the Second Person of the Trinity against the Third. Instead, it highlights the inseparable work of the Spirit and the Son in the redemptive mission. It is partly in this sense that Paul writes, "Anyone who does not have the Spirit does not belong to him" (Rom 8:9). God the Father, the Son, and the Spirit never act independently of each other.

The Spirit and Son are the Father's two hands, while the Spirit is the bond between the Father and the Son. Believers are, therefore, sacraments of the Father, the Son, and the Spirit. Therefore, the sacramentality of believers has a Trinitarian outlook. In keeping with this, the Bible describes the Holy Spirit as "the Spirit of Jesus" (Acts 16:7), "the Spirit" (Rom 8:9; 1 Pet 1:11), "the Spirit of Jesus Christ" (Phil 1:19), and the "Spirit of Christ" (Rom 8:9).

The Spirit is indivisibly linked to the Father and Son (1 Cor 2:12; Gal 4:6). To signify the Spirit is to signify the Father and the Son concomitantly. It implies that believers are sites, signs, or symbols of the Trinity. Fee alludes to this when he says, "the first location of God's clothing presence in the new covenant is within his people individually."[29] The believers render God's clothing presence visible in this present world, the "already," and the one to come, the "not yet." This proleptic act awaits fulfillment in the eschatological kingdom (Rev 6:11; 7:9, 13, 14).

The Spirit's clothing presence offers a pneumatological foundation for the sacramentality of the believers. It is partly in this sense that all the believers are "the people of God's immediate presence"[30] in the here and now and the *eschaton*. Seen in this light, believers are sacramental in their character as they experience the future in the present. In fact, believers signify the Spirit of Christ. As embodied signs or symbols of the Spirit,

---

29. Fee, *Paul*, 20.
30. Cross, *People of God's Presence*, 166.

believers render tangible the reality of God in Christ. However, it is in and through Christ that the Spirit of God's presence is fully manifested.

It is in and through Christ's words and deeds that he rendered God's presence tangible or visible. This is because the Spirit acted in and through the humanity of Christ. The same Spirit who acted in and through Christ now acts in and through the humanity of believers. In this sense, believers are sacraments of God's dynamic presence. The Spirit becomes tangible in and through believers as they live out the Christian teachings. Thus, believers' sacramentality necessitates discipleship that aims at their growth and maturity in the image of Christ's likeness. Growth and maturity assume that the sacramentality of believers takes seriously human responses to Christ.

In sacramental events, there are two sides: divine action and human response. The divine action is primary, while the human response is secondary. Divine action is what God does to the believer, while the human response is what the believer does based on the divine action. Knowledge of the Word shapes and informs the believers' sensitivity to divine action and their response to the same. Divine actions are seen in and through human responses. That is to say, the former gives concrete expression to the latter. Put more pointedly, believers' activities disclose God's activities. For example, when God tells Moses to stretch his rod over the Red Sea (Exod 14:16), it is because God has already stretched his hand over the Red Sea. This is why God wonders why Moses cries out to him (Exod 14:15). Moses' action reveals God's action.

Believers as Means of Grace (the Spirit)

Paul writes that, "And how are they to hear without someone to proclaim him (Rom 10:14)? This text points to the role believers play in spreading the Gospel of Christ and bolsters their sacramentality. A sacramental principle maintains that sacraments are means of grace. Put in another way, sacraments cause or mediate grace. In keeping with this view, believers are means of grace. That is to say, believers cause or mediate grace. It is by manifesting or acting by the Spirit that believers are means of grace as in preaching the Gospel. This reflects the view that grace is God's visible presence. Jesus Christ is God's visible presence par excellence. For this book, grace is God's presence becoming visible via believers.

To clarify this thinking, let us reflect on Moses's actions before the Israelites cross the Red Sea. Moses by himself did not part the Red Sea. It is God through Moses (Exod 14:21). Precisely, as Moses lifts his rod and stretches his hand over the Red Sea, he acts by God's Spirit. By so doing, Moses appears to cause or to mediate grace. Moses is thus not a direct cause but a derivative cause of grace. As any disease's symptoms announce its existence or presence, but are not its cause, Moses's actions show outwardly that God is already in action but invisibly.

Moses does not cause God to act. God causes Moses to act and gives him specific instructions. By lifting his rod and stretching his hand, Moses allows God to manifest. Moses thus mediates or causes grace in a derivative sense. Those who act based on Scripture or the Spirit's instructions thus cause or mediate grace. This is not a magical causation of grace but rather a partnership with God's Spirit.

To use another example, believers do not heal the sick in a direct sense when they lay hands upon the sick. Believers who lay hands upon the sick allow God's healing presence to flow in and through them to the sick. Seen in this light, those that lay hands on the sick mediate God's healing grace. As those who lay hands upon the sick do not act arbitrarily but obey Scripture or the Spirit, they cause grace through their acts of mediation.

Moses does not act arbitrarily when he lifts his rod and stretches his hand over the Red Sea (Exod 14:16). Based on God's instructions, he lifts his rod, and stretches his hand symbolizing acts of mediation, and thus causes grace. His visible actions manifest God's invisible actions. Moses does not cause grace directly but indirectly through mediation.

Mediation helps clarify how believers cause grace since to mediate is to act between two parties. Moses mediates grace between God and Israelites (Exod 14:15); and also between Israelites and Egyptians (Exod 14:13). Manifestation and mediation belong together as they explain how believers fit as sacraments.

Believers are means of grace when their actions enable other believers and unbelievers to become aware or more aware of God's presence in the here and now. As believers act in ways that signify the Spirit of God's presence, and inspire, deepen or enhance others' faith, hope, and love for God fully revealed in Christ.

Like Moses, believers are concrete signs of grace as God works in and through them. The Spirit acts in and through the believers and thereby discloses his presence tangibly. When the believers reflect Christ in word and deed, or character and charisma, they show that God works in and through them by the Spirit. Such believers are sacraments of God's presence, for they render him tangible. This is not a magical expression of God but requires active participation in the Spirit. The new birth gives believers the right to participate in the Spirit. From conversion, God inhabits believers so that the latter share in the life of the former by the Spirit (Heb 6:4). The Spirit not only regenerates sinners but remains in them to facilitate their transformation in Christ.

CHAPTER 2

Manifesting the Regenerating Spirit

Baptized Believers

> What is born of the flesh is flesh, and what is born of the Spirit is spirit.
>
> (JOHN 3:6)

WHEN THE UNREGENERATE RESPOND to the call of salvation, they manifest the Spirit who convicts and leads sinners to repentance (John 8:46). By accepting Jesus as Lord and Savior, they become new creation (2 Cor 5:17). God declares them righteous (Phil 3:9). That is to say, they are not condemned (Rom 8:1) but are justified (Rom 3:24). The Spirit transforms them as God's children (John 1:12–13; 3:6) who render Christ their Savior visible (Acts 11:26).

Converts are signs of personal encounter with the converting Spirit of Christ (Rom 10:9; Phil 2:11; 1 John 4:3). Since the Spirit is invisible, the reborn individuals render him visible by responding to the altar call of salvation (Rom 10:9). The reborn individuals are a lens for discerning the Spirit's convicting and converting presence (1 Tim 2:4–5). Notably, sinners make God's grace and mercy visible. For example, the three thousand who repent of their sins at Pentecost publicly manifest God's grace and mercy (Acts 2:37).

The Spirit who confronts the human heart as the Gospel is proclaimed finds concrete expression through sinners' positive response to altar call. Response to altar call happens in variety of ways, like stepping forward to the front of a church meeting or raising a hand from one's seat to publicly commit to Christ. The altar call conceived this way creates space for the unregenerate to render the Spirit's converting presence tangible.

The altar therefore functions as a context for a visible encounter with God's presence.[1] It is not necessarily a physical location but wherever one encounters God. In the Old Testament, for example, encounters with God often precede the building of altars. One built an altar after an encounter with God (Gen 12:7; 26:25; Exod 17:15). In the same way, sinners may encounter God's grace of salvation as they sit and listen to the gospel preached. Thus, their conversion would be complete without going to the front of a church meeting. The altar is not a space in the front of a church but a place one encounters God.

As such, one can have an altar at home to encounter with God. Sinners respond to the altar call of salvation to express what they have already encountered, i.e., the Spirit's converting presence. To be sure, salvation is not the only reason people respond to the altar calls. In many churches, people are invited to the altar for prayer for diverse needs. Prayer can be offered for emotional, physical, psychological, marital, academic, and other needs. Response to the altar call is a sign of awareness of God's presence.

With regard to the altar call of salvation, converts are known by their public response to the altar of salvation. By responding to the altar call of salvation, sinners reveal that they have been translated from darkness to light. The practice of calling sinners to the altar for repentance supports the sacramentality of believers. In this sense, the converts are sacraments of a personal encounter with the Spirit of Christ. It is through Christ's vicarious death that people are saved.

The Spirit convicts a sinner primarily through hearing the gospel preached at church, on television, radio, etc. The concrete steps one takes upon hearing the gospel of salvation render the Spirit visible. Conversion is a life-giving event of the Spirit (John 3:6; 2 Cor 3:6). One is saved through repentance and faith in Jesus all occurring within the heart (John 4:42; 14:6; Acts 4:12; Eph 5:23; 1 Tim 2:5). Jesus told the thief crucified alongside him that he would be with him in Paradise (Luke 23:43). The thief was transformed from condemnation to commendation. Jesus implies that this thief is not condemned before God. By asking Jesus to remember him (Luke 23:42), he manifests the convicting

---

1. Tomberlin, *Pentecostal Sacraments*.

and converting Spirit. The sinners come face to face with God at the moment of conversion.

In keeping with this, Saul comes face to face with Christ at the moment of his conversion (Acts 9:4) and so does the criminal on the Cross (Luke 23:42). This encounter with God leads to a radical turnabout of a sinner's life trajectory. Seen in this light, this criminal and Saul of Tarsus are sacraments of a personal encounter with God's regenerating presence. Although the two do not physically raise their hands in prayer for salvation as typically done at the altar of salvation, their disposition of surrender is difficult to miss (Luke 23:40; Acts 9:5). The raising of one's hands at the altar of salvation signifies surrender to God who confronts the unregenerate. Thus, converts at the altar disclose the Spirit of God's regenerating presence to believers and also unbelievers.

The Spirit gives the repentant new life in Christ (John 3:3, 5–6; 2 Cor 3:6). While human beings are created in God's image, they do not adequately reflect him in their sinful state. Thus, the idea that "my neighbor stands before me as God's sacramental presence"[2] though he or she is not saved is inadequate. However, converts adequately reflect God's image primarily because of the gift of the Spirit who indwells them (Acts 2:38) through Christ. In his humanity, Christ is the image of God *par excellence*. It is in this sense that the reborn human beings reflect God's image more than unbelievers since the latter do not have the indwelling Spirit of God's presence. This is why the regenerated signify and point others to the reality of God in Christ by the Spirit.

Consequently, reborn individuals exhibit a fundamental character of sacraments as they make visible God's presence. The redeemed are sacraments of God's reality not the reality itself. The redeemed do not become gods (*theosis*) but point to God. As sacraments, believers reflect the creator-creature distinction. The converts are signs of the grace of new life in Christ by the Spirit (Rom 8:1–2, 6; 2 Cor 3:6). More theologically robust, the converts are those crucified with Christ (Gal 5:24); raised with Christ (Rom 6:4; Col 3:1); live in Christ by faith (Rom 7:6; Gal 5:25); and manifest newness of life in Christ (2 Cor 5:17), through the Spirit's enabling presence.

To confess Jesus as Lord is to point others to his hidden but living presence. Furthermore, to confess Christ is to point others to the Spirit. This is because no one can confess Jesus as Lord except by the Spirit (1

---

2. Hughes and Lösel, *Reformed Sacramentality*, 63.

Cor 12:3). In a typical evangelistic service, believers pray for the Spirit's convicting and converting presence to minister to sinners' hearts. Those ready to make a decision are asked to step forward for prayer. By so doing, sinners publicly acknowledge their encounter with God.

Stepping forward for the prayer of repentance allows persons to express outwardly what they experience inwardly. The altar is charged with the Spirit's presence. Those who step forward to the altar are mobile sites of the grace of the Spirit's regenerating presence. It is when responding to the altar call for salvation that one renders the Spirit tangible. It implies that the altar-call responders are signs of the grace of the Spirit's convicting and converting presence. The Spirit of God's redeeming presence normatively works in and through the preached Word.

At Pentecost, the three thousand people who repented of sin and accepted Christ as their Savior are signs of the grace of the Spirit's convicting and converting presence (Acts 2:41). The Spirit convicted them when they heard the 120 disciples speak about the wonders of God in their native languages (Acts 2:8), but also when they heard the gospel preached by Peter (Acts 2:37). In addition, the Spirit of Christ manifested in and through each of the three thousand converts as they submitted to Water Baptism (Acts 2:41). Sacraments not only reveal but also mediate, and draw others into an encounter with the divine. This is what the 120 disciples did at Pentecost.

Not only did all the 120 disciples exhibit essential characteristics of sacraments, but they also inspired others to exhibit the same. These 120 disciples mediated God's redeeming grace when they inspired the three thousand individuals' conversion. Against this backdrop, the 120 disciples and the three thousand converts are sacraments of encounter with God's saving grace.

The Convert as Sacraments of the Spirit

> But you are a chosen race, a royal priesthood,
> a holy nation, God's own people.
>
> (1 PET 2:9)

The regenerate also manifest signs of transformation or translation from the kingdom of darkness to light. More specifically, transformed regenerates signify a radical departure from the life of evil or darkness to the life of righteousness or light (Col 1:13; cf. Luke 16:8; John 1:9; 1 John 2:8). The relation of light to the transformed converts stresses their visible character (Matt 5:14–16; John 8:12; 9:5). In this sense, conversion is not cerebral but concrete. Saul, the former murderer of believers in Christ, exemplifies the sacramentality of the transformed regenerates.

Luke describes Saul as breathing threats and murder against the disciples (Acts 9:1). Saul was on his way to Damascus to arrest and kill the disciples of Jesus (Acts 9:1–2). Nonetheless, his radical change of lifestyle confirms that he truly encountered the risen Christ by the Spirit. In other words, Saul was transformed or translated from the kingdom of darkness to the kingdom of light (John 3:5–8). His soteriological encounter shows in his radical break with his sinful past life (Acts 9:4–9). Thus, Saul is a sign of salvific grace. Notably, the transformed Saul enables others to see the transformative power of the Spirit of the ascended Christ (Rom 11:13; 2 Tim 1:11).

Saul's profound and dramatic conversion can only be attributed to the work of Christ by the Spirit. The life of Jesus Christ is the standard for authenticating claims of conversion. In other words, Christ is the reality at work within regenerated believers by the Spirit (Col 1:15, 18; Heb 12:23). By manifesting the Spirit, the reborn render Christ visible or tangible. Seen in this light, believers, reflect *imago Dei,* or God's image, not unbelievers. In functional terms, believers' image-bearing function after Pentecost supersedes the image-bearing role of human beings after the fall. More precisely, the sending of the Spirit to indwell believers enables them to reflect the image of God effectively. Notably, Christ is, in his humanity, the image of God-bearing Man *par excellence* (Col 2:29).

The experience of conversion or rebirth restores one as *imago Dei* or image of God (Gen 1:26–27). All human beings lost the *imago Dei* because of the fall of Adam (Gen 3). However, the life, death, and resurrection of Christ opened the door to the restoration of human beings into *imago Dei*. This *imago Dei* is not an abstraction but a concrete expression of the life of God.

The converts are those at peace or one with God as Adam and Even were before the fall. The converts are *imago Dei* to the degree that the life of Christ, the Last Adam, finds concrete expression in and through them. The reborn concretely express God's mercies in Christ due to Adam's sin (Rom 3:23) and reverse the effects of sin that distorted *imago Dei* in all humanity. The Spirit facilitates the conversion of sinners to *imago Dei* (Rom 3:24; 5:17).

In his conversation with Nicodemus, Christ relates conversion to the Spirit (John 3:5–10). This is because the Spirit convicts and prompts sinners to repent (John 16:8–9). Conviction of sin occurs within one's heart (2 Sam 24:10; Ps 119:11; Prov 20:9). It is those the Spirit convicts of sin who are born again. Therefore, the reborn render the Spirit's converting presence tangible. In other words, the reborn are signs of the Spirit's converting presence. Also, the reborn point others to the reality of the Spirit's converting presence. As sinners respond to the call to repentance, they make the Spirit's converting presence tangible at the altar. Seen in this light, the converts are sacraments of an encounter with the Spirit's converting presence in Christ.

Whenever people confess Jesus as Lord and Savior, they render him tangibly present. It makes no difference if this confession is made within or outside ecclesial contexts. The Spirit prompts people to confess Christ as Lord and Savior (1 Cor 12:3). The Spirit is not invisible in and of himself but becomes tangible in and through the converts' confessions. To confess Jesus as Lord and Savior is to concomitantly acknowledge the Spirit (Acts 9:5; 22:8; 26:15; Rom 8:1; 2 Cor 5:17). Thus, we can plausibly conceive converts as sacraments of the regenerating Spirit.

To the extent that God's converting presence is tangible in and through the reborn, they serve as signs of grace. Conversion is neither esoteric nor cerebral but concrete. Sacramentality of the reborn intensifies with maturity. Converts show signs of the regenerating Spirit as they grow in Christ's likeness (Eph 4:13, 15; 2 Pet 3:18). The Spirit who indwells converts from the moment of conversion enables them to grow into the likeness of Christ (1 Cor 11:1). Converts' growth also requires other spiritual disciplines, like studying the Word and effective discipleship.

This does not mean that the reborn necessarily live sinless lives. Instead, the Holy Spirit reminds the reborn to stay on the path of righteousness (Ps 51:3). Conversion does not render the reborn invincible to sin but helps them overcome desires of the flesh and aids them in achieving God-pleasing ways of life (Rom 7:18–20; 8:26). While salvation is mostly attributed to the work of Christ, notably his life, death, and resurrection, the Spirit also plays a vital role (2 Thess 2:13).

Elsewhere, Paul notes the joint role of the Son and the Spirit when he writes: "But you were washed, you were sanctified, you were justified in the name of the Lord Jesus Christ and in the Spirit of our God" (1 Cor 6:11). Elsewhere, Paul writes, ". . . so that the offering of the Gentiles may be acceptable, sanctified by the Holy Spirit" (Rom 15:16). To say that conversion is by the Spirit is simply to recognize the role of the Trinity, that is God the Father, God the Son, and God the Holy Spirit (Rom 8:3–4; 15–17; 1 Cor 1:4–7; 2:4–5, 12; 1 Cor 6:11; 19–20; 2 Cor 1:21–22; Gal 3:1–5; Col 3:16; Eph 1:17; 2:18; 2:20–22; Phil 3:3).

Next, the Bible refers to the Holy Spirit as the Spirit of Christ (Rom 8:9; 1 Pet 1:11), the Spirit of Jesus (Acts 16:7; Phil 1:19), and the Spirit of God (Gen 1:2; Matt 3:16; 12:28; Rom 8:9,14; 15:19; 1 Cor 2:11; 7:40; 12:3; Eph 4:30; Phil 3:3; 1 Pet 4:14; 1 John 4:2). The Spirit is God's personal presence on the earth and within believers. As the Spirit is incorporeal in nature, he finds concrete manifestation in and through the believers both in word and deed (3 John 1:11).

Conversion turns humans into signs of the grace of the Spirit through his indwelling presence. The converts are the Spirit's hosts both individually and communally (1 Cor 6:19; 2 Cor 6:16). Christ draws on this motif when he says: "I am able to destroy the temple of God and to build it in three days" (Matt 26:61). More robustly, Christ is the temple of God's presence *par excellence* (John 2:19–22). Likewise, the believers are individually and communally temples of God's presence. They receive the Spirit at conversion (John 4:10; Acts 2:38; 2 Cor 1:22; 5:5).

The Spirit's indwelling presence in believers captures the idea of sacramental ontology. Precisely, this sacramental ontology can be described as pneumatological-participatory ontology. This links to the biblical view that believers are temples of God by the indwelling Spirit (Rom 8:9, 11; 1 Cor 3:16; 6:19). This implies that the converts are signs of the Spirit of God's presence in the same sense that Christ in his humanity is the primordial sign of the Spirit of God's presence.

According to the New Testament, the humanity of Christ is what brought the full and concrete manifestation of the Spirit of God's presence. For example, Luke presents Christ as the full bearer of the Spirit (Luke 1:35; 4:18–21; Acts 4:27). Consequently, everything that Christ does flows from the power of the Spirit (Matt 12:23; 13:54–55; Luke 4:32; 9:42–43; Acts 10:38).

Believers' words and deeds also flow from the indwelling Spirit. It does not mean that their words and deeds always reflect Christ's life. In fact, the regenerated remain susceptible to sin while in this world. Thus, they remain in need of reconciliation with God throughout their lives. Notwithstanding this susceptibility to sin, the Triune God declares converts as justified from the moment of conversion based upon Christ's work in the Spirit (Rom 5:1, 9; 1 Tim 3:16).

The Justified as Sacraments of the Spirit

> You were justified in the name of the Lord Jesus Christ and in the Spirit of our God.
>
> (1 COR 6:11)

While I do not intend to engage in a full-scale theology of justification, it suffices to say that converts are justified before God (Rom 4:1–5:21). One is justified by grace through faith and repentance (Rom 3:24). God does not give the justified a license to live as they please but to live according to Christ's teachings (Gal 5:13). He declares converts justified upon conversion (Rom 8:1). This act of justification sets the believers apart from the unbelievers in their relation to God.

The Spirit indwells the justified as a guarantee (2 Cor 1:22; 5:5; Eph 1:13–14). As Paul also observes, the Spirit in believers distinguishes them from unbelievers (1 Cor 2:6–16; 12:3; Rom 8:9). Paul refers to believers as spiritual and unbelievers as natural persons (1 Cor 2:6–16).

Believers, but not unbelievers, have the Spirit indwelling them. The believers' public confession of Christ as Lord and Savior makes the Spirit visibly present (1 Cor 12: 3). Confession that Jesus Christ is Lord and Savior enables the converts to point others to the reality of God by the Spirit.

In this way, those who publicly confess Jesus as Lord are sacramental in their character. Of course, the confession of Jesus as Lord and Savior also needs to reflect in converts' lifestyle. To the extent that they show signs of Christ-likeness, the converts render God's presence visible.

As noted, one remarkable story of conversion in the New Testament is that of Saul. Luke reports Saul's encounter with Christ in the Spirit on the road to Damascus to kill those of the Way (Acts 9:5). As a known killer of Jesus' followers, it is understandable that many were reluctant to see Saul as a convert (Acts 9:13–14). It is only after Saul begins to manifest signs of conversion that his testimony persuades others. The fact that Saul begins to preach the gospel not long after his conversion signifies his encounter with God's presence. The Spirit works in and through Peter to the Jews as in and through Saul to the Gentiles (Gal 2:8). This shows that the Spirit of Christ convicted and radically transformed Saul into a sacrament of God's presence.

The Reconciled as Sacraments of the Spirit

> Now when they heard this, they were cut to the heart and said to Peter and to the other apostles, "Brothers, what should we do?"
>
> (ACTS 2:37)

The Spirit of God grips the human heart and makes it realize its depravity. This is what brings about the conviction of sin. Its remedy is in Christ through God's redeeming grace. The convicted of sin signify to others about their personal encounter with God's reconciling presence. Reborn individuals are signs of the reconciliation with God (Rom 5:10; 2 Cor 5:18). In contrast, sinners are separated from God and therefore need reconciliation. This separation traces back to Adam, whom God evicted from the Garden due to sin (Gen 3:23).

Adam was the first to be separated from God. It is in and through the First Adam that all are separated from God. In and through Jesus, the Last Adam, all are reconciled with God (1 Cor 15:45). The reconciled receive the gift of the Spirit as a guarantee (2 Cor 1:22; 5:5). The giving of the Spirit therefore attests to one's reconciliation with God. The reconciled prodigal son and his father exemplify how God reconciles with his lost children.

The prodigal son adequately depicts conversion as reconciliation (Luke 15:11–32). This is particularly evident in how the Father responds to the Son's return: he runs toward him (Luke 15:20, 22–23). This is what happens when sinners are called to the altar in response to the call of salvation. Approaching the altar echoes the prodigal son's approach to the father. A sinner's response to God's invitation to salvation renders the Spirit's converting presence visible.

Similarly, the prodigal son's return makes tangible the Spirit's converting presence (Luke 15:10). The prodigal son is a sign of the grace of God's forgiveness and reconciliation. As the once-prodigal son is now reconciled with his Father, so are the reborn reconciled with the Father and are, hence, signs of the grace of forgiveness. In this sense, the reconciled prodigal son is a sacrament of his father's love. Drawing from this, the reconciled sinners are sacraments of an encounter with God's salvific love. That is to say, they make God's grace of forgiveness visible.

Reconciliation brings peace between God and the reborn (Rom 5:1). God's relation with humanity was broken due to Adam and Eve's disobedient act in the garden of Eden (Gen 3:24; Rom 5:12). Consequently, all humans are born in need of reconciliation (Rom 3:23). Conversion is the most fundamental experience of reconciliation as it delivers sinners from condemnation. It is the Spirit who initiates reconciliation with sinners by convicting them. Sinners respond to the primary act of the Spirit. Reconciliation is an act of grace as it issues in the Spirit's conviction.

While the conviction of sin is an interiorized act of the Spirit in the hearts or spirits of the sinners, their act of surrendering to Christ through a prayer of repentance led either by clergy or laity enables the reborn to provide concrete expression to the convicting Spirit. In other words, God's convicting presence in Christ becomes tangible as sinners or believers respond to God's invitation for reconciliation by the Spirit.

Reconciliation is both a one-time and an ongoing event (Luke 15:17; 2 Cor 5:18; 1 John 1:9). Conversion is basically reconciliation with God. This reconciliation is rooted in Christ's life, death, resurrection, and ascension. The most significant reconciliation happens when Christ saves sinners in the power of the Spirit through the drama of the Cross (Eph 2:16; Col 1:20). In particular, Christ made this reconciliation possible when he asked his Father to forgive those who nailed him to the Cross (Luke 23:34). This does not mean that all humans are automatically saved. It is the sinners who turn to Christ in faith and repentance that are saved (2 Cor 7:10). All humans are born sinners due to Adam's sin (Rom 3:23). After initial reconciliation with God at the moment of conversion, believers still need to be reconciled with him by confessing their sins whenever they sin before God (1 John 1:9). Reconciled believers remind others that there is enough room at the foot of the Cross of Christ for one to encounter God's grace of reconciliation.

Further, reconciled individuals point to the reality of God's redemptive presence in Christ and participate in this reconciling presence by the indwelling Spirit. In this way, the reconciled reflect the principle that sacraments participate in the reality they point to, signify, or symbolize. The indwelling Spirit enables believers to get back in line with God in Christ when they stumble (Prov 24:16; Heb 4:16). As hinted earlier, the reconciliation that believers experience is not a one-time event. By seeking reconciliation with God, believers show that they have encountered the Spirit who convicts from sin. The Spirit brings sinners to Christ, who pleads with the Father on their behalf (1 John 2:1).

In some church traditions, ordained clergy or priests act *in persona Christi* or on Christ's behalf. Therefore, they play a role in a believer's forgiveness and reconciliation with God. For example, in the Roman Catholic Church, the ministry of reconciliation rests with ordained priests. This is where the Roman Catholic Sacrament of Reconciliation intersects with the sacrament of the holy orders, or ordination. Generally, the Roman Catholic Church officials point to the text that, "If you forgive the sins of any, they are forgiven them; if you retain the sins of any, they are retained" (John 20:23). Drawing from this, they insist that Christ assigned the role of forgiving post-baptismal sins to ordained priests as the apostles' successors. But other churches disagree.

Pentecostals, Protestants, and others who dispute this Catholic position and hold that one does not need to confess sins to an ordained priest or a church official to be forgiven of original sin or post-water-baptismal sins to be reconciled with God. Among other texts, they point to James, who says, "Therefore confess your sins to one another" (Jas 5:16). But the priesthood of believers (1 Pet 2:5–9) seems to suggest otherwise. Precisely, Pentecostals and Protestants argue that the clergy have no special access to God compared to the laity. Believers in need of God's forgiveness and reconciliation can approach God through Christ in the Spirit. After all, the Father and the Son indwell believers by the Spirit (John 14:20). All believers can approach Christ.

Pentecostals and Protestants insist that believers can confess sin to God and be reconciled with him directly or without priestly mediation (Heb 4:16). Notably, confessing sins to others reinforces or demonstrates one's sincerity and accountability. For example, Saul experiences his conversion or reconciliation with God from the moment he encounters Jesus by the Spirit (Acts 9:5). This is before he is prayed for and baptized by Ananias (Acts 9:18). Here Saul is reconciled with God without confessing his sins to any human being. By presenting himself to Ananias (Acts 9:4–6, 9–15), the reborn Saul renders the redemptive grace of Christ tangible by the Spirit.

Moreover, Saul's forgiveness and reconciliation with God find concrete manifestation in and through his actions, including his submission to Ananias for prayer, his recovery of sight, and his Water Baptism. Thus, it seems plausible to advance that forgiveness and reconciliation with God are bolstered as one manifests concrete signs that bear witness to the redemptive encounter. In short, Saul is a human site or sign of the grace of God's redeeming presence.

The Bible teaches about confessing sins to one another (Jas 5:16). This suggests that one should share some details about specific areas of failure. In some churches, one may simply respond to an altar call for a prayer of forgiveness. Response to a call for a prayer of forgiveness proposes that one has been encountered by the Spirit. Responding to the call for a prayer of forgiveness at the altar manifests surrender to God of one's body as a living sacrifice and as an act of worship (Rom 12:1). In fact, to respond to an altar call for repentance and conversion is to stand in God's presence (1 Kgs 17:1; Acts 13:2).

In conversion, people encounter the presence of God by the Spirit. An encounter with the Spirit can occur while seated in pews during teaching or preaching of the Word, or through sung worship, prayer, and intercession. Those seated near such persons may pray for them as directed either by church officials or as led by the Spirit. Both the convicted and those who pray with them are channels for the concrete manifestation of God's redemptive presence. That is to say, both the convicted of sin and those who pray with them enable the Spirit to be visible or tangible.

The grace of God's redeeming presence in Christ is revealed in and through actions of the reborn and others that lead them in prayer. Of course, one can request a prayer of forgiveness in sacred settings like a worship service or a secular environment like a social event. The reborn person's affective expressions at an altar bolster the claim that the convicted, the converted, the saved, the reconciled, or the transformed serve as signs of God's redeeming grace.

As signs of God's redemptive grace, the reborn enable others to see the Spirit's reality at work in transforming societies one soul at a time. For example, the Samaritan woman at Jacob's well functions as a concrete sign of God's redemptive grace to her community (John 4:39–42). It is God's Spirit who worked in and through her witness to the encounter with Christ. Likewise, the redeemed are themselves signs of the grace of God's redeeming presence.

The Spirit transforms converts into agents of reconciliation with God within their society. Seen in this light, the reborn or reconciled are sacraments of encounters with the Spirit. For non-sacramental church traditions, this is not difficult to grasp, unlike sacramental church traditions, like those of the Roman Catholic tradition. For example, reconciled believers themselves are sacraments not just the rite of reconciliation itself. Let's use the analogy of a vehicle to illustrate this.

In the analogy, when one sees a repaired vehicle, it makes visible the repairer's skill. But, it is also true to say that the repaired vehicle reveals the repairer himself or herself. The Roman Catholic view accents the repairing process (the rite of reconciliation or penance). It is inevitable for believers to sin in this world, just as it is inevitable for a vehicle to need repairs. Thus, there will always be a need for a believer to get back in line or be reconciled with God. This does not mean that believers intentionally commit sins because of God's readiness to forgive in the same way that one does not need to drive a vehicle recklessly just because it can be repaired. However, if the vehicle develops a problem, it is advisable to have it checked. In fact, sometimes, a vehicle may have to be pulled off the road to avoid further damages.

Once the repairs are done, the vehicle is restored to normalcy. The owner takes it back on the road with more assurance and peace than before the repairs. The repairs do not necessarily guarantee that the vehicle will not experience other problems. To be sure, repairing a vehicle is costly in terms of money, time, etc. Thus, there is no incentive to deliberately wreck or recklessly drive a vehicle. Even those with deep pockets must drive carefully lest they cause a crash, resulting in loss of life. It is essential to continually check that one's vehicle functions well and have it repaired when necessary.

The Christian life is similar to this analogy, as it requires deliberate and constant self-examination in terms of one's relationship to God. As the creator of human beings, God fits as the repairer of broken human beings *par excellence*. Whenever believers fall short, they typically confess the sin, seek forgiveness, and reconcile with God in Christ through the Spirit. God's desire to forgive and reconcile with his children is difficult to miss in the biblical text, especially as demonstrated via Christ's death (Rom 5:10; 2 Cor 5:18, 20; Eph 2:16; Col 1:20).

In this sense, Christ is the preeminent sacrament of God's forgiving and reconciling presence by the Spirit. To be sure, conversion experiences or Water Baptism do not make a convert invincible to sin (Heb 3:12; 2 Pet 3:17). This is why Christ is the advocate for those who fall into the trap of sin (John 14:16, 26; 15:26; 16:7; 1 John 2:1). Life on this side of the *eschaton* requires believers to be on guard lest they fall prey to the enemy who roars like a lion (1 Pet 5:8).

Spiritual disciplines like prayer, fasting, Scripture studying, fellowship, etc., enhance the sacramentality of believers by, for instance, heightening their spirituality. Thus, Christ warns his disciples to pray lest they enter into temptation (Matt 26:41; Mark 14:38; Luke 22:40, 46). If and when believers fall short, they can be reconciled with God when they earnestly confess and repent their sins (Jas 5:16; 1 John 1:9). Reconciliation enhances the believers' conversion into Christ's likeness and engenders them as signs of God's redeeming presence through the Spirit.

In some churches, those who seek to be reconciled with God are invited forward for prayer. In this way, they manifest the reconciling presence of God by the Spirit. For example, David commits adultery with Bathsheba and sets up Uriah, her husband, to be killed in battle but reconciles with God after repentance (2 Sam 12:13; Psalm 51). Thus, David is a sacrament of an encounter with God's reconciling presence because he makes it tangible through the Spirit.

Accordingly, the Spirit enables believers to reconcile with each other (horizontally) (Matt 5:24; 1 Cor 7:11; 2 Cor 5:18–19). Another notable case of reconciliation occurs between Christ and Peter as the latter denies the former just before his crucifixion (Matt 26: 60–75; Mark 14: 66–72; John 18:15–27). This horizontal reconciliation serves as an example to all believers. In fact, that Christ has reconciled with Peter can be inferred from his appointment to lead the other disciples after his ascension (John 21:15–17).

It follows that believers who reconcile with others manifest God's reconciling presence by the Spirit. For example, Paul and Barnabas have different opinions about John Mark's service (Acts 15: 36–38). This contention becomes so sharp that they separate from each other. Paul goes with Silas and Barnabas with Mark (Acts 15:39–40). They reconcile later through the Spirit of Christ. In this way, they make God's reconciling presence tangible (1 Cor 9:6; Col 4:10).

Theological conviction about the sacramentality of the reconciled is strengthened when the reconciled person manifests signs of transformation. Generally, transformed individuals show signs linked to the Spirit's fruit, one of this book's themes in a later chapter. In other words, the converted, reconciled, and transformed are like Christ as they reflect him in word and deed. Let's explore further the claim that the transformed believers are sacraments of encountering the Spirit.

The Transformed as Sacraments of the Spirit

> . . . being transformed into the same image from one degree of glory to another; for this comes from the Lord, the Spirit.
>
> (2 COR 3:18)

Transformation herein is meant to be changed into the likeness of Christ in words and deeds. The Spirit transforms sinners into Christ-likeness and bearers of God's image (2 Cor 3:18; Eph 1:5). Transformation begins, but continues beyond, the moment one repents of sin and accepts the gift of salvation in Christ. The gift of the Spirit one receives at the moment of conversion enables the reborn to be continually transformed into Christ-likeness (John 14:17). The converts are justified at the moment of conversion (Rom 8:1; 2 Cor 5:17). However, transformation into Christ-likeness is a lifetime process. In other words, transformation intensifies as the reborn individuals to grow in their faith and knowledge of God.

Transformation is both an event and a process of "already or realized," or "not-yet or unrealized." Put another way, transformation occurs in the past (transformed), in the present-continuous (being transformed), and in the future (will be transformed) (1 John 3:2–3; 4:17). Though the Spirit indwells persons from the moment of conversion, it does not mean those persons do not struggle with old habits linked to a past life of sin. Seen in this light, noticeable differences between one's past life and the regenerate person's new life manifest the extent of one's transformation.

This visibility of transformation underscores one's sacramental character because it is the Spirit who transforms into Christ-likeness. To the extent that the reborn show distinct levels or degrees of transformation relative to Christ, they exhibit different levels or degrees of sacramental intensity. As temples of the divine, the reborn manifest the presence of the Spirit in words and deeds. Of course, the reborn do this in different, albeit related, ways and in varying degrees of sacramental intensity.

Transformed converts are temples of the Spirit inasmuch as they render Christ tangible (1 Cor 6:19). Transformed reborn individuals point to the reality of the Spirit. Specifically, their bodies are signs of the redemptive grace of the Spirit. When the reborn show signs of radical or marked changes in words and deeds, they manifest the Spirit's reality. But, transformed converts point toward the reality of the Spirit only in part. This does not trivialize the fact that the converts are a new creation (2 Cor 5:17). From the moment of conversion, the reborn serve as bearers of God's image as their lifestyles reflect Christ. As transformation takes time, one cannot be faulted for expressing skepticism about another's claim of conversion, especially without any noticeable marks of transformation.

For example, Ananias was right to express surprise when Jesus asked him to meet with Saul: "Lord, I have heard from many about this man, how much evil he has done to your saints in Jerusalem" (Acts 9:13). The disciples in Judea were also startled at Saul's testimony of conversion as Paul writes, "The one who formerly was persecuting us is now proclaiming the faith he once tried to destroy" (Gal 1:23). Paul's transformation persuaded others to believe he had indeed encountered Jesus by the Spirit.

The skepticism of other disciples about Saul's conversion seems justified given his past manner of life. It shows that the reborn render tangible the converting and transforming presence of God. The reborn function as embodied signs that point others to the reality of God's presence. The reborn person's ability to render God's presence tangible issues in the Spirit. Put another way, the Spirit of conversion, who is invisible by nature, finds concrete expression in and through the transformed converts.

In this way, the transformed believers can impart the grace of God's transforming presence by the Spirit. Transformed converts function as signs and means of grace. However, transformed converts are the means of convicting and transforming the Spirit's grace only by manifesting his presence. Transformed converts are means of grace of the Spirit in a derivative, not direct sense.

It is challenging to dismiss signs of a radical departure from a past lifestyle of sin. A concrete testimony of transformation authenticates one's conversion. Transformation attests to others that one has encountered the reality of God. Transformed converts delight in righteousness (1 John 3:9) and the fruit of repentance (Matt 3:8; Acts 26:20; 2 Cor 7:10). By bearing fruits of repentance, they function as sacraments of encountering the transforming Spirit. Transformation manifests renewal of the mind (Rom 12:2). Renewal of the mind is cerebral until it manifests concretely in words and deeds. An inward transformation that does not reflect in words and deeds renders a claim of conversion suspect (2 Cor 5:17). As the author of Hebrews admonishes:

> Therefore, let us go on toward perfection, leaving behind the basic teaching about Christ, and not laying again the foundation: repentance from dead works and faith toward God, instruction about baptisms, laying on of hands, resurrection of the dead, and eternal judgment. (Heb 6:1–2)

Of course, the most extraordinary transformation occurs when one repents of sin and is born again (2 Cor 5:17). The new person in Christ differs significantly from the former sinful person. Transformation increases with maturity. Transformed believers make God's cleansing presence tangible and are, thus, signs of grace. In this light, Christ is the transforming Man *par excellence*. Christ assumed the human body and was transformed to become like his brethren (Heb 2:17). It is by following

Christ that converts manifest their transformation as new creations (2 Cor 5:17). Transformed believers are identified by their Christ-likeness or God-pleasing lifestyle. The term "disciple" adequately captures this characterization of Christ-likeness or a God-pleasing lifestyle.

The Disciples as Sacraments of the Spirit

> So it was that for an entire year they met with the church and taught a great many people, and it was in Antioch that the disciples were first called "Christians."
>
> (ACTS 11:26)

It is not a coincidence that the first disciples to be called Christians were in Antioch. As both Saul and Barnabas were full of the Spirit and grounded in the Word, they took time to teach the Antioch disciples about Christ (Acts 11:24, 25; 13:9). Certainly, one would not be called a Christian unless there are marked signs that relate to his life in word and deed (John 8:31; 13:35; 15:8).

To be a disciple is not merely to follow someone. Instead, to be a disciple is to reflect or embody the life or values of the person you are following. Drawing from this, being a disciple of Jesus requires reflecting or embodying his teachings and values. Jesus alludes to this when he says that a student cannot be above his teacher (Matt 10:24–25; Luke 6:40). Jesus' disciples came from diverse communities and social-economic backgrounds. Nevertheless, Jesus challenged them to seek to reflect on his life. It is only by reflecting on the life of Jesus that they can be considered his disciples.

To the extent that they reflected his life, the disciples are sacraments of God's presence. By following Jesus, the disciples dramatically changed the course of their lives (Matt 19:27; Mark 10:28; Luke 18:28). For example, Levi, a tax collector, abandoned his financially rewarding but corrupt career to follow Jesus (Luke 5:27–32). Levi manifested to others the transforming Spirit. At Pentecost, the three thousand newly reborn confessed Jesus as Lord and Savior by the Spirit (Acts 2:38).

The three thousand baptized reborn at Pentecost are of historical significance as they manifested to others that they encountered the Spirit. These were added to the church and devoted themselves to the apostles' teachings, fellowship, breaking of bread, and communal prayer (Acts 2:42). The Great Commission emphasizes making disciples of Christ

(Matt 28:19). The disciples have confessed and repented from sin, turned to Jesus as their Lord and Savior, and committed to his teachings. Water baptism enables the baptized to publicly identify with the life, death, burial, and resurrection of Christ. Reborn individuals effectively identify themselves with Jesus by undergoing the rite of Water Baptism and being taught its biblical grounding.

Furthermore, the disciples at Antioch were the first to be called Christians (Acts 11:26). It is noteworthy that Barnabas and Saul taught them for a year. It seems reasonable to suggest that these teachings contributed to their growth into the likeness of Christ. By reflecting Christ, they enabled others to see them as followers of Jesus. The Antioch disciples are, therefore, signs of God's transforming grace. The Antioch disciples likely saw Barnabas and Saul as embodying the Spirit of Christ.

Specifically, Barnabas and Saul's teachings informed and shaped them as followers of Christ. The transformed disciples at Antioch likely persuaded others to refer to them as Christians. Seen in this light, these Antioch disciples are sacraments of God's presence as they rendered his presence tangible. It would make no difference if these were baptized in water or not. This is so because conversion occurs when one repents from sin through Christ.

The Regenerating Spirit and Believers' Death to Sin

> So you also must consider yourselves dead to
> sin and alive to God in Christ Jesus.
>
> (ROM 6:11)

The converted ones are those who have died to sin and made a commitment to live a life that is pleasing in God's sight. This does not mean that converts cannot sin, but rather that they crucify their flesh with its ungodly desires. This death to sin is signified by the rite of Water Baptism (Luke 23:39–43; Acts 2:38). As a post-conversion experience, Water Baptism allows converts to make a public commitment to eschew sinful lifestyle. As the baptized arise from baptismal waters, they signify that they have buried a past life of sin and are alive to righteousness in Jesus (Matt 10:33; Luke 12:9; Rom 10:9). Through Water Baptism, converts publicly identify with Jesus' death, burial, and resurrection (Rom 6:4; Col 2:12) in keeping with the Great Commission (Matt 28:19).

While conversion occurs in the heart, the Spirit concretely manifests his presence in and through the Christ-like lives of the baptized. It is through conversion that one dies to sin. If persons undergo the water-baptism rite without a conversion experience, they have not truly died to sin. Thus, the water-baptized are, personally, signs of God's redeeming grace only to the extent that they live in ways that show that they are dead to sin. Those that are dead to sin render God's presence tangible. Water baptism opens space for public testimony of death to sin.

Converts testify to others of their salvific encounter with God. By so doing, they render tangible God's converting presence. As such, testifying converts serve as signs of God's salvific grace. Pentecostals encourage public testimonies, especially about one's salvation. Importantly, Pentecostals insist that salvation is not esoteric or abstract but concrete with God's saving presence. In particular, those who claim to be saved are expected to manifest concrete or tangible signs of a salvific encounter with the Spirit.

Salvation is held as multidimensional in that it affects all aspects of one's life. To be sure, non-Pentecostals also expect believers to manifest signs of the grace of salvation. Salvation ought to reflect concretely in all areas of life such as the religious, moral, affective, intellectual, professional, vocational, etc. To the extent that the character of Christ reflects in these multidimensional aspects of one's life, such a person can be held as a sacrament of a personal encounter with God's salvific grace by the Spirit.

Reborn individuals show signs of salvific grace beyond worship contexts; they are sacraments of God's presence. As the primordial sacrament, Christ shapes this holistic sacramentality of the reborn; his life, death, resurrection, and ascension influence all areas of life. Sacramentality of the reborn reflects the Spirit's fluidity as one who cannot be domesticated or confined to ecclesial settings. Converts are unlike sacraments or rites administered or celebrated mostly in ecclesial settings. Contrariwise, the dead to sin manifest the Spirit wherever they interface with others. In other words, converts or the born again hold the world as their parish (Luke 9:6; Acts 8:4).[3]

Interestingly, the reborn, especially in Pentecostal church settings, commonly introduce themselves with phrases like: "Praise the Lord," "I'm born again," "I'm saved," "I'm heaven bound," "I'm sanctified," "I'm blessed," and "I'm highly favored." These are not to be held as religious

---

3. Martin, *Pentecostalism*.

clichés. Such phrases are intended to make concrete their salvific encounter with God in Christ by the Spirit. The utterance of such phrases enables believers to manifest God's saving grace. Sinners render God's grace of forgiveness tangible as they respond to the altar call of salvation.

Typically, sinners lift their hands when they stand at the altar to signify surrender to God. By lifting hands at the altar to receive Christ, one manifests a personal encounter with the Spirit. It is noteworthy that lifting hands at an altar does not in itself suggest that one has encountered the Spirit's saving grace. Likewise, those with a form of disability preventing them from raising hands or repeating words in prayer of salvation may nonetheless be genuinely saved. I discuss in-depth sacramentality of the suffering or disabled believers in a later chapter.

Pentecostals hold that people are saved the moment they repent from sin and turn to Christ for salvation. This can happen as one sits in or stands by pews without necessarily going to the altar. Physical gestures or acts may be a response to the Spirit's convicting presence, thus a lens that signifies an encounter with God in Christ. For example, standing by a church altar, lifting hands in prayer, or crying while sitting or standing by a pew may signify a personal encounter with God.

Stepping to an altar without conviction of sin by the Spirit leading to salvation is like descending into baptismal waters without conviction of sin by the Spirit, which does not magically translate to salvation. To be sure, there are diverse signs that signify an encounter with God's salvific grace. Of course, some signs may be overt while others are covert. For example, Zacchaeus, who committed to give up almost half of his wealth to the poor, is a clandestine (covert) sign of a personal encounter with God's saving grace (Luke 19:8).

Sacramentality of the reborn depends to no small extent on the ability of others to recognize or discern signs of a personal encounter with God's saving grace. Therefore, sacraments are not an end in and of themselves. Sacraments are signs that point to the reality of God. As sacraments, the converts are signs of God's forgiving grace as they point others to the reality of God's grace of forgiveness in Christ through the Spirit.

By making God's grace of forgiveness tangible, the reborn inspire others to seek God. By so doing, the reborn function as means of grace of God's forgiveness. The reborn in themselves do not save. Instead, they inspire others toward a relationship with Christ. As discussed earlier, to testify to salvation is to manifest God's saving grace. Testifying persons are human channels of the saving grace of God.

In this way, the story of one's salvation may inspire others to embody the same experience. When reborn persons testify about their conversion, they inspire others toward God and serve as "derivative" means of grace. This is not a magical cause of grace. The converts are means of grace only by manifesting signs of saving grace. When the reborn show signs of conversion, they render the Spirit tangible. Thus, the reborn manifest the Spirit's converting presence.

The Regenerating Spirit and Believers' Sanctification

But you were washed, you were sanctified, you were justified in the name of the Lord Jesus Christ and in the Spirit of our God.

(1 COR 6:11)

Water baptism symbolizes a person's bonding, or union, with Christ by the Spirit. This union with Christ in the Spirit is not possible without sanctification. Baptized believers make their sanctification visible in and through Water Baptism although this sanctification begins at the moment of conversion. Union with Christ implies sanctification by Christ and confirmed by the Spirit of God's indwelling presence. Precisely, as believers are immersed in baptismal water, they signify their bond in soul, body, and spirit with the death and burial of Jesus. As they emerge from baptismal waters, the baptized signify the bond of their soul, body, and spirit with the resurrection of Jesus. This bonding or union is in the same sense as the Three Persons of the Trinity's bonding.

Although there are different theological views about Water Baptism, most churches practice this rite. Sacramental churches hold Water Baptism as the beginning of salvation. Thus, Water Baptism and salvation are inseparably linked. Non-sacramental churches like Pentecostals conceive Water Baptism as a symbol of repentance. In other words, one must repent first and put faith in Christ before submitting to Water Baptism. Luke records several instances where faith in Christ precedes baptism (Acts 2:38; 8:8, 12; 16:31).

Pentecostals insist that Water Baptism merely symbolizes but does not initiate salvation. For Pentecostals, Water Baptism is an outward sign of an inward and spiritual grace. Given the notion of grace as God's personal presence, I posit that believers who submit to Water Baptism are signs of grace as they render God's converting presence tangible. It is in this sense that the water-baptized are sacraments of an encounter with the Spirit. Remember, sacraments manifest or disclose the divine. In this way, water-baptized individuals inspire others to encounter God as they manifest God's presence in Christ, which they encounter through the Spirit's conversion.

We can infer from this that Water Baptism creates space for baptized believers to publicly identify with the death, the burial, and the resurrection of Christ. In this way, the water-baptized testify about their personal encounters with God's salvific grace thus can draw others to encounter God. Among other things, the water-baptized are saved, in a covenantal relation, circumcised in heart, sanctified, and incorporated into the body of Christ by the Spirit.

At Pentecost, the disciples baptized their first converts after the ascension of Jesus. Thus, the baptized reborn were incorporated into the new community of believers. Their Water Baptism was a sign that they were cleansed from signs and were no longer under condemnation (Rom 8:1). To be sure, public identification with Christ, let alone Water Baptism in his name, was a huge risk that could dearly cost one their life.

The baptized are signs that point to the reality of God in Christ, who commissioned his disciples to preach the good news of salvation (Matt 28:19). It implies that the Spirit who drives the Great Commission is tangibly manifest in and through baptized disciples of Christ. The baptized publicly commit to following the teachings and life of Jesus. The baptized are signs of the willingness and readiness to die for Christ.

This thinking is firmly rooted in Christ, the baptized Man *par excellence*. His Water Baptism shows his willingness and readiness to die for God's redemptive mission (Matt 3:15). Baptized believers are means of grace inasmuch as their lives reflect Christ by the Spirit. Thus, Paul can say "imitate me as I imitate Christ" (1 Cor 11:1). This is partly what Paul means when he says that he died with Christ (Rom 6:8; Col 2:20; 3:3).

Baptized individuals are signs of martyrdom (Gal 2:20). The baptized are signs of a desire to lose one's life to gain Christ's life (Matt 10:39; 16:25; Mark 8:35; Luke 9:24; 17:33; John 12:25). The baptized leave their old life in the baptismal waters and arise with the newness of life in Christ. In this light, the three thousand baptized at Pentecost are sacramental in character (Acts 2:38).

Next, Water Baptism is a public event. Those who submit to Water Baptism make their conversion experience visible. Since the Spirit convicts a person to submit to Water Baptism, it is an act of grace. That is to say, it is a divinely initiated act to which the baptized individuals respond. This resonates with the principle that in every sacramental event, there is divine action and human response.

The divine action is by the Spirit who convicts individuals of sin and righteousness, whereas the human response is submission to Water Baptism. The baptized individual is a concrete sign who manifests God's grace of forgiveness. Put another way, the baptized provide concrete expression to the grace of God's forgiveness. Thus, the water-baptized are sacraments of an encounter with the grace of the Spirit of forgiveness in Christ.

The water-baptized Christ shows that God's grace of forgiveness is linked to his death, resurrection, and ascension by the Spirit. By submitting to Water Baptism, Christ invites all of humankind to follow his lead. The baptized manifest the death, resurrection, and ascension of Christ (Rom 6:4; Col 2:12). Notably, they are signs that Christ has taken away their sin by the Spirit. In this way, the baptized publicly and personally abandon their past life of sin and embrace new life in Christ by the Spirit (Acts 2:38; Eph. 4:22–24).

In this sense, the three thousand converts (Acts 2:41), the converted Saul (Acts 9:18), and the converted Cornelius (Acts 10:44–48) are sacraments of encounters with the Spirit. The Spirit imparts new life (John 3:1–8; Titus 3:5), confirms new status (Rom. 8:15–17), and incorporates believers into the universal family of God by the Spirit (1 Cor. 12:13). As believers mature, they show a radical break with their past life of sin. Such changes reflect in believers' words and deeds.

Further, Water Baptism reveals those who have died to the old life of sin and have risen to a new life of righteousness in Christ by the Spirit. The Greek word for Water Baptism is βαπτίζω, pronounced as *baptizein* or *baptize*, translated as "to dip under" or "immerse." Interestingly, this term was also used in ancient non-Christian literature to mean plunge, drench, sink into, or overwhelm. Some proponents of Water Baptism by immersion point to the biblical passage which states: "John also was baptizing at Aenon near Salim because water was abundant there; and people kept coming and were being baptized" (John 3:23). Notably, Water Baptism through sprinkling does not require much water. Consequently, this text supports Water Baptism by immersion.

Additionally, Jesus' baptism seems to support this view. For example, Mark writes, "And just as he was coming up out of the water . . ." (Mark 1:10). Proponents of the mode of baptizing through immersion observe that Jesus emerged from the waters, which rules out sprinkling.

Water baptism by immersion connects to the biblical idea of the believers dying and rising with Christ (Rom 6:3–5). The baptized are signs of the New Covenant in Christ by the Spirit. Water baptism by immersion requires one to be dipped into the waters just as the dead are buried in the ground. By this visible act of being immersed in water, the baptized believers make visible the reality of dying to sin, being buried in the ground, and being raised in righteousness by the Spirit of Christ.

Those who advocate Water Baptism by immersion generally reserve it for believers or the regenerated. They argue that conversion requires sinners to acknowledge their sins, repent, and profess faith in Christ. In other words, the faith in Christ which leads to repentance and salvation precedes Water Baptism. The requirement of belief or conversion before Water Baptism is seen in Acts 8:12; 18:8, and 19:1–7. Water baptism by immersion mirrors the death and the resurrection of Christ himself. In this sense, the Water Baptism by immersion seems to adequately picture the believers' death, burial, and resurrection with Christ through the power of the Spirit's presence.

Although believers inwardly identify with the life, death, and resurrection of Christ from the moment of repentance from sin (regeneration), Water Baptism by immersion allows them to identify with the death, burial, and resurrection of Christ outwardly (1 Cor 15:23). This justifies the theological view that the baptized Christ is the primordial sacrament of God's presence. By descending into and emerging from the Jordan River's waters, the baptized Christ makes the Spirit visible (Matt 3:16; Mar 1:10). Thus, Christ is the most concrete human site or sign of the Spirit's presence. That is to say, he manifests the Spirit in the most concrete way relative to others.

By descending into and emerging from baptismal waters, baptized individuals make the convicting and radically-transforming Spirit tangible. The people who step into baptismal waters signal to others that they have abandoned past life of sin and embraced new life of righteousness in Christ. As John required repentance and confession of sin from those that sought his baptism (Matt 3:2, 6), candidates for baptism outwardly demonstrate repentance and confession of sin. In the same way, Peter required repentance first and Water Baptism second, from three thousand individuals convicted at Pentecost by the Spirit (Acts 2:37–41). It implies that the baptized are themselves signs of spiritual change the Spirit produces (Matt 3:7; Luke 3:7). Further, baptized believers are themselves visible signs of the invisible Spirit of Christ who works from within.

Seen in this light, baptized persons are primary while the rite of baptism itself secondary. Those who descend into baptismal waters and emerge from them the same, without conversion, can not manifest the regenerating Spirit: "No one can enter the kingdom of God without being born of water and Spirit" (John 3:5). While some churches practice other forms of Water Baptism, such as sprinkling, biblical data seems to firmly endorse immersion. Besides, it fully preserves and accomplishes the meaning of Water Baptism (Rom 6:1–4). Water baptism by immersion captures believers' participation in the death, the burial, and the resurrection of Christ through the Spirit's power. Some who argue for Water Baptism by sprinkling often point to the text that speaks about God sprinkling water upon Israel's restored nation (Ezek 36:25).

Notwithstanding this, it seems unreasonable to suggest that believers baptized through sprinkling have a questionable salvific experience. Interestingly, church traditions that practice Water Baptism by immersion, like Pentecostals, often espouse the theological conviction of Water Baptism as a post-conversion or post-regeneration experience. Accordingly, they would likely be the last group to question those who claim to be saved, albeit they are not baptized or baptized through sprinkling. Even so, what is more significant is the *genuineness* of repentance and expression of faith in Christ in one's heart before than the outward expression of Water Baptism.

The Regenerating Spirit and Circumcised Believers

> Rather, a person is a Jew who is one inwardly, and real circumcision is a matter of the heart—it is spiritual and not literal.
>
> (ROM 2:29)

Paul relates Water Baptism to the circumcision of the heart by Christ (Col 2:11–12). In the Old Testament, the circumcised manifested that they were participants in God's covenant with Abraham (Gen 17:7, 10–11; 17:12, 23–27). God's covenant with Abraham preceded circumcision (Gen 12; 17). Thus, circumcision confirmed the covenant relationship with the God of Abraham. But God expected the circumcised to reflect the faithfulness of Abraham. The circumcised of the foreskin manifested God's presence only to the extent that their lives reflected Abraham's (John 8:39; Rom 4:12). Importantly, circumcision did not cause a relationship but signified it. To be sure, Abraham was declared to have faith in God, hence he was righteous, before he was circumcised (Rom 4:11).

In the same way, the Water Baptism confirms but does not cause one's faith in God. Put differently, Water Baptism reveals a person's faith rather than initiates a person's faith in God. A believer's faith finds concrete expression in and through participation in baptismal rite. It follows that baptized believers are concrete signs of a covenant relationship with God. Although female Jews, both adults and infants, were exempted from circumcision, they were nonetheless God's covenant children just as circumcised males were (adults and infants). In contrast to circumcision of foreskin, circumcision of heart is egalitarian, as it includes male and female as God's covenant children. God who sees the heart (1 Sam 16:7) validates one's inward circumcision.

Seen in this light, inward circumcision of the heart precedes outward circumcision of the foreskin as the latter only confirms the former. Outward circumcision without inward circumcision is less pleasing to God than inward circumcision without outward circumcision. Therefore, Paul rightly shows, "For neither circumcision nor uncircumcision is anything; but a new creation is everything!" (Gal 6:15). The outward circumcision presupposes the inward circumcision. The rite of Water Baptism (outward) presupposes regeneration or conversion of heart (inward).

As cutting off one's foreskin manifests taking away of sin, Water Baptism manifests the washing away of one's sin (Deut 10:16; 30:6; Jer 4:4; 9:25–26; Ezek 44:7,9; Acts 2:38). Because circumcision involves hidden parts of the body (foreskin and heart), the life of the circumcised is what indeed identifies him or her as a child of God. Christ replaced circumcision of the foreskin (flesh) with spiritual circumcision (Col 2:11–12). As Paul notes, "a person is a Jew who is one inwardly, and real circumcision is a matter of the heart—it is spiritual and not literal" (Rom 2:29). The Old Testament circumcision of the flesh identifies one, at least outwardly, as Jewish.

Notwithstanding this, faithful Jews are neither circumcised nor baptized outwardly but are inwardly circumcised or converted. The inwardly circumcised believers are heirs of God and joint-heirs with Christ by the Spirit (Rom 8:17). By the inward circumcision of the heart, God extends the covenant with Abraham and Jews to Gentiles through Christ in the Spirit (Acts 2:39; Rom 4:13–18; Gal 3:13–18; Heb 6:13–18). Thus, baptism conceived as circumcision bolsters the claim that the circumcised are sacraments of a personal encounter with God. As circumcision is a personal experience, Water Baptism is also a personal experience. One cannot be circumcised on another's behalf in the same way that one cannot be baptized on another's behalf.

The Regenerating Spirit and Sanctified Believers

> How much worse punishment do you think will be deserved by those who have spurned the Son of God, profaned the blood of the covenant by which they were sanctified, and outraged the Spirit of grace?

(HEB 10:29)

The person circumcised was deemed cleansed or sanctified (Col 2:11). As circumcision involves the shedding of blood, it pointed to the sanctification of believers through Christ's blood (Heb 9:10; 10:29). No one could claim sanctification through another person's circumcision. Likewise, baptized persons are deemed sanctified. More appropriately, they embody God's sanctification. In this sense, the baptized are concrete signs of God's cleansing grace. The cleansing of sinners is by grace, as it results from God's initiative as one repents and puts faith in Christ (Heb 10:10).

The Bible speaks of being sanctified by the blood of the covenant in Christ. Precisely, one is sanctified because of Christ's shed blood. Christ's blood is not sprinkled upon a sinner but is spiritually applied. It is similar to being sanctified through the Water Baptism. For example, Paul clarifies baptism as sanctification (1 Cor 10:1) when he relates it to the Israelites' Red Sea crossing. Precisely, it signifies sanctifying or setting the Israelites apart from the Egyptians (Exod 14:21–31). By crossing over the Red Sea, God manifested the Israelites as people set apart for His glory.

To be sure, this was not the first time that God distinguished the Israelites from the Egyptians (Exod 11:7). Specifically, baptism reveals those who the Spirit sanctifies through faith in Christ (Acts 26:18). In other words, sanctification begins when a person repents of sin and accepts Jesus as Lord and Savior (John 17:16–19; Acts 26:18; Rom 15:16). The Bible often describes the Spirit as water, commonly used for washing, cleansing, purifying, etc. (Isaiah 44:3; John 4:14; 7:37–39; 1 Cor 12:13).

Consequently, baptism symbolizes sanctification or purification from sin. Sanctification begins from the moment sinners are reborn, and the Spirit indwells them. Water-baptized persons signify to others that the Spirit is sanctifying them. This is precisely why the Spirit relates to believers' sanctification (Rom 15:16; Acts 26:28; 1 Cor 6:11). It is noteworthy that teachings contribute to believers' sanctification (John 17:19; Acts 20:32).

The sanctification of believers occurs by the self-giving act of God in Christ through the Spirit. Remarkably, the use of water in baptism manifests grace in that water is God's creation. It is God who created water used in baptism; hence sanctification is an act of grace. The baptized signify to others that they have encountered the Spirit's sanctifying presence via Water Baptism. Also, the use of water created before humankind (Adam and Eve) in believers' baptism signals to others that the baptized are brought back to God's primordial relation, as before the fall. In other words, the baptized signify God's desire to save the lost. In this sense, the baptized thus provide a concrete manifestation of the presence of the lost-seeking God.

If Water Baptism symbolizes the converts' cleansing, then the baptized are, in their persons, signs that reveal God's desire to cleanse lost humanity. Right from the fall of Adam and Eve in the Garden of Eden, God sought them out as they hid in the bushes covered in leaves (Gen 3:7–8). The merciful God clothed them with animal skin as an embryonic act of sanctification at his own initiative (Gen 3:21). Notably, God clothed them with animal skin despite their disobedient act. It was not a coincidence that he clothed them after pronouncing "curses," as this enabled them to know how much they had fallen from grace.

It is only in God's presence that sinners derive their righteousness (2 Cor 5:21). Seen in this light, baptized believers are sanctified and render tangible the Spirit's sanctifying presence through Christ. During baptism, baptized believers mediate and inspire others to encounter God. Water-baptized believers make visible their incorporation into the body of Christ by the Spirit.

The Incorporated as Sacraments of the Spirit

> For in the one Spirit we were all baptized into one body—Jews or Greeks, slaves or free.
>
> (1 COR 12:13)

When people are born again, they are baptized into the body of Christ (1 Cor 12:13). That is to say, converts are incorporated into the body of Christ (2 Cor 5:17). The ecclesial rite of the Water Baptism symbolizes this spiritual incorporation. Put more succinctly, those incorporated into the body of Christ are revealed through the rite of Water Baptism (Rom 6:3; Gal 3:27). The moment people are born again; they are incorporated into the body of Christ by the Spirit.

People do not have to undergo the rite of Water Baptism before they are incorporated into the body of Christ. It is conversion following faith and repentance that leads to incorporation into the body of Christ and not the rite of Water Baptism by itself. When people are saved, they are immediately incorporated into the family of God in Christ through the act of the Spirit (John 1:12; Gal 3:26).

"Adoption" is another biblical term that bolsters the notion of incorporation into the body of Christ as God's family. Water baptism depicts this adoption or incorporation. At the least, the baptized believer is depicted as incorporated into God's family through the instrumentality of the one who baptizes the person. It is noteworthy that no one self-baptizes. Put another way, no one can baptize himself or herself. Typically, church officials baptize and welcome the reborn into a church family by extending the fellowship's right hand. In this sense, the baptized themselves are signs of the grace of incorporation into the body of Christ. Notably, those who are the water-baptized are sacraments of the indwelling Spirit.

At Pentecost, the three thousand reborn were incorporated into the body of Christ, signified by their baptism (Acts 2:41). Since no one can call Jesus Lord except by the Spirit (1 Cor 12:3), these three thousand reborn function as signs of the grace of God's incorporating presence. By submitting to the rite of Water Baptism, the three thousand reborn signified to others they had personally encountered the presence of the Spirit working in and through them (Gal 2:20). The question that arises is the relation of Water Baptism to conversion. It appears that the three thousand accepted Christ before they were baptized in water (Acts 2:41).

Similarly, the thief crucified along with Jesus was reborn apart from Water Baptism. This does not negate the significance of Water Baptism. In fact, Luke records several instances of baptizing the reborn in the early church at Pentecost (Acts 2:41), in Samaria (Acts 8:12), the Ethiopian eunuch (Acts 8:38), Paul (Acts 9:18), Lydia (Acts 16:15), the Philippian jailer (Acts 16:33), in Corinth (Acts 18:8), and in Ephesus (Acts 19:5). Proponents of Water Baptism of believers insist that this ritual is rooted in unambiguous teaching of Scripture. Precisely, they argue that infant baptism is based upon available evidence of biblical narratives about baptizing households (Acts 10:47–48; 16:15; 18:8; 1 Cor 1:16).

Those that hold Water Baptism as a means of grace that affects or facilitates salvation point to biblical passages like: "The one who believes and is baptized will be saved; but the one who does not believe will be condemned" (Mark 16:16). While the first part of the verse links belief to Water Baptism, the second part does not. Precisely, it merely says that persons who do not believe are condemned. The condemnation arises due to the absence or lack of belief, not of being baptized. Those who are exegetically sensitive would also argue that verses 9–20 of Mark 16 do not appear in most original manuscripts.

Also, they point to Nicodemus' discussion with Christ as linking conversion to the rite of Water Baptism. Though Christ indeed speaks of being born of water and Spirit in the same breath as being born again (John 3:5), he does not do so in the next verse: "What is born of the flesh is flesh, and what is born of the Spirit is spirit" (John 3:6). Christ stresses being born of the Spirit, which is difficult for Nicodemus to grasp (John 3:4, 9).

The new birth experience is not esoteric. Christ concretizes being born of the Spirit by pointing to water, to which Nicodemus can relate. Besides, one cannot sincerely seek Water Baptism unless the Spirit convicts him/her. The desire to be baptized makes visible the Spirit of God's convicting and converting presence. This experience precedes the rite of Water Baptism.

Another appealing passage is by Peter, who tells those convicted by the Spirit following his preaching, "Repent, and be baptized every one of you in the name of Jesus Christ so that your sins may be forgiven; and you will receive the gift of the Holy Spirit" (Acts 2:38). Though Peter mentions repentance and Water Baptism in the same breath, he does so after he has ministered the Word to the multitudes. Further, the Spirit poured out at Pentecost inspired Peter's sermon.

Notably, the Spirit also engenders the Word, "because no prophecy ever came by human will, but men and women moved by the Holy Spirit spoke from God" (1 Pet 2:21). In keeping with this, it is worth pointing out that Peter's sermon is about interpreting Joel's prophecy (Joel 2:28–29; Acts 2:16–20). Drawing from this, it is inadequate to say that one is saved through Water Baptism. In fact, the three thousand souls saved and baptized following Peter's sermon cannot be separated from the Spirit poured upon the disciples (Acts 2:41).

In sacramental terms, the three thousand souls saved and baptized are signs that make the Spirit poured out visibly present. It is inadequate to say that the Water Baptism is a sacrament. Instead, the water-baptized are sacraments as they render tangible God's cleansing presence. The Water Baptism only confirms one's cleansing encounter with God but does not initiate it. Conversion is an inward encounter with God that finds concrete expression in Water Baptism. Typically, converts express the new birth experience when they step forward in response to the altar call of salvation. Conversion engenders one as a host of God's presence (John 14:17).

In contrast, the Ethiopian eunuch makes visible God's converting presence as he asks Phillip to baptize him in water (Acts 8:36). These are signs of the grace of the converting Spirit. Conversion enables individuals to receive the Spirit (John 1:12; 3:5–7; Acts 2:38). Often, believers signify conversion by submitting to Water Baptism. The relation of the sacramentality of believers to Water Baptism finds particular significance in the water-baptized Christ.

It is because of the sin of all humanity laid upon Christ that leads him to John's baptism (2 Cor 5:21; 1 Peter 2:22, 24; 1 John 3:5). Thus, Christ shows that all humanity needs cleansing. Others seeking cleansing through John's baptism are rightly convicted of sin. By submitting to John's baptism, Christ reveals his desire to sanctify all sinners (Matt 3:13; Mark 1:9; Luke 3:21; John 1:29–34; Acts 1:22). Notably, John introduces Christ as the Lamb of God who takes away the sin of the world (John 1:29). John acknowledges that his baptism which symbolized washing of sin finds fulfillment in Jesus. It is Jesus who takes away the sin of humanity, not water. In this light, Jesus fits the theological view of the primordial sacrament of God's sanctifying presence.

Drawing from this, water-baptized believers are those from whom the Lamb of God has taken their sin away. When the Spirit convicts the sinners upon hearing the gospel, and they turn to Christ for forgiveness, God declares them righteous immediately (2 Cor 5:21). Water Baptism only concretizes God's declaration of righteousness. When believers step into baptismal waters, Christ welcomes them as those un-condemned. This partly explains why the Ethiopian eunuch asks Phillip, "Look, here is water! What is to prevent me from being baptized?" (Acts 8:36). Water-baptized believers are concrete signs of grace as they provide concrete expression to God's sanctifying presence in Christ. In other words, they make visible God's invisible grace of cleansing. In this way, the Water-baptized believers are concrete signs of God's sanctifying presence. Water-baptized believers can inspire others to submit to Water Baptism to make their encounter with Christ's cleansing presence visible. As such, water-baptized believers are human sites or signs of God's sanctifying grace. Notably, they are sacraments of a personal encounter with God's sanctifying grace by the Spirit of Christ.

Further, the baptized are sanctified to be incorporated into the family of God. The baptismal rite allows believers to confess Christ as their Lord and Savior publicly and identify with his death and resurrection (Rom 6:4; Col 2:12). Further, baptized believers manifest their abandonment of past life of sin (darkness) and embrace of new life (light) (Acts 2:38; Eph 4:22–24). In this sense, each of the three thousand reborn at Pentecost (Acts 2:41), Saul (Acts 9:18), and Cornelius (Acts 10:44–48) are sacraments of encounter with the Spirit.

The Spirit imparts new life into the believer (John 3:1–8; Titus 3:5). It confirms to the believer of the new status as God's child and joint-heir with Christ (Rom 8:15–17) and incorporates the believer into the universal family of God by the Spirit (1 Cor 12:13) etc. As believers grow in the knowledge and the likeness of Christ, they exhibit a radical break with a sinful past life. Believers' inspiring words and deeds are windows to discern a radical break with the past life. Furthermore, this radical break with a sinful past life points to the work of the indwelling Spirit.

Reborn individuals receive the gift of the Spirit (John 1:12; 3:5–7; Acts 2:38). This conversion occurs when one confesses with the mouth and believes in their heart that God raised Christ from the dead (Rom 10:9–13). In this way, conversion allows believers to host the Spirit (John 14:17). The converts are as signs of God's saving presence by the Spirit. The Spirit becomes visible as people respond to an invitation to receive Christ as their Lord and Savior.

Salvation occurs when one is convicted of sin by the Spirit (John 16:8). As the conviction of sin occurs within one's heart, it only becomes apparent to others when it finds concrete expression (Jas 2:9). When one is convicted of sin by the Spirit and turns to Christ for repentance and forgiveness, that person is born again (John 3:6, 8).

As noted, salvation begins when one confesses Christ with mouth and believes in the heart that God raised him from the dead (Rom 10:9–13). For example, Zacchaeus tells Christ that he would give up to half of his wealth to the poor (Luke 19: 8–9). In this way, Zacchaeus shows he is repentant. Comparing Zacchaeus to the rich young ruler, the former gladly decides to pay back four times those he cheated and also the poor, while the rich young ruler is sad when Jesus tell him to share his wealth with the poor to inherit eternal life (Matt 19:16-22; Mark 10:17-22; Luke 18:18-23). Zacchaeus is a sign of the grace of God's forgiveness.

Conviction of sin is the foundation of the sacramentality of believers. It is possible for one to be convicted of sin but remain unrepentant. Indeed, not all people who heard Jesus teach or preach were reborn (Matt 11:21; 13:57–58; 28:17; Mark 6:4–6; Luke 10:13; John 8:8–11).

Another way to stress the sacramentality of the baptized is to think about those baptized in anti-Christian societies. Precisely, those who are baptized in public risk persecution or death. Therefore, the baptized in anti-Christian communities signify to others that they have indeed encountered the Spirit's converting presence in Christ. Seen in this light, the baptized in anti-Christian societies render visible God's consoling presence. Hence, the baptized believers in such anti-Christian faith communities merit as sacraments of a personal encounter with Christ. The experience of Spirit baptism empowers believers to act boldly even in hostile circumstances.

CHAPTER 3

Manifesting the Empowering Spirit
Charismatic Believers

> But you will receive power when the Holy Spirit has come upon you . . .
>
> (ACTS 1:8)

THIS CHAPTER USES THE term "charismatic" to refer to believers empowered by the Spirit's overwhelming presence. Such believers show outward signs of grace. Here, I limit my focus to diverse spiritual gifts or charismata as outward signs of the Spirit's empowering presence. Before his ascension, Christ instructed his disciples to await the Spirit's empowerment (Luke 24:49–51; Acts 1:8). Among other things, the empowering Spirit would render them effective witnesses to the Great Commission (Matt 28:18–20).

The empowering Spirit finds full manifestation in and through Christ. Thus, Christ is the Spirit-empowered or the charismatic Man *par excellence*. Consequently, Christ is also the spiritual-gifted Man *par excellence*. When Christ manifested the empowering Spirit, he drew or inspired people toward personal encounters with God. The empowered Christ is the primordial sacrament of the personal encounter with the Spirit's presence. Similarly, the Spirit-empowered believers render the ascended Jesus tangible to others. In this way, the Spirit-empowered believers are concrete signs of God's presence in Christ. By manifesting God's empowering presence, they witness the redemptive mission of Christ.

Thus, they fit as sacraments of the Spirit of Christ. Spirit empowerment is characterized by concrete, tangible, visible, discernible, or outward signs.

The descent of the Holy Spirit at Pentecost was characterized by tangible phenomena that included wind, tongues of fire, and tongues-speech (Acts 2). Apart from speaking in tongues, all these phenomena occurred or happened outside the bodies of the disciples. In other words, these pneumatic signs were exteriorized rather than internalized or esoteric. Seen in this light, it seems theologically plausible to conceive the Pentecost disciples as signs of grace. Put directly, these empowered disciples are sacraments of a personal encounter with the Spirit's presence in Christ.

Pentecost inaugurated the disciples and subsequent believers as sacraments of the Spirit. Sacramentality of the empowered resonates with the biblical notion of being clothed with power from on high (Luke 24:49). To be clothed with power from on high is to be empowered by the Spirit (Acts 1:8). Since people can tell whether one has put on clothes or not, the idea of being clothed with power hints that others can also tell if a believer is Spirit-empowered. The term which adequately captures this experience of being clothed with the power from on high is "Spirit baptism," or baptism in/of/with the Spirit. As the Father sent the Son in the power of the Spirit on a redemptive mission (Matt 3:16; Mark 1:10; Luke 3:22; John 1:32), the Son sends believers in the power of the Spirit (Matt 28:18–20; Luke 24:49; Acts 1:8; 2:1–4).

At Pentecost, the Spirit endued the 120 disciples with power. They revealed the Spirit's power in their service to both believers and unbelievers. Believers manifest the Spirit in words and deeds, or in charismata and character. In this way, believers mirror Christ, who fully revealed God's empowerment (Matt 11:21–23; Mark 6:2, 14; Luke 10:13; 24:19; Acts 10:38). He shapes the view that empowered believers are sacraments of the Spirit. Empowered believers effectively witness to Christ's mission through the Spirit (Matt 28:18–20; Luke 24:49; Acts 1:8; 2:1–4).

Scholars describe Spirit-empowerment differently. For example, Macchia links it to Spirit baptism, held as a divine act that draws believers into God's charismatic enrichment presence, resulting in renewed power.[1] Some conceive it as an experience of "new birth, sanctification, empowerment for witness, and giftedness."[2] Others insist that Spirit baptism encompasses the saving, sanctifying, and empowering aspects of

---

1. Macchia, *Baptized in the Spirit*, 258.
2. Brand et al, *Perspectives on Spirit Baptism*, 118.

the Spirit.³ Notwithstanding this, scholars agree that the believers experience spiritual empowerment owing to the Spirit's indwelling presence. The Bible uses different phrases to speak about believers' experience of the empowering Spirit.

Next, Spirit empowerment is implied in biblical phrases such as "baptized in the Spirit" (Acts 1:5; 11:16); the Spirit "comes upon" (Acts 1:8; 19:6); believers are "filled with the Spirit" (Acts 2:4); the Spirit is "poured out" (Acts 2:17, 18, 33; 10:45); believers "receive the Spirit" (Acts 2:38; 8:15, 17, 19; 10:47; 19:2); the Spirit is "given" (Acts 8:18; 11:17); and the Spirit "falls upon" (Acts 8:16; 10:44; 11:15). Such descriptions suggest tangible encounters with the Spirit of God's presence. Stronstad sees parallels between the Old and New Testament experiences of the Spirit affecting prophetic and charismatic activities.⁴ In short, regardless of how one defines Spirit baptism, it links to tangible effects in the life of believers.

For the purpose of this book, Spirit empowerment in general, and the Spirit baptism in particular, enhances the sacramentality of believers, and empowers, indwells, baptizes, fills, comes, or falls upon them for service. Schillebeeckx posits that "The *pneuma* or the Spirit, as the fullness of power in the messianic mission, becomes visible in the acts of those who have been confirmed."⁵ Schillebeeckx relates Spirit baptism to the Sacrament of Confirmation in Roman Catholicism aimed at empowering and endowing believers with charismatic grace or gifts.

Based upon this understanding, the empowered believers are sacraments of encountering the Spirit. They manifest signs of grace of the Spirit and thereby render God's presence tangible. In keeping with this, Dunn states: "The baptism in the Spirit, as always, is primarily initiatory, and only secondarily an empowering."⁶ On his part, Hemphill adds that "Pentecost marks the beginning and the empowering of the New Testament church. It marks a unique transformation in the lives of the members of the early church."⁷ Pentecost engenders high-voltage Christianity of bold witnesses and supernatural church growth.⁸ Also, it is "a deep and a personal experience in which the regenerated and sanctified

---

3. Keener, *Gift & Giver*, 143–46, 151, 159; Menzies and Menzies, *Spirit and Power*, 201–2.

4. Stronstad, *Prophethood of All Believers*, 16.

5. Schillebeeckx, *Christ, the Sacrament of the Encounter with God*, 165.

6. Dunn, *Baptism in the Holy Spirit*, 54.

7. Hemphill, *Antioch Effect*, 27–28.

8. Hemphill, *Antioch Effect*, 27–28.

believer receives in an unprecedented encounter with the Spirit empowerment for the Christian life."[9] However, Spirit baptism or Spirit empowerment is simultaneously believers' personal encounter with the Father and the Son, or simply the Trinity.

The Spirit Baptism as Encountering the Trinity

> And when Jesus had been baptized, just as he came up from the water, suddenly the heavens were opened to him and he saw the Spirit of God descending like a dove and alighting on him.
>
> (MATT 3:16)

God the Father, God the Son, and God the Spirit were all involved at Jesus' Pentecost (Matt 3:16; Mark 1:10; Luke 3:22; John 1:32, 33). The Pentecost experience of the disciples also involved the Triune God. Spirit baptism is not an experience of the Spirit only but the Trinitarian community. The Spirit-baptized encounter the Father, the Son, and the Spirit. A Trinitarian view of the Spirit's baptism resonates with empowered believers' sacramentality based upon Christ's prayer to the Father to send the Spirit to his disciples (John 14:26). The four Gospels portray this Trinitarian picture as the Father sends the Spirit upon the Son at the Jordan (Matt 3:16; Mark 1:10; Luke 3:22; John 1:32).

To be sure, the empowering presence of God is entirely tangible in and through the Spirit-baptized Christ. The Spirit's manifestation glorifies the charismatic Christ (John 16:14). Christ is the primordial site or sign of the Spirit's empowering presence (Col 2:9). Likewise, empowered believers as charismatic believers function as signs of the grace of the Spirit's empowering presence. Empowered believers point to the reality of the Spirit and render him tangible to others. Through Spirit manifestation, empowered believers facilitate fresh encounters with God's presence.

When the Spirit's empowering presence becomes tangible in and through believers, they function as means of grace. Turner says that "the Spirit is the self-manifesting and empowering presence of both the Father and the Son."[10] It is noteworthy that the Spirit self-manifests this empowering presence of the Father and the Son in and through believers. Thus, Spirit baptism implies that the empowered take part in the Spirit's

---

9. Vondey, *Pentecostal Theology*, 84.
10. Turner, *Holy Spirit*, 170.

empowering presence. Precisely, Christ-like words and deeds of the empowered attest that they experience the Spirit's empowering presence.

The Spirit primarily acts in and through empowered believers. In this way, empowered believers reveal, mediate, and inspire others to personal encounter with God. Seen in this light, empowered believers are Spirit-baptized, Spirit-filled, Spirit-gifted, or simply Spirit-empowered.

The Believer and the Empowering Spirit

> . . . filled with the Holy Spirit and spoke
> the word of God with boldness.
>
> (ACTS 4:31)

It is noteworthy that Jesus is the baptizer in or with the Spirit (Matt 3:16; Mark 1:8; Luke 3:16). However, Jesus was himself Spirit-baptized (Matt 3:16; Mark 1:10; Luke 3:22; John 1:32). His Spirit baptism pointed to the descent of the Spirit upon all believers beginning at Pentecost. The theme of Spirit baptism is a critical theological theme especially in Pentecostalism.[11] To be sure, there is no universally agreed-upon definition of the Pentecostal experience of baptism in or with the Spirit even in global Pentecostalism. Unlike the *Magisterium*, the teaching office of Roman Catholicism, Pentecostals have no such office for clarifying their theological positions.

Notwithstanding this, Pentecostals hold Spirit baptism as distinct and subsequent to the new birth experience (Acts 8:12–17; 10:44–46; 11:14–16; 15:7–9). The Old Testament invokes this image when blood and oil are applied to symbolize cleansing (Lev 14:14, 17). Likewise, believers are cleansed through shed blood at Calvary after repenting and professing faith in Christ (Heb 9:22). Only after this primordial cleansing are believers anointed with oil (the Holy Spirit) in the same sense as prophets, kings, and priests (2 Cor 1:21; 1 John 2:20).

For this reason, following his death on the Cross, Jesus instructs his disciples who are cleansed to wait for the anointing or the empowerment of the Spirit. Pentecostals link Spirit baptism to empowerment and bestowal of spiritual gifts for ministry work (Luke 24:49; Acts 1:4, 8; 1 Cor 12:1–31). Spirit baptism is normative for all believers, both Jews and Gentiles, men and women. Pentecostals hold Spirit baptism as analogous

---

11. Macchia, *Baptized in the Spirit*.

to Water Baptism practiced by immersion.[12] Specifically, believers come to Christ to be baptized in the river of the Spirit just as water surrounds water-baptized individuals. Thus, believers are immersed in the river of the Spirit as they are immersed in rivers of natural waters. The laying on of hands for baptism in the Spirit typically symbolizes immersing one in the Spirit.

Pentecostals hold Spirit baptism as "a deep, personal experience in which the regenerated and sanctified believer receives in an unprecedented encounter with the Spirit empowerment for the Christian life."[13] The empowerment motif is critical for the Pentecostal view of baptism in the Spirit as "the sound of a mighty wind suggests conveying power upon the disciples for service."[14] Spirit baptism unleashes a new dimension of power that grants believers extraordinary power for service.[15]

Pentecostals often use terms such as "Spirit-filled," "Spirit-endowed," "possessed by the Spirit," and "investiture with the Spirit" about Spirit baptism.[16] As in Water Baptism, the church is the agent, water is the element, and the water-baptized individual is the object; in Spirit baptism, Christ is the agent, the Spirit is the element, and the Spirit-baptized person is the object.[17] The Spirit's dynamic presence links to the power of God being active in the lives of believers.[18]

Spirit baptism can thus be summarized as "a post-regeneration, visible, outward, and miraculous manifestation of the Spirit."[19] Pentecostals recognize that conversion and Spirit baptism is sometimes synchronized.[20] The Bible uses different phrases to speak about the experience of Spirit baptism. Spirit baptism is implied in the same verses that refer to Spirit empowerment.

Though Spirit baptism is a one-time event, Spirit infilling is continuous. The disciples were Spirit-baptized at Pentecost and were later Spirit-filled (Acts 2:1–4; 4:31). The purpose of Spirit baptism is to empower

12. Kay, *Pentecostalism*, 232.
13. Vondey, *Pentecostal Theology*, 84.
14. Horton, *What the Bible Says*, 140.
15. Menzies and Menzies, *Spirit and Power*, 104.
16. Burgess and van der Maas, *New International Dictionary*, "Baptism in the Holy Spirit," 356.
17. Du Plessis, *Spirit Bade Me Go*, 30.
18. Menzies and Menzies, *Spirit and Power*, 171.
19. Mittelstadt, *Reading Luke-Acts*, 72.
20. Kay, *Pentecostalism*, 233.

believers to be effective witnesses to Christ. Jesus, the Spirit baptizer,[21] told the disciples to wait in Jerusalem for their Spirit empowerment (Luke 24:49–51; Acts 1:8).

The descent of the Spirit at Pentecost was characterized by tangible phenomena, including a mighty rushing wind, tongues of fire, and speaking in tongues (Acts 2:1–4). Luke states that on each of the disciples sat tongues of fire (Acts 2:3), and they were each filled with the Spirit and spoke in tongues (Acts 2:4). The Spirit caused the disciples to manifest his presence in and through their bodies. Seen in this light, each of the 120 disciples became a concrete site or sign of the grace of the Spirit's empowering presence through Christ the Spirit baptizer.

Sacramentality of Spirit-baptized believers mirrors the motif of being clothed with power from on high (Luke 24:49). To be clothed with power is to be endued with the Spirit (Acts 1:8). Just like Jesus was clothed with the power from on high by the Spirit upon him at the Jordan (Matt 3:16; Mark 1:10; Luke 3:22; John 1:32), the disciples were clothed with power from on high by the Spirit at Pentecost (Matt 28:18–20; Luke 24:49; Acts 1:8; Acts 2:1–4).

Likewise, Spirit-baptized believers are clothed with power from on high. As the Spirit-empowered Man *par excellence*, Christ shapes Spirit-baptized believers (Matt 11:21–23; Mark 6:2, 14; Luke 10:13; 24:19). Through Spirit baptism, Jesus manifested God's power in words and deeds (Acts 10:38).

The Disciples and the Empowering Spirit

> With great power the apostles gave their testimony to the resurrection.
>
> (ACTS 4:33)

Holy Spirit empowerment is meant for effective witness to Christ and centers upon his resurrection (Acts 1:8; 4:33). Pentecostals and Charismatics generally agree that speaking in tongues is a biblical sign of Spirit baptism or empowerment. However, little is known about the sacramentality of Spirit-empowered believers. On his part, Macchia postulates that "Pentecostals regard tongues as a kind of primary sacrament or Kairos event that signifies, while participating in, the empowerment of the

---

21. Macchia, *Jesus the Spirit Baptizer*.

Spirit in the Christian life."[22] Menzies also holds tongues-speaking as a Pentecostal sacrament.[23] But I argue that it is less accurate to conceive tongues-speaking itself as a sacrament. It is relatively accurate to conceive the believers who speak in tongues as sacraments. This is so because tongues-speaking believers encounter the Spirit within their total being rather than merely in the vocal parts of their bodies.

Spirit baptism is a direct and intense encounter with God's empowering presence. Therefore, believers are human agents for manifesting the tangible presence of the Spirit. In this light, Spirit empowerment and Spirit manifestations linked to Spirit baptism can help explore believers' sacramentality. As Horton postulates, "the sound of a mighty wind suggests conveying power upon the disciples for service."[24] However, there is no Spirit baptism without the direct activity of Christ.[25]

Generally, Spirit baptism is an experience of Christ distinct from regeneration or conversion.[26] Menzies asserts that Spirit baptism unleashes a new dimension of the Spirit's power, granting a believer power for service.[27] Williams relates Spirit baptism to Water Baptism in that one is submerged within the reality of Christ, engendering a vivid sense of the Spirit's power.[28]

Du Plessis states that in Water Baptism, the church is the agent, the water is the element, and the new Christian is the object. Regarding Spirit baptism, Christ is the agent, the Spirit is the element, and a believer is the object.[29] Thus, the power motif features heavily in a Pentecostal view of Spirit baptism. This dynamic presence and power of God are active in the lives of believers.[30] This partly explains why Pentecostals relate speaking in tongues to Spirit baptism. This is unsurprising given the role of Lukan pneumatology in Pentecostal theology and spirituality.

22. See Macchia, "Tongues as a Sign," 69.

23. Menzies, *Speaking in Tongues*, 157–58.

24. Horton, *What the Bible Says*, 140.

25. Burgess and van der Maas, *New International Dictionary*, "Baptism in the Holy Spirit," 356.

26. Macchia, *Baptized in the Spirit*, 20; Atkinson, *Baptism in the Spirit*, 3; Hunter, *Spirit–Baptism*, 227–31.

27. Menzies and Menzies, *Spirit and Power*, 104.

28. Burgess and van der Maas, *New International Dictionary*, "Baptism in the Holy Spirit," 353–63.

29. Du Plessis, *Spirit Bade Me Go*, 30.

30. Menzies and Menzies, *Spirit and Power*, 171.

The experience of Spirit baptism by the disciples at Pentecost and by Cornelius and his household fulfilled Joel's prophecy (Joel 2:28–29; Acts 2:16), In both instances, those baptized spoke in tongues. Notably, the Gentiles' ability to speak in tongues also demonstrates God's love. Moreover, their tongues-speech was an expression of worship and intimacy with the Spirit of God's presence in Christ.[31]

The Gentiles' experience, previously thought of as a privilege of Jews only, suggests an intimacy with God. The Gentiles' experience of the Spirit is *mystērion* or a mystery because this was previously thought to be an exclusive privilege of Jewish believers (Acts 10: 45, 47). This is why the tongues-speaking Gentiles are sacramental in character. Cornelius and his household reflect the two basic characteristics of sacraments (God doing something and human responding). More precisely, God pours out the Spirit and Cornelius and his household speak in tongues.[32] The tongues-speaking Cornelius and household are Spirit empowered in the same sense as the Jewish disciples.

The Empowering Spirit and Tongues-Speaking Believers

> But you will receive power when the Holy Spirit has come upon you.
>
> (ACTS 1:8)

At the Pentecost event, prayer, praise, and tongues signify Spirit baptism (Acts 2:1–4; 10:45–47; 19:6). Nonetheless, Macchia maintains that "Pentecostals regard tongues as a kind of primary sacrament or *Kairos* event that signifies, while participating in, the empowerment of the Spirit in the Christian life."[33] More relevantly, Menzies holds tongues-speaking as a Pentecostal sacrament.[34] But to say that tongues-speech by itself is a sacrament seems inadequate. This is so because tongues-speech is not a disembodied experience. Instead, it is more accurate to say that the tongues-speaking believers themselves are sacraments. That is to say, the believers who speak in tongues provide concrete expression to the Spirit's empowering presence and hence are sacraments.

---

31. Cartledge, *The Mediation of the Spirit*, 115.
32. Horton, *What the Bible Says*, 229.
33. See Macchia, "Tongues as a Sign," 69.
34. Menzies, *Speaking in Tongues*, 157–58.

At Pentecost, the disciples speak in intelligible tongues about the remarkable works of God, considered an act of praise, in the languages of the dazed or bewildered crowd (a prophetic act) (Acts 2:8–11). Specifically, the disciples spoke in tongues in part to signify to the crowd that God would do great works by taking the gospel as far as their native countries or nations. Granted this assertion, the notion that the act of speaking in tongues by itself is a sacrament seems inadequate. In keeping with this, Peter signifies the Spirit's boldness when he addresses the bewildered crowd (Acts 2:6–13).

Seen in this light, one could say that the praising, prophesying, or boldly witnessing believers are sacraments of a personal encounter with God's presence in the same sense as speaking in tongues. Therefore, it is inadequate to call speaking in tongues by itself a sacramental act. Instead, it is adequate to say that the tongues-speaking disciples are themselves sacraments of encountering the Spirit. At the Pentecost event, the 120 tongues-speaking disciples praise, prophesy, and boldly witness to Christ, and thereby concretely manifest God's Spirit.

Similarly, the Spirit-baptized are themselves sacraments inasmuch as they provide concrete manifestation to the Spirit. The view of tongues-speaking as a sacrament by itself fails to account for the sacramentality of Spirit-baptized individuals adequately. This thinking does not undermine the Pentecostal belief that tongues are an initial sign of Spirit baptism. Instead, it acknowledges that the whole person, not isolated parts of a believer, participates in the act.

Rahner bolsters this argument when he says, "in every human expression, mimetic, phonetic, etc. in nature, the whole man is somehow present and expressing himself, though the expressive form is confined to start with to one portion of the body."[35] This clarifies that speaking in tongues is not confined to the tongue, lips, mouth, or vocal faculties but involves the totality of the person who speaks in tongues. Hence, it is more accurate to refer to the tongues-speaking believers as sacraments of the Spirit than the act of tongues-speaking by itself.

Other charismata can also illustrate sacramentality of the Spirit-baptized. Christ shapes the sacramentality of gifted believers, for it is in him that the fullness of God dwells bodily (Col 2:9). Even though the Spirit indwells believers from the moment of conversion, Spirit baptism intensifies the Spirit's manifestation. Pentecostals believe the Spirit's gifts

---

35. Rahner, *Theological Investigations*, 51.

did not cease with the early church or at any time in history. To the extent that believers exercise gifts of the Spirit, they provide concrete expression to his presence.

In this way, they can mediate and draw others to encounter the Spirit. By so doing, the gifts-exercising believers also function as signs of the grace of the Spirit. Seen in this light, the gift-exercising believers are sacraments of an encounter with the Spirit's empowering presence. As such, gifts-exercising believers inspire others' faith, hope, and love toward God. For example, the Spirit-baptized Peter manifested, mediated, and drew people into an encounter with God's therapeutic presence (Acts 5:16) and salvific grace (Acts 5:14). In this way, the empowered Peter is a visible *significant* or sacrament as he rendered tangible the *signifié* or empowering Spirit.

The Empowering Spirit and Charismatic Pentecost Disciples

> All of them were filled with the Holy Spirit and began to speak in other languages, as the Spirit gave them ability.
>
> (ACTS 2:4)

As all the 120 disciples speak in tongues as the Spirit enables them, they individually and communally manifest God's presence. Thus, they can be held as sacraments of the Spirit. Luke is clear that their tongues-speech outwardly signifies their personal encounter with God (Acts 2:2–4). To be sure, Luke also mentions sound, wind, and tongues of fire as accompanying the Spirit's descent (Acts 2:2, 3). Peter interprets this experience as a prophetic fulfillment (Joel 2:28–29). The Spirit gives each of these disciples the ability to speak in tongues (Acts 2:4).

This suggests that they each encounter God. In particular, the Spirit works in and through the tongues-speaking disciples to draw the attention of Jews from the diaspora. As tongues-speech is Spirit-initiated, it is a divine speech. Heaven and earth meet in temples of the flesh of the tongues-speaking disciples. The tongues-speaking point others to the ascended Christ (Acts 2:33). Also, tongues-speech is missiological in that it hints at God's desire to pour the Spirit upon non-Jewish believers.

The Empowering Spirit and Charismatic Samaritans

> Then Peter and John laid their hands on them,
> and they received the Holy Spirit.
>
> (ACTS 8:17)

Luke reports about the Samaritans' remarkable Spirit baptism. It is quite impressive that they received the message of salvation through Phillip's preaching but were not yet Spirit-baptized (Acts 8:5). This narrative justifies the doctrine of subsequence (Acts 8:15–16). But they are Spirit-baptized after apostles Peter and John pray and lay hands on them (Acts 8:17). The text does not state that they speak in tongues, but something tangible happens in and through them, which leads Peter and John to conclude that they are Spirit-baptized.[36] These Samaritans function as sacraments of a personal encounter with the Spirit of God's empowering presence.

The Empowering Spirit and Charismatic Cornelius

> . . . for they heard them speaking in tongues and extolling God.
>
> (ACTS 10:46)

Similarly, Cornelius experiences Spirit baptism reminiscent of Pentecost (Acts 10:44, 46). This Gentile Pentecost breaks cultural borders as Cornelius renders the Spirit visible beyond the Jewish land (Acts 10:47). Cornelius and his household speak in tongues as the Jewish disciples; are empowered as the Jewish disciples; and Spirit-indwelled as the Jewish disciples. This implies that if the missiological Spirit of God in Christ transcends ethnic borders, the disciples are left with no choice but to fall in line (Acts 10:47).

The empowered Cornelius and his household can witness to their counterparts about their personal encounter with the Spirit of God in Christ. It flows from this that Cornelius and his household can manifest God's presence in the same ontological sense as Jewish disciples (Acts 10:35). The Ephesus disciples experience the Spirit in a similar manner.

---

36. Bruner, *Theology of the Holy Spirit*, 179; Sullivan, *Charisms*, 67; Menzies, *Speaking in Tongues*, 33.

The Spirit-Baptized Ephesians

> When Paul had laid his hands on them, the Holy Spirit came upon them, and they spoke in tongues and prophesied, altogether there were about twelve of them.
>
> (ACTS 19:6–7)

Like the Samaritan disciples, the twelve disciples at Ephesus had only experienced Water Baptism until they met with Paul (Acts 19:4–5). After Paul prays and lays hands on them, they are Spirit-baptized accompanied by a sign of speaking in tongues and prophecy (Acts 19:6–7). This passage depicts Spirit baptism as a post-conversion experience and apart from Water Baptism. More relevantly, these Spirit-baptized Ephesians signify to Paul and others that they have encountered God's empowering presence. Like the 120 disciples at Pentecost and the Samaritan disciples, the twelve Ephesians are signs of the grace of God's empowering presence through the Spirit of Christ.

By providing concrete manifestation to God's empowering presence, the twelve Ephesians fit as sacraments of an encounter with the Spirit. Sacraments, you will recall, reveal, mediate, and draw others into a fresh encounter with God. In keeping with this, the Spirit-baptized Ephesians enabled Paul to encounter God afresh. Therefore, he witnessed boldly about Jesus to both Jews and Greeks (Acts 19:8–10).

The Empowering Spirit and Gifted Believers

> Serve one another with whatever gift each of you has received.
>
> (1 PET 4:10)

Spirit baptism results in the endowment of spiritual gifts for serving each other (1 Pet 4:10). Thus, Paul says that the Spirit bestows gifts for the common good (1 Cor 12:7). Jesus taught his disciples to serve and not to be served (Matt 20:28; Mark 10:45). Whenever believers minister to others in need through spiritual gifts, they function as means of grace of the Spirit. Thus, it is no coincidence that Christ heals two blind men immediately after teaching his disciples about serving freely (Matt 20:29–34).

Spiritual gifts enable believers to effectively witness to the redemptive mission of God in Christ (Acts 1:8). By ministering to others through diverse spiritual gifts, believers render the Spirit concretely present. Seen in this light, such believers are human locations or signs of grace. In effect, believers who serve others via spiritual gifts are sacraments of God's presence. To be sure, let me illustrate how different spiritual gifts give rise to the sacramentality of believers.

The Empowering Spirit and Gifts-Manifesting Believers

> To each is given the manifestation of the Spirit for the common good.
>
> (1 COR 12:7)

Spiritual gifts are "the action and utterance which demonstrate the Spirit's presence and activity."[37] Thus, spiritual gifts point to the Spirit at work in and through believers. Indeed, "each charisma is a manifestation of the Spirit."[38] The gifted believers are endowed with the grace of the Spirit. Gifted believers manifest and draw others into an encounter with the Spirit.

Therefore, it is "important to realize that in Paul's view the sort of charismatic action and utterance which he lists in 1 Cor 12:8–10 are in some sense an evidence, a disclosure, a making-visible of the Spirit."[39] That is to say, the gifted believers enable the Spirit to be visible. Hocken notes that "spiritual gifts are distinctive works of the Spirit."[40] Though believers act in exercising spiritual gifts, they only respond to the Spirit at work in and through them (Phil 2:13).

The Empowering Spirit and Wisdom-Manifesting Believers

> To one is given through the Spirit the utterance of wisdom.
>
> (1 COR 12:8)

The utterance of wisdom relates to Christ as the very wisdom of God (1 Cor 1:24). More precisely, the utterance of wisdom refers to recognizing the message of salvation in and through the crucified Christ. According to Fee, "this recognition comes only to those who have received the Spirit."[41] Specifically, one who acknowledges Christ as the crucified savior

37. Dunn, *Jesus and the Spirit*, 212.
38. Dunn, *Jesus and the Spirit*, 212.
39. Dunn, *Jesus and the Spirit*, 212.
40. Hocken, "Jesus Christ and the Gifts of the Spirit," 10.
41. Fee, *God's Empowering Presence*, 166–67.

is enabled by the gift of wisdom. Since it is the Spirit who gives this wisdom, this gift's exercise renders the Spirit tangibly present. This gift can manifest via preaching. For example, Paul says that his preaching about the Cross did not originate in human wisdom but in Christ (1 Cor 1:17).

Paul adds that his preaching was backed by the Spirit's demonstration (1 Cor 2:4). This means that the utterance of wisdom is linked to the power of the Spirit. Echoing this view is Schatzmann, who writes: "From 1 Cor 1–3 it is almost certain that Paul identified the wisdom from God with God's saving deed in the crucified Christ."[42] The utterance of wisdom reflects divine inspiration.

In particular, "the Spirit may so move upon a person as to impart depth-understanding to a truth of the gospel. As he speaks this forth, a word of wisdom is exercised."[43] This does not suggest that the Spirit bypasses human faculties. In fact, the Spirit uses human faculties to manifest wisdom. In other words, the utterance of wisdom reflects divine-human cooperation inasmuch as the Spirit who bestows this gift reveals his tangible presence in and through wisdom-uttering believers.

It is worth pointing out that other scholars interpret the gift of the utterance of wisdom differently. For example, Horton holds the gift of wisdom as a revelation of God's purpose concerning people, things, or future events.[44] The Spirit enables believers to reveal and communicate God's purpose about people, things, or future events. Thus, such believers point others to the reality of the Spirit. For example, Joseph demonstrated wisdom when he told the pharaoh his dream and gave its interpretation (Gen 41:14–38).

This could not have happened except by the Spirit at work upon Joseph (Gen 41:8). Seen in this light, believers who utter words of wisdom as Joseph did are sacraments of the Spirit.

The Empowering Spirit and Knowledge-Manifesting Believers

> . . . and to another the utterance of knowledge according to the same Spirit.
>
> (1 COR 12:8)

---

42. Schatzmann, *Pauline Theology of Charismata*, 36.
43. Williams, *Renewal Theology*, 354.
44. Horton, *Gifts of the Holy Spirit*.

Drawing on the situation in the Corinthian church, Dunn holds the utterance of knowledge as "a word spoken under inspiration giving an insight into cosmic realities and relationships."[45] The Spirit grants believers insight into cosmic realities and relationships in space and time. Thus, believers who exercise the gift of knowledge provide concrete expression to the Spirit. This is so because the knowledge or insight that is communicated originates from the Spirit, not from human faculties. Christ showed this gift of knowledge when he ministered to people through the Spirit.

The Empowering Spirit and Knowledge-Manifesting Peter

Peter also exemplifies the sacramentality of believers arising in the exercise of the gift of knowledge. For example, Peter tells Ananias (Acts 5:3) and Sapphira (Act 5:8) about their lying scheme. There is no reasonable basis to explain how Peter knew details of the couple's lie about their transaction except through the Spirit and, particularly, the gift of knowledge. By manifesting the Spirit via the gift of knowledge, Peter is a sign and means of God's grace. Notably, Peter is a sacrament of an encounter with the Spirit.

The Empowering Spirit and Faith-Manifesting Believers

> . . . to another faith by the same Spirit, by the one Spirit.
>
> (1 COR 12:9)

The gift of faith is widely considered as an attendant gift because it works alongside others. The gift of faith is "that assurance that God is speaking or acting through the words or actions."[46] Believers who exercise the gift of faith experience a "mysterious surge of confidence that God is about to act either by word or action."[47] Likewise, Schatzmann states that the gift of faith is "a sense of 'mysterious surge of confidence' that God will grant a healing or miracle."[48]

---

45. Dunn, *Jesus and the Spirit*, 218.
46. Dunn, *Jesus and the Spirit*, 211.
47. Dunn, *Jesus and the Spirit*, 211.
48. Schatzmann, *Pauline Theology of Charismata*, 37.

Fee adds that the gift of faith "refers to a supernatural conviction that God will reveal his power or mercy in a special way in a specific instance."[49] Confidence surges in a specific time as the Spirit leads. Drawing from Heidegger,[50] believers' actions in exercising faith are secondary to the Spirit. It follows that believers who exercise the gift of faith reveal the faith-gifting Spirit.

The Empowering Spirit and Faith-Manifesting Elijah

Similarly, Elijah inspires the people of Israel when "the fire of the Lord fell and consumed the burnt offering, the wood, the stones, and the dust, and even licked up the water that was in the trench" (1 Kgs 18:38). In this way, Elijah manifests, mediates, and draws the Israelites to encounter God's presence as they confess: "The Lord indeed is God; the Lord indeed is God" (1 Kgs 18:39). Thus, the faith-exercising Elijah fits as a sacrament of God's presence.

The Empowering Spirit and Healing Believers

> . . . to another faith by the same Spirit, to another gifts of healing by the one Spirit
>
> (1 Cor 12:9)

According to Dunn, "gifts of healing are cures for which no natural or rational explanation would suffice—they could only be put down to the action of God."[51] For Dunn, "the charisma is not a healing power which is effective for all [sorts of] illnesses . . ."[52] The persons gifted with the grace of a healing function are signs of divine grace.[53] The gifted in healing does not become a healer but "only passes on the healings to others."[54] Believers gifted in healing are concrete signs and means of grace that can draw other people into an encounter with the Spirit's therapeutic presence.

---

49. Fee, *God's Empowering Presence*, 168.
50. Heidegger, *Being and Time*, 51–52.
51. Dunn, *Jesus and the Spirit*, 210.
52. Dunn, *Jesus and the Spirit*, 211.
53. Fee, *God's Empowering Presence*, 169; Turner, *Holy Spirit*, 266–68; Yong, "Spirit, Body, and Sacraments," 263.
54. Williams, *Renewal Theology*, 367.

It should also be pointed out that even those who benefit from healing gifts contribute to providing concrete manifestation of God's healing presence. Healed individuals signify and point others to the Spirit of God's healing presence at work in and through their lives (John 9:25).

The Empowering Spirit and Healing Elisha

The healing of Naaman from leprosy after dipping himself seven times into the river Jordan is a sacramental event that shows Elisha as a sacrament of a personal encounter with God revealed in Christ through the Spirit (2 Kgs 2:14). Notably, Naaman expresses faith in Israel's God, who signifies the bestowal of grace upon him (2 Kgs 2:15). The narrative shows that Elisha was conscious of the grace bestowed on him by the Spirit. Additionally, this sacramental healing event's impact arises because Naaman comes from another country that worships another god. For Naaman, then, his encounter with Elisha is a concrete encounter with the healing God of Israel. That is to say, Elisha is to Naaman a sacrament of an encounter with God's presence.

The Empowering Spirit and Healing Peter

The New Testament also features several individuals who fit as sacraments of an encounter with the Spirit of God's healing presence. For example, Peter healed a man bedridden for eight years (Acts 9:34). Peter relates the man's healing experience to the Spirit of God through Christ. In this way, Peter manifests God's presence and draws Lydda and Sharon's residents to the Lord (Acts 9:35). Indeed, many people confessed Jesus as Lord owing to this healing event.

Likewise, Peter ministers to Dorcas (Tabitha), whose death deeply affected her community (Acts 9:36). In exercising the healing gift, Peter commands the dead woman to get up, and she does (Acts 9:40). Upon seeing this miracle, "many believed in the Lord" (Acts 9:42). Since Peter enables others to encounter the Spirit of Christ by exercising the healing gift, he is a sacrament of an encounter with God. Peter, gifted in grace of healing, rendered the Spirit tangible.

The Empowering Spirit and Healing Pentecostals-Charismatics

> Cure the sick, raise the dead, cleanse the lepers, cast out demons. You received without payment; give without payment.
>
> (MATT 10:8)

The Pentecost event democratized the healing experience so that apostles and ordinary disciples could minister healing to the sick (Acts 3:1–10; 5:12; 6:8). For Pentecostals, healing did not cease with the early church or during the early decades of church history. Thus, Pentecostals oppose the notion of cessationism but favor continuationism. The Pentecostals expect encounters with God's gifting presence, including healing. Pentecostalism is synonymous with spiritual gifts.

The gift of healing is most popular among Pentecostals, especially in the Global South. Inadequate health facilities in developing countries partly contribute to the popularity of healing gifts in Pentecostal churches. The churches that do not create space for encounters with God's healing presence are difficult to classify as Pentecostal. In the West, Pentecostal churches also emphasize encounters with God's healing presence. The tangibility of God's presence in and through the gifted in healing is a pneumatological foundation for the sacramentality of believers.

Early modern Pentecostalism also stressed encounters with the healing presence of God by the Spirit. Typically, early Pentecostals sent out anointed handkerchiefs or cloths, laid hands on the sick and anointed them with oil, etc. Such practices are widely held as evidence of an implicit sacramental outlook in Pentecostalism. To be sure, such practices were also employed in the early church, where healing was given pride of place following the outpouring of the Spirit at Pentecost. The *telos* of healing is to bring people to the saving knowledge of Jesus by the Spirit.

Healed individuals manifest the redemptive intent of God in Christ. Put another way, divine healing of the human body points to the human soul's ultimate healing. It implies that the Spirit-healed believers bestow the grace of God's redemptive presence as they make this grace visible and thereby inspire unbelievers to move toward salvation. To the extent that the Spirit-healed point others to the reality of God's redemptive grace in Christ, they reflect a sacramental character. To be healed, one takes part in God's healing presence. By testifying to healing, one manifests, mediates, and can draw others to encounter God's presence.

By testifying to healing, Pentecostals render visible the presence of God. Seen in this light, both those empowered to heal and the healed are signs of God's presence in Christ. To be sure, those endowed with healing gifts never operate independently from God. Instead, as with all gifts of grace, the Spirit himself manifests in and through believers who pray for others to be healed as well as those who are healed. It follows that the empowered to heal are signs of the grace of God's healing presence. For example, people would line up the sick so that Peter's shadow should fall upon them for a healing experience (Acts 5:15).

This is incredible because it shows a critical sacramental principle: that sacraments participate in the reality they represent. Put directly, the empowered in Christ to heal join in God's healing presence by the Spirit. Through tarrying in prayer and fasting, believers participate in the Spirit's healing presence in Christ. This participation in the Spirit disposes believers to the same empowering presence of God.

For this reason, Pentecostals expect to encounter God's presence in tangible ways. The saturation of God's presence in Pentecostal meetings is most attractive to outsiders. To be sure, Pentecostals do not consider Jesus as one who healed only in the past during his earthly ministry, but that Christ continues to heal today through Spirit-empowered believers.

Thus, whenever a person is healed, the healing presence of God by the Spirit becomes tangible in and through both the healers and the healed. For example, when the people of Lystra witness a miracle of the healing of a man born disabled through the empowered Paul and Barnabas, they conclude, "The gods have come down to us in human form!" (Acts 14:8). In other words, Paul and Barnabas provided tangible manifestation to the gods.

It is remarkable in that even the priest of Zeus decides to offer sacrifices to Paul and Barnabas. It is this kind of tangible manifestation of God's healing presence that Pentecostals yearn for. Therefore, the sacramentality of believers shaped by Jesus as the healer seems reasonable. Pentecostals allow those who encounter the Spirit's healing presence to testify. It is not uncommon for Pentecostals to publish periodic magazines that feature testimonies of people that encounter God's healing presence.

Interestingly, some people testify to encountering the healing presence of God after reading another's testimony. This shows that the healed are themselves means of healing. Specifically, the healed inspire others to seek the healing presence of God. The sacramental principle helps to clarify how testimonies of healing, whether written or oral, can cause fresh encounters with God's healing presence. Precisely, the sacramental principle insists that sacraments signify and make present the invisible reality to which they point. In this light, the healed, as sacraments, not only point to or signify God's healing presence but are enabled, as it were, to be visible and accessible to others.

Consequently, people sought to touch Jesus because of healing reports in his ministry (Matt 14:36; Mark 1:41; 6:56; Luke 8:47; 22:51). In this way, the healer and the healed serve as concrete signs of the healing presence of God. In keeping with this, Pentecostals conduct healing campaigns and expect God's healing presence to manifest in and through both testimonies shared by the healers and those healed. Those empowered to heal do not act apart from the Spirit's healing presence but partner with the Spirit in ministering healing to the sick.

Thus, healers have no ontological significance but are only means of grace. Certainly, healers, just as all sacraments, are nothing apart from God's presence. Sacraments are natural, while the reality they reveal is divine. To be sure, the Spirit can use believers with questionable conduct to manifest his healing presence for the benefit of the sick or the afflicted.

While this is not meant to condone sinful conduct or behavior among those endowed with the gift of healing, it merely shows that it is indeed God who works in and through sacraments. To be sure, it is even common to find that those healed do not have a salvific relationship with God but may sometimes surrender their lives because of their healing experiences. This is an essential point in that it shows that believers' sacramentality emphasizes the witnessing function or *telos* of the manifestation of God's presence by the Spirit. In other words, the ultimate goal of the self-disclosing presence of God in and through believers is to draw humankind to the saving knowledge of God. Thus, the healed are sacraments of an encounter with God's healing presence by the Spirit for others, both believers and unbelievers.

The Empowering Spirit and Healing
Pentecostal-Charismatic Believers

Healing is synonymous with Pentecostalism.[55] Pentecostals stress "the manifestation of divine power through healing, deliverance, prophecy,

---

55. Alexander, *Pentecostal Healing*.

speaking in tongues, and other Pentecostal phenomena."[56] Such Pentecostal phenomena signify concrete expressions of the Spirit in the Pentecostal community. In fact, the Spirit empowers believers "to prophesy, speak in tongues, heal, exorcise demons, have visions and dreams, and live 'holy' lives."[57] Believers who minister healing to the sick are signs of grace as they manifest the Spirit, theologically described as the Divine Person without a face.[58] Typically, Pentecostals and charismatics lay hands on the sick to signify impartation or mediation of God's healing grace through the therapeutic Spirit.

The Empowering Spirit and Healing Anointing

> They will lay their hands on the sick, and they will recover.
>
> (MARK 16:18)

The rite of laying hands upon the sick has a biblical root. Pentecostals practice laying on of hands in ways that suggest a sacramental worldview of themselves. Thus, it is the one who lays hands who is the primary channel of the Spirit's grace, not the oil that he or she might use in the process. A sacramental view in early North American Pentecostalism can be inferred from an *Apostolic Faith* publication about the Azusa Street revival, which reported that "Handkerchiefs are sent in to be blest, and are returned to the sick and they are healed in many cases."[59]

Thus, early Pentecostals at the Azusa Street revival espoused a sacramental outlook. They believed that the grace of the Spirit could be bestowed through material channels. To be sure, Luke reports similar experiences in Paul's ministry (Acts 19:11–12). This shows that early disciples had a sacramental outlook wherein the Spirit's grace could be encountered in and through material objects and human channels.

Thus, sacramentality was not viewed as antithetical to dynamic life in the Spirit in the early Church and during early modern Pentecostalism, as some Pentecostal scholars seem to suggest.[60] Even early African Pentecostal leaders espoused a sacramental outlook. While Africa is a vast

---

56. Anderson, *Introduction to Pentecostalism*, 234.
57. Anderson, *Introduction to Pentecostalism*, 197.
58. Smail, *Giving Gift*, 30–55; Congar, *I Believe in the Holy Spirit*, 5.
59. See Seymour, "Beginning of World Wide Revival," 1.
60. See Macchia, "Tongues as a Sign, " 61–62.

continent with distinct cultures and languages, a sacramental worldview was common among early African Pentecostal pioneers. This sacramental view is supported by the belief that the spiritual and physical realms are inseparably linked, or the visible and the invisible realms interweave.[61] For example, African Pentecostal believers often hold Spirit-filled believers as "human channels of God's grace which followers seek after."[62]

Thus, African Pentecostals readily embrace a sacramental worldview[63] often seen during prayer sessions for deliverance from "spiritual strongholds" of demonic powers.[64] It is not uncommon for African Pentecostals to use a variety of objects as channels, as it were, of the grace of God. Prayer for healing is what brings many people to the Pentecostal altar. This does not mean that the healing presence of God only flows from the altar to the pew. From the early days of Pentecostalism, there was a firm conviction that anyone could pray and lay hands on the sick for healing.[65]

Lekganyane of South Africa laid hands on ill persons and blessed objects like strips of cloth, strings, papers, needles, walking sticks, and water to heal and protect and for use by his ministers.[66] Like Paul and Peter, God's healing power flowed in and through Lekganyane. In the same way, Wade Harris of Liberia was a sign of healing grace. For example, he would invite people possessed by evil spirits and traditional deities to touch his staff and be sprinkled with holy water, after which ecstatic manifestations reportedly followed.[67] Ecstatic manifestations were seen as confirmation that these anointed objects had mediated God's healing grace. Thus, both Lekganyane and Wade Harris demonstrated a sacramental worldview in their ministry.

According to Perry, early Pentecostals conceived believers baptized with the Spirit as channels for carrying out the works of Christ.[68] This demonstrates that early Pentecostal leaders had an embedded sacramental

---

61. Kalu, *African Pentecostalism*, 175–78; Asamoah-Gyadu, *Contemporary Pentecostal Christianity*, 44–57.

62. Asamoah-Gyadu, *Sighs and Signs of the Spirit*, 66.

63. Anderson, *African Reformation*, 26.

64. See Kärkkäinen, "The Spirit in the World," 192–94; Asamoah-Gyadu, *Contemporary Pentecostal Christianity*, 35–57.

65. Alexander, *Pentecostal Healing*, 108.

66. Anderson, *Introduction to Pentecostalism*, 108.

67. Anderson, *African Reformation*, 72.

68. See Perry, "There Are Other Things as Well," 3.

view of believers. It is noteworthy that this understanding resonates in many ways with the critical biblical text at the center of this exploration: "how God anointed Jesus of Nazareth with the Holy Spirit and with power; how he went about doing good and healing all who were oppressed by the devil, for God was with him" (Acts 10:38). That is to say, the Spirit upon Jesus Christ is the same upon the early disciples and modern believers.

On his part, Boddy is reported to have administered what he called the anointed touch.[69] This partly mirrors James's appeal for elders to minister by praying and anointing the sick with oil (James 5:14). In short, Boddy espoused a sacramental view about the anointing oil. To be sure, even Christ himself laid hands on sick people or the dead (Matt 8:3; 20:34; Mark 1:41; 7:33; 16:18; Luke 5:13; 7:14; 22:51; Acts 28:8). Thus, the laying on of hands upon the sick fits as a sacrament.

On the one hand, sacraments are defined primarily as a rite or ritual that mediates God's presence. This characterization views grace as a thing, substance, or something that someone, especially clergy or a church official, does, such as administering Water Baptism or the Lord's Supper. On the other hand, sacraments can also be viewed as a person who mediates God's presence, holding grace as the gift of the Holy Spirit. In this light, Jesus, as the bearer of the Spirit *par excellence* and the Spirit baptizer, is the primordial sacrament. This is the definition I follow in this book. God's promise to impart the Spirit upon all flesh opens space for the sacramentality of believers.

In this light, Christ is the primordial sacrament of the personal encounter with the Spirit. The sacramental being of Christ inspired a response from those that followed him. Specifically, he manifested the Spirit's presence and thereby drew multitudes into an encounter with God. Most of his followers deemed his actions as sacramental as they flowed out of his sacramental being. For instance, the woman with the issue of blood presses through the crowd to touch the hem of Jesus' garment (Matt 9:21; 14:36; Mark 6:56). This woman is not the one who imparts the healing presence of God by the Spirit; Christ is.

To conceive the laying of hands itself as a sacrament fails to take into full account the fact that it is the one who lays hands who imparts the Spirit of Christ's healing grace. This is why Jesus is reported to have asked "Who touched me?" rather than "Who touched my cloth?" Thus, we can

---

69. See Boddy, "Anointing with Oil," 21.

conceive believers who lay hands, resulting in the healing of the sick, as signs of healing grace. The hands cannot move independently without the full participation of other aspects of the believer who lays the hands. As signs of healing grace, believers who lay hands participate in the grace of God's healing presence. They impart the Spirit of God's healing grace upon the sick.

Moreover, it is God's primary action by the Spirit that brings about healing, while humans only respond as they cooperate with him when they lay hands. God's action in all sacraments is primary, while the one who lays hands to this primary action is secondary. It is Christ and, indeed, all those who lay hands upon the sick that serve as the primary sign of an encounter with God's healing presence by the Spirit. Focusing on the rite of laying hands apart from the person laying hands mirrors the classic sacramental principle of *ex opere operato*.

This sacramental principle, held by the Roman Catholic Church tradition, insists that sacraments' efficacy is independent of the person administering or receiving a sacrament. It is merely by the work performed by a priest. The spiritual merits of the minister and recipients are considered irrelevant. This does not seem to resonate with Pentecostal thinking which gives pride of place to spiritual disciplines like tarrying, praying, fasting, Bible study, righteous living, etc., to enhance one's spiritual disposition or spirituality. While *ex opere operato* may be true about Water Baptism and the Lord's Supper, it seems difficult to relate it to Christ and believers as sacraments of a personal encounter with the Spirit of God's presence.

The principle that rightly captures the Pentecostal thinking that stresses appropriate spiritual dispositions as determinants of sacramental efficacy is *ex opere operantis*. For example, disposition of faith plays a role in salvation, healing, Water Baptism, participating in the Lord's Supper, foot washing, and laying on of hands. To suggest otherwise is to hold these rites as self-contained rites that convey the grace of the Spirit. This is not in keeping with Pentecostal beliefs and mainstream Christianity. This thinking also applies to the practice of anointing with oil.

The Empowering Spirit and the Anointed with Oil

> They cast out many demons, and anointed with
> oil many who were sick and cured them.
>
> (MARK 6:13)

The oil used to anoint the sick does not have built-in power. The oil only symbolizes the Spirit who indwells believers. When James admonishes church elders to pray and anoint the sick with oil (Jas 5:14), it enables the sick to respond to God's healing grace by the Spirit. The efficacy of the rite of anointing the sick requires faith, especially of the one who offers a prayer. Therefore, it is inadequate to call the rite of anointing with oil by itself "sacrament."

The rite of anointing the sick resonates with the principle of *ex opere operantis* and not *ex opere operato*. In fact, it is more acceptable to call one who anoints than the rite of anointing by itself a "sacrament." Those who anoint the sick with oil make the grace of God's healing presence tangible, not the rite of anointing the sick in and of itself. God's anointing works in and through believers.

The Empowering Spirit and Miracle-Working Believers

> . . . to another the working of miracles.
>
> (1 COR 12:10)

The Bible records extraordinary miracles God performed through ordinary people. For example, Elijah prayed that it should not rain, and it did not rain (1 Kgs 17). Elijah prayed again, and it rained (1 Kgs 18; Jas 5:17). This is a feat that defies human ingenuity. It can only be attributed to God's presence that worked in and through Elijah. Paul lists the workings of miracles as gift of the Spirit.

Miracles attest that God is at work in and through a person. Seen in this light, persons in and through whom God performs miracles render his presence tangible. Such people render God's presence tangible and deepen the faith, hope, and love of others toward God. It follows that the gifted in working miracles function as means of grace. Indeed, they are, in their persons, signs of the grace of the Spirit of God's miracle-working power.

To be sure, the gift of workings of miracles is for "demonstrations of supernatural power."[70] But, miracles only happen when people step out in faith.[71] To step out in faith is to partner with the Spirit for the manifestation of God's miracle-working presence. Arrington describes this gift of workings of miracles as a "profound encounter with God's

---

70. Williams, *Renewal Theology*, 375.
71. Williams, *Renewal Theology*, 377.

sovereign action and the Spirit's power to do supernatural works."[72] Schatzmann holds this gift as "powerful displays of God's power in humanity's environment."[73] Peter and Paul are examples of people God used to perform extraordinary miracles. Thus, they fit as sacraments of an encounter with God's presence.

The Empowering Spirit and Miracle-Working Peter

After the Pentecost event, Peter and John ministered to a 40-year-old man born lame (Acts 3:2). He was laid daily at the Beautiful Gate leading to the temple where the disciples met for prayer (Acts 3:1). Peter commands the lame man to rise and walk, and he miraculously does (Acts 3:6, 16). Significantly, Peter exercises the gift of working miracles and manifests the Spirit at work in and through him.

In fact, Peter points others to Jesus as the one who performs the miracle (Acts 3:6, 16). In this way, Peter renders the ascended Jesus tangible by the Spirit and thereby draws the other disciples and unbelievers to encounter God's presence. The gift of working miracles in and through Peter was so overwhelming that people lined up the sick along streets for his shadow to mediate healing upon them (Acts 5:15). Thus, Peter serves as a sacrament of a personal encounter with the Spirit's miracle-working presence in Christ.

The Empowering Spirit and Miracle-Working Paul

The Spirit empowered Paul to work extraordinary miracles (Acts 19:11). For example, people were healed by contact with handkerchiefs or aprons from Paul (Acts 19:12). Paul thus functioned as a concrete site of divine grace. By performing miracles, he drew many people into an encounter with God's redemptive grace in Christ through the Spirit. The miracle-working Paul serves as a sacrament of an encounter with the Spirit's empowering presence.

---

72. Arrington, *Encountering the Holy Spirit*, 331.
73. Schatzmann, *Pauline Theology of Charismata*, 38.

The Empowering Spirit and Prophesying Believers

> ... to another prophecy.
>
> (1 COR 12:10)

The gift of prophecy speaks of a "believer's confidence that God's Spirit is speaking in the very words he is uttering."[74] The Spirit leads those who prophesy. "Spontaneity marks such an occasion, and the words are divinely inspired."[75] Precisely, a person "speaks to the needs of God's people and offers them edification, exhortation, and consolation."[76] Since prophecy is communicated through an inspired human intermediary,[77] it engenders the prophesying person as a human sign of grace. Through prophecy, God self-reveals his presence amid his people.[78] Often a pophecy has a futuristic element so that those prophesying are called "predictors."

Others claim that all believers can prophesy.[79] Since in prophesying, believers speak by the Spirit, they manifest God's presence. In this way, they draw others into an encounter with God's presence. It is in the course of prophesying that one is a sacrament of encountering the Spirit. The sacramentality of prophesying believers intensifies when a prophetic utterance is fulfilled shortly after its declaration, like when Jesus cursed a fig tree, and it dried the next day (Matt 21:20–22; Mark 11:20–24).

By so doing, Jesus rendered God's presence tangible to the disciples who heard him utter the prophecy. The disciples' faith in God was strengthened by witnessing this prophetic act. In this light, Jesus is the prophesying Man *par excellence* and primordial sacrament of the personal encounter with the Spirit of God's prophesying presence. Christ shapes sacramentality of all prophesying believers.

The Empowering Spirit and Prophesying Elijah

Elijah manifests God's presence when he challenges the prophets of Baal (1 Kgs 18:24). This was after the prayer of the prophets of Baal yielded

---

74. Dunn, *Jesus and the Spirit*, 212.
75. Williams, *Renewal Theology*, 382.
76. Arrington, *Encountering the Holy Spirit*, 335–36.
77. Aune, *Prophecy*, 339.
78. Turner, *Holy Spirit and Spiritual Gifts*, 225–26.
79. Williams, *Renewal Theology*, 381; Menzies, *Speaking in Tongues*, 101.

no result (1 Kgs 18:30). When he prays, God answers him by sending fire upon the sacrifice (1 Kgs 18:38–39). In this way, Elijah enables the Israelites to encounter God's presence. Seen in this light, Elijah serves as a sacrament of an encounter with the presence of the God of Israel.

The Empowering Spirit and Prophesying Paul

Next, Paul speaks prophetically about the danger ahead (Acts 27:9–10). Interestingly, his prophetic advice is dismissed with 276 people on board a ship (Acts 27:11, 37). Later, Paul is proven right, and his advice is heeded (Acts 27:21–25; 33–36). Paul did not speak out of his own volition but by the inspiration of the Holy Spirit. By exercising the prophetic gift, he rendered the Spirit tangible to the other sailors. Hence, Paul fits as a sacrament of an encounter with the Spirit.

The Empowering Spirit and Discerning Believers

> . . . to another the discernment of spirits.
>
> (1 COR 12:10)

Concerning the gift of discernment, it is the phenomenon of distinguishing, differentiating, or correctly judging prophecies.[80] In other words, it "provides a test of prophetic utterance and a control against its abuse."[81] It can also be held as "the Spirit-given ability to distinguish the Spirit from a demonic spirit."[82] Precisely, "it is by the illumination of the Spirit through the spirit of a particular individual that spirits are perceived."[83] It is often applied when dealing with demon-possessed individuals.[84] Whenever believers discern, they concretely manifest the Spirit of God's presence.

To the extent that they do this, they enable others to know something or someone's true nature and function as means of grace. Put another way, the discerning believers facilitate fresh encounters with God's presence as they render the Spirit tangible to others. Thus, discerning believers are sacraments of a personal encounter with the Spirit of God's

---

80. Fee, *God's Empowering Presence*, 171.
81. Dunn, *Jesus and the Spirit*, 233.
82. Schatzmann, *Pauline Theology of Charismata*, 41.
83. Williams, *Renewal Theology*, 389.
84. Arrington, *Encountering the Holy Spirit*, 339.

The Empowering Spirit and Discerning Peter

Some scholars argue that Peter used the gift of discernment to expose or detect the spirit underlying Ananias and Sapphira's actions. This seems reasonable, since the couple did not disclose to Peter details of the sale of their property. Precisely, the Spirit empowers him to discern the lying spirit at work in and through the couple (Acts 5:3, 9). By exercising this gift, Peter demonstrates that the Spirit is at work in the early church community.

Additionally, Peter reveals and therefore enables other disciples in the early church community to encounter God. The God who punished Achan and the household once again manifested his presence resulting in loss of life (Josh 7). Accordingly, the discerning Peter is a human sign and means of grace. More fittingly, Peter is a sacrament of an encounter with the Spirit of God's presence in Christ.

The Empowering Spirit and Discerning Paul

Likewise, Paul uses the gift of discernment to detect a spirit of divination in a slave girl (Acts 16:16). However, the evil Spirit recognizes Paul and Silas as servants of God (Acts 16:17). Paul and Silas cast the spirit out and the infuriated authorities kick them out (Acts 16:19–24). By so doing, Paul reveals the Spirit's empowering presence to the community and draws some to encounter Christ.

The Empowering Spirit and Diverse Tongues-Speaking Believers

> . . . to another various kinds of tongues.
>
> (1 COR 12:10)

Next, the gift of varieties of tongues differs from tongues related to Spirit baptism.[85] Paul describes this gift as Spirit-inspired and incomprehensible

---

85. Williams, *Renewal Theology*, 397.

to the speaker (1 Cor 14:14) and others (1 Cor 14:16).[86] It can be held as inspired utterances where the Spirit speaks through believers.[87] Because those who exercise this gift of diverse tongues manifest the Spirit, they thus mediate and draw others into an encounter with God. This gift typically requires another person to provide an interpretation and allow for understanding among the worshiping community.

The Empowering Spirit and Diverse Tongues-Interpreting Believers

... to another the interpretation of tongues.

(1 COR 12:10)

The gift of interpreting tongues is a companion to that of the tongues' varieties due to the latter's unintelligibility.[88] Notably, the gift of interpreting tongues conveys a message understandably. By so doing, the interpreter reveals the Spirit and facilitates fresh encounters with God's presence in a worship community. To be sure, "what is 'interpreted' is not speech directed toward others, but the 'mysteries' spoken to God."[89] Put in another way, the "mysteries spoken in the Spirit, while addressed not to men but to God (1 Cor 14:2), may contain a message to people when interpreted by the same Spirit."[90] Thus, Turner concedes that "Paul probably thought of tongues-speech as *xenolalia* and (possibly) heavenly languages."[91]

The nine-fold gifts discussed above create space for believers to partner with the Spirit for their concrete expression. To the extent that the gifted act as they are led and enabled by the Spirit, they function as concrete sites, signs, or means of grace. More adequately, exercising any spiritual gift manifests the Spirit, as he bestows the gifts. Accordingly, believers who serve others through spiritual gifts, either within or outside worship contexts, can be conceived as sacraments of a personal encounter with the Spirit of God's empowering presence in Christ.

---

86. Fee, *God's Empowering Presence*, 172–73.
87. Dunn, *Jesus and the Spirit*, 245.
88. Fee, *God's Empowering Presence*, 173.
89. Fee, *God's Empowering Presence*, 173.
90. Williams, *Renewal Theology*, 405.
91. Turner, *Holy Spirit and Spiritual Gifts*, 224.

The Empowering Spirit and Servanthood

> Like good stewards of the manifold grace of God, serve one another with whatever gift each of you has received.
>
> (1 PET 4:10)

Believers also render the Spirit tangible through other diverse areas of service. For example, the deacons appointed to serve at tables in the early church manifest the Spirit as their service brings peace into the early church community (Acts 6). The Spirit who manifests in and through the apostles also manifests in and through the deacons serving at tables (Acts 6:2–6). Therefore, both the apostles and deacons are signs of the grace of the Spirit.

In the same way, the believers who serve others render the Spirit tangible. For example, the women who provide for Jesus and his disciples (Luke 8:3), Barnabas who encourages others in the early church community (Acts 4:36), and Dorcas, who serves others through her works of charity (Acts 9:39) all fit as sacraments of God's presence.

The Empowering Spirit and Ministering

> The gifts he gave were that some would be apostles, some prophets, some evangelists, some pastors and teachers.
>
> (EPH 4:10)

The five-fold ministers are God's gifts to the church through Christ by the Spirit (Eph 4:10). Fundamentally, ministry is a call to serve others. To be sure, ministry-related gifts are not limited to the fivefold ministries: an apostle (ἀπόστολος or *apostolos* in Greek), a prophet (προφήτης or *prophetes* in Greek), an evangelist (*euaggelistes* or εὐαγγελιστής in Greek), a pastor or shepherd (ποιμήν or *poimen* in Greek), and a teacher (ῥαββί in Greek or *rhabbí* in Hebrew) (Eph 4:10–11).

Paul establishes the purpose of these ministry gifts to build and equip the saints and strengthen the body of Christ (Eph 4:12–13). It is noteworthy that it is the one called to a particular office who is the gift. For example, Jesus is an apostle (Heb 3:1), a prophet (Deut 18:15–19; Matt 13:57; 14:5; 21:10–11; Luke 13:33; 24:19; Acts 3:22), an evangelist (Matt 18:11; Mark 1:14–15; Luke 19:10; 1 Tim 1:15), a pastor (Ezek 34:11–16; John 10:11, 14; 1 Pet 2:25; 5:4), and a teacher (Matt 13:54; Mark 1:22; John

1:38; 3:1–2). This depicts the empowered Christ as the most visible or concrete sign of the presence of God by the Spirit. The Christ is the primordial sacrament of the encounter with the empowering Spirit (Acts 10:38).

Following his ascension, Jesus calls some to be apostles, prophets, evangelists, pastors, or teachers (Eph 4:11). The Spirit manifests in and through those who exercise charismata; he also manifests in and through those who serve in the body of Christ, including apostles, prophets, evangelists, pastors, and teachers. Different church traditions use other designations, including, but not limited to, pope, cardinal, archbishop, bishop, priest, father, reverend, overseer, elder, deacon, deaconess, nun, etc.

To the extent that those who occupy such offices are divinely appointed and serve as such, they provide concrete expression to the Spirit. It is worth pointing out that the priesthood of all believers suggests that every Christian contributes to rendering God's presence tangible or visible by the indwelling Spirit. For example, Mother Theresa is a sacrament of God's presence in Christ inasmuch as her works of charity to the poor or marginalized manifested, mediated, and drew others into an encounter with God's presence. This included the poor, marginalized, and others inspired in faith, hope, and love toward God in Christ because of Mother Theresa's worldwide charity works.

In keeping with this, believers called to the offices of an apostle, a prophet, an evangelist, a pastor, and a teacher, are themselves signs that point to God's presence. Indeed, these ministers participate in, manifest, and thus impart upon others the presence of God by the Spirit. By serving others, empowered believers provide concrete manifestation to God's presence by the Spirit. For example, Peter and Paul provided tangible expression to the Spirit's empowering presence in their service to Jews and Gentiles, respectively (Gal 2:8).

Peter and Paul represented means of grace to the Jews and Gentiles (2 Cor 12:11–12) and indeed sacraments of the Spirit. Lastly, believers are also means of grace when they manifest the fruit of the Spirit in dealings with others. In this way, they witness to Christ's redemptive mission.

CHAPTER 4

Manifesting the Relational Spirit
Fruit-Bearing Believers

> You will know them by their fruits.
>
> (MATT 7:16)

THE FRUIT OF THE Spirit portray the Triune God's character in relation to mankind. Significantly, love is the foundation of the Triune God's dealings. Jesus states that the greatest commandment is to love God (Matt 22:38). This resonates with John, who describes God as love (1 John 4:8, 16). Love speaks of the relational character of God. Moreover, Jesus says that the second greatest commandment is for one to love their neighbor (Matt 22:39). Love defines God's dealings with humans and also humans' dealings with each other. Thus, it is unsurprising that the apostle Paul mentions love first in describing the fruit of the Spirit (Gal 5:22).

All dimensions of Pauline fruit of the Spirit flow from love or are shaped and informed by love (the Triune God). Put another way, love engenders and validates all other dimensions of the fruit of the Spirit. Among other things, Paul describes love as patient, long-suffering, selfless, hopeful, enduring, and kind, not envious, boastful, arrogant, or rude (1 Cor 13:4–7). Love characterizes the life of the age to come. In this light, by bearing the fruit of the Spirit, believers render God's presence tangible to others.

Drawing from this, I postulate that the fruit-bearing believers are sacraments of personal encounters with the Spirit of God fully manifested in and through Christ. The fruit of the Spirit reflects the Triune God's relational character in Christ through the Spirit.[1] It functions like light, which illuminates its surroundings or brightens darkness (John 1:5). Paul speaks of fruit as light consisting of goodness, righteousness, and truth (Eph 5:9). Fruit of the Spirit is a lens for discerning the presence of God at work in and through believers.

Those believers in and through whom any dimension of the Spirit's fruit manifests can be held as sacraments. This is partly so because the fruit of the Spirit is God's relational character toward his children and God's children toward others. Believers who manifest fruit show participation in the relational nature of God. Notably, the fruit of the Spirit points to a transforming, personal, and intimate relationship between God and believers. Christ primordially points to God's relational character through the fruit of the Spirit climaxed by love (John 17:26).

Next, Christ is the fruit-manifesting Man *par excellence* because he reveals the fullness of God's relational character by the Spirit. Thus, Christ renders God tangible with the degree of intensity that no one else has ever done and will ever do. This implies that the Spirit inspires all fruit-manifesting believers. The Spirit, who enables Christ to reflect God's primordial character, also encourages believers to reflect the nature of Christ. Fruit of the Spirit is an identity marker of followers of Christ. This partly explains why Jesus says fruit distinguishes the true prophets from false ones (Matt 7:21).

The Spirit opens up believers to the Father, the Son, and one another.[2] Fruit of the Spirit has eschatological import in that fruit-manifesting believers signify to others that "heaven is already present on earth."[3] Since fruit issues in the Spirit, it allows believers to point others to the Spirit at work in and through them. In essence, the fruit of the Spirit reflects God's holiness (Rom 12:1; 1 Pet 5:3). Consequently, fruit-manifesting believers inspire others toward holiness and fit as means of grace and sacraments of God's presence.

To illustrate the sacramentality of fruit-manifesting believers, let us reflect on the following dimensions of the fruit of the Spirit: love, joy, peace, patience, kindness, generosity, faithfulness, gentleness, self-control (Gal

---

1. Fee, *Paul, the Spirit*, 114.
2. Smail, *Giving Gift*, 184.
3. Boersma, *Heavenly Participation*, 5.

5:22–23), humility, forgiveness (Col 3:12–13), and hospitality. Let us first look at how loving believers render God's presence tangible to others.

The Relational Spirit and Loving Believers

It is not a coincidence that Paul mentions love first when describing the Spirit's fruit (Gal. 5:22–23). This is because love is God's essential character.[4] Love is the ground upon which all other virtues of the fruit of the Spirit rest and manifest God's grace in a significant way. Thus Keener writes, "Many of the expressions of the Spirit relate to this fruit of love, e.g., peace, patience, meekness."[5] Similarly, Boff maintains that "love is this pristine capacity to freely communicate oneself to another who is different."[6]

Seen in this light, Christ fits as the primordial sacrament of God's presence of love epitomized by his sacrificial death on behalf of humankind (Rom 5:7–8). Christ is the primordial sign of the Spirit's loving presence. This is the love God pours into the heart of a believer by the Spirit (Rom 5:5). Likewise, loving believers are locations, sites, and signs of grace as they render the Spirit of love tangibly present to others.

To be sure, believers play an active role in the concrete manifestation of God's love in their dealings with others. Precisely, the loving believers are concrete signs of the relational Spirit. As such, they make the relational Spirit visibly present. Seen in this light, the loving fit as sacraments of the relational Spirit. The love which God pours into believers' hearts by the Spirit finds manifestation in diverse ways. Diverse manifestations of God's love via believers bolster the assertion that they are sacraments of God's love, e.g., the women who provided for Christ (Luke 8:1–3). A joyful attitude often accompanies believers who love both God and others (believers and unbelievers).

The Relational Spirit and Joyful Believers

Joy is God's character (Neh 8:10) and finds full expression in Christ (Luke 6:22–23; 10:21; John 15:11). Christ is the primordial sacrament of God's presence of joy. Believers are joyful, knowing that God is with them (Ps

---

4. Fee, *God's Empowering Presence*, 446–47.
5. Keener, *Gift & Giver*, 78.
6. Boff, *Liberating Grace*, 167.

5:11; 9:14; 13:5).⁷ Joy defies adverse life circumstances (Phil 4:4–7; 1 Thess 5:16–18; Jas 5:13). As Fee notes, "the presence or absence of joy is quite unrelated to one's circumstances."⁸ Joy thrives on awareness of God's immanence. Seen in this light, the joyful are signs of the relational Spirit and render him visibly present.

More robustly, they are sacraments of encountering the relational Spirit. For example, Paul encourages others to rejoice in the Lord while he sits in prison (Phil 4:4) and sings hymns of praise (Acts 16:23–30). The joyful Paul and Silas are sacraments of encountering the relational Spirit. The joyful are signs of the grace of the Spirit and inspire others to encounter Christ. Often, joyful persons also experience and manifest peace in their dealings with other people.

The Relational Spirit and Peaceful Believers

Human beings generally desire to live in peace. The peace I reference here derives from the Spirit. It finds its concrete expression in and through Spirit-indwelled believers. At the individual and collective levels, believers make a difference by living and relating peaceably to their neighbors. Similarly, peaceful believers are concrete signs of the grace of God's relational presence by the Spirit. This is so because peace is within God's character (1 Thess 5:23; 2 Thess 3:16; 1 Cor 14:33; 2 Cor 13:11; Rom 15:33; 16:20; Phil 4:9).

God's peace is visible in peaceful believers in their relation to others. It is rooted in God, and thus its manifestation concomitantly manifests the Spirit. By living peaceably, believers reflect an essential characteristic of sacraments, i.e., disclosing God's relational presence by the Spirit (Rom 14:17; 15:13). Christ is the peace-manifesting Man *par excellence* as he reveals the fullness of God's peace in his dealings with others. Thus, Christ is the primordial sacrament of the personal encounter with the Spirit of God's peaceful presence (Eph 2:13–17). Peace relates to patience, especially in dealing with people that may be unjustifiably hostile toward you.

---

7. Keener, *Gift & Giver*, 78.
8. Fee, *God's Empowering Presence*, 448.

The Relational Spirit and Patient Believers

Patience is the fruit of the Spirit and characterizes God's tolerance of humanity (Rom 2:4; 9:22).[9] It sets a standard of how believers ought to deal with each other (Col 3:12–13; 1 Thess 5:14). The Christian life requires tolerance, especially toward those who need long and patient love and kindness (Col 1:11; Jas 5:10–11). In fact, long-suffering is having patience with people who deliberately try to upset or harm you. Patient believers make the relational Spirit visible.

More adequately, patient believers participate in the Spirit of God's patience. Hence, the patient believers are concrete signs of the grace of God's relational presence. It is partly in this sense that patient believers are sacraments of God's relational presence. The synoptic Gospel shows how Christ related patiently to both his disciples and those who opposed him (Matt 12:24; Mark 3:2–22; Luke 11:15). In this light, Christ is the primordial sacrament of the encounter with the Spirit's relational presence.

The Patient Paul and the Relational Spirit

This section takes seriously the theological conviction that Christ is the primordial sacrament of a personal encounter with God through the Spirit of patience. Christ shapes the sacramentality of patience-bearing believers. Hence, Paul testifies about bearing the fruit of patience as he spreads the message of salvation through Christ (2 Cor 6:4). By so doing, Paul renders Christ visible. This is so because Christ is the fruit of patience-bearing Man *par excellence*.

To be sure, Paul bore the fruit of patience only in a derivative sense. Precisely, Paul bore the fruit of patience by the empowering grace of the Spirit's presence. Seen in this light, the fruit of patience-bearing Paul signifies divine-human cooperation, which is key to believers' sacramentality. Thus, Paul demonstrated divine-human cooperation by bearing the fruit of patience as he faced numerous and varieties of hardships. By doing so, Paul reflected the patience of Christ and rendered him visible. Paul fits as a sacrament of the patience of Christ.

---

9. Keener, *Gift & Giver*, 80.

The Relational Spirit and Kind Believers

The fruit of kindness expresses God's character toward humankind (1 Kgs 3:6; 2 Chr 1:8; Ruth 2:20; Joel 2:13). It is directed especially toward those who don't deserve it (Luke 6:35; Rom 11:22). The fullness of God's kindness is evident in the sending of Christ to bring salvation to humankind (Titus 3:4). Even more, Christ demonstrates God's kindness in the way he deals with others. His willingness to assume the body of flesh and to identify with sinful humankind is the utmost manifestation of the kindness of God.

The fruit of the Spirit also expresses God's character in how he deals with humankind. Thus, Keener asserts that "In Paul's letters, kindness most often represents God's kindness toward those who don't deserve it."[10] This kindness of God is seen in and through the humanity of Christ, especially when he is dealing with those who opposed his redemptive mission. As an example, Jesus healed the person whose ear was cut off (Luke 22:50).

It is noteworthy that one would not expect such an act of kindness to be performed toward one seeking your death. Fee partly clarifies this when he writes: "The Spirit not only empowers us to endure the hostility or unkindness of others; he also enables us to show kindness to them, actively to pursue their good."[11]

Notably, Christ is the kindness-bearing Man *par excellence* and the primordial sacrament of God's kindness. As they originate in God, kind believers express the kindness of God by the Spirit. To be sure, it is not natural for people to show kindness or compassion to those who are hostile toward them. Precisely this behavior is foreign to the natural human until one is made new in Christ (Rom 3:12).[12] Kindness is not a disembodied experience but originates in the Spirit and manifests in believers. Thus, kind believers are sacraments of the Spirit of kindness.

The Relational Spirit and Christ's Kindness

It is also true that Christ manifests this kindness in the way he deals with his brethren. For example, he touches a leper and cleanses him (Matt

---

10. Keener, *Gift & Giver*, 80.
11. Fee, *God's Empowering Presence*, 450.
12. Keener, *Gift & Giver*, 80.

8:1–4); spends time with tax collectors well-known as sinners in society like Zacchaeus (Luke 19:5); ministers to people out of compassion (Matt 9:36; 14:14; 15:32; 20:34; Mark 1:41; 5:19; 6:34; 8:2; 9:22; Luke 7:13; 8:48). Such events depict Christ as the kind Man *par excellence,* and primordial sacrament of God's kindness.

In keeping with this, believers are expected to show kindness to others (2 Sam 9:3; Eph 2:7; 4:32; Col 3:12; 1 Pet 3:8; 2 Pet 2:7; 1 John 3:17; Jude 1:22). This kindness is of the same nature as the kindness of God. Thus, kind believers are sacraments of encountering the Spirit's relational presence. By so doing, kind believers are concrete signs of the relational Spirit (Luke 23:34; Acts 7:60). As it is not natural for people to show kindness, especially to those who are hostile toward them, the Spirit enables believers to make God tangible. Since God's kindness is not esoteric or abstract, believers who show kindness toward others by the Spirit are like Christ.

The Kind Stephen and the Relational Spirit

The events in the life of Stephen indeed confirm that he was full of the Spirit. For example, Stephen reacts kindly toward those stoning him to death. One would expect Stephen to respond in a vengeful way, yet he shows kindness. This kindness is not humanly engendered but is an act of the Spirit working in and through Stephen. Notably, Stephen shocks his captors by asking God to forgive them (Acts 7:60).

To be sure, this kindness mirrors the kindness of Christ, who forgives his captors as he dies on the Cross (Luke 23:34). By forgiving those stoning him to death, Stephen expresses God's kindness and renders Christ visible by the Spirit's presence. This kindness relates to generosity.

The Relational Spirit and Generous Believers

Generosity speaks of the goodness of God toward all creation, especially humankind. As the fruit of the Spirit, generosity entails doing good to others. This goodness or generosity does not exist apart from its active and concrete expression. Generosity points to the relational presence of God by the Spirit who works in and through believers. Generosity or goodness is often directed to the underserving and thereby points to God's unmerited gift-giving character. For example, God sends rain upon both the just (believers) and unjust (unbelievers) (Matt 5:45). The most generous act of God toward humankind is his self-giving of Christ (John 3:16). The most generous act of Christ is his self-giving death on the Cross for others (John 12:27; 1 John 3:8).

Seen in this light, Christ merits as the primordial sacrament of God's generosity by the Spirit. Similarly, believers who act generously toward others are like Christ. Such believers function as signs of God's generosity. Because generous believers make the relational Spirit visibly present, they fit as sacraments of God's presence.

The Relational Spirit and Faithful Believers

Faithfulness is God's character that points to how he deals with all his creation (Deut 7:9; Hos 11:12; 1 Cor 1:9; 10:13; 2 Cor 1:18). The faithfulness of God finds full manifestation in and through the life of Christ (Matt 8:8; John 8:29; 1 John 1:9). As the fruit of the Spirit, it has the same character as the faithfulness of God. It points to the reality of God's faithfulness and makes him visibly present. Thus, Christ, who does not give up in the face of the cruel death on the Cross, is the preeminent sign of God's faithfulness. To be sure, the Spirit enables Christ to remain faithful to God's redemptive mission (Matt 26:39; Mark 14:36; Luke 22:42; Heb 12:2).

Faithfulness is a stance of utter trust in God. Christ is the faithful Man *par excellence*. A faithful believer always speaks from a position of truth. Put another way, faithfulness finds expression in and through believers who speak truthfully or speak truth. For instance, David spoke honestly, truly, and faithfully when he told his men, "The Lord forbid that I should do this thing to my lord, the Lord's anointed, to raise my hand against him; for he is the Lord's anointed" (1 Sam 24:6). This was when David only cut off a corner of Saul's cloak against the former's advisors urging that David should kill Saul (1 Sam 24:4). Thus, David manifested God's presence at work in and through him. Significantly, David is a sign and means of grace of God's faithfulness or truthfulness. The fruit of faithfulness or truthfulness manifests in one's relationship to others, both believers and unbelievers.

Drawing from this, faithful believers are concrete signs of the grace of God's relational presence by the Spirit. Notably, the Spirit enables believers to live out faithful lives notwithstanding storms of the Christian life. The faithful believers point to the reality of the Spirit. In this sense, these believers can be held as sacraments of God's faithfulness by the

Spirit. For example, Stephen does not renounce his faith in God as he is stoned to death (Acts 7:57–60). Therefore, he fits as a sacrament of an encounter with the Spirit of faithfulness.

The Faithful Disciples and the Relational Spirit

That the early church disciples manifested faithfulness as the fruit of the Spirit is difficult to miss. Though it is beyond this book's scope to provide details that support this claim, the Lukan narrative in his second volume suggests so. As discussed previously, faithfulness as the fruit of the Spirit refers to unwavering trust in God's trustworthiness.[13] For example, despite being beaten and facing death threats, the disciples continued to preach and teach in the name of Jesus.

Certainly, their faithfulness can be seen in their response to the leaders who warned them neither to preach nor to teach in the name of Jesus: "But Peter and the apostles answered, 'We must obey God rather than any human authority" (Acts 5:29). This Spirit manifestation via the fruit of faithfulness reflects the faithfulness of their Lord, Jesus. Notably, by bearing this fruit of faithfulness in the face of hostility, they rendered Jesus visible.

In fact, their response of joy or indeed of faith, hope, and love after being flogged render Christ the flogged Man *par excellence* visible (Acts 5:40; cf. Acts 16:23; 22:24; 2 Cor 11:23). For this reason, these faithful disciples are sacraments of personal encounters with Christ through the Spirit of God's presence.

The Faithful Stephen and the Relational Spirit

Luke describes Stephen as a man full of grace and power who performed great wonders and signs among the people (Acts 6:8). To be sure, the only way to explain the source of the ability to perform great wonders and signs is Spirit empowerment. Spirit empowerment partly reflects in exercising spiritual gifts and bearing spiritual fruit. Precisely, Stephen manifested the fruit of faithfulness. A believer's unwavering trust marks this fruit of faithfulness in God despite adverse circumstances. For example, Luke indicates that Stephen maintained his faith until his last

---

13. Fee, *God's Empowering Presence*, 451.

breath. Notably, Stephen prayed to God to forgive those who stoned him to death (Acts 7:60).

Similarly, Stephen's posture of looking up to heaven and kneeling in prayer depict faith, hope, and love toward God (Acts 7:54–59). Indeed, Stephen demonstrates to his persecutors that he is faithful to Christ. Precisely, the faithful Stephen signifies cooperation with the Spirit of God in Christ. The Spirit inspires Stephen's words and deeds that depict faithfulness to God in Christ.

In turn, Stephen inspires others because he remains faithful to Christ until his death. In this way, he manifests Christ who also remained faithful until his death on Calvary's Cross. Seen in this light, the faithful Stephen is a sign and means of grace. More adequately, Stephen is a sacrament of a personal encounter with the Spirit of God's presence through the faithful Christ.

The Faithful Shadrach, Meshach, and Abed-Nego and the Relational Spirit

Shadrach, Meshach, and Abed-Nego manifest the concrete presence of the Spirit by bearing the fruit of faithfulness. Precisely, King Nebuchadnezzar enacts a law that requires all people in his kingdom to worship the golden image he has set up (Dan 3:7–10). Violators are threatened to be thrown into a burning furnace (Dan 3:11). Fully aware of this threat, Shadrach, Meshach, and Abed-Nego remain faithful to their God. The conspirators bring their violations to the attention of the King, "these men, O king, have not paid due regard to you. They do not serve your gods or worship the gold image which you have set up" (Dan 3:12). They admit the charge and choose to die rather than disobey their God (Dan 3:17–18).

God delivers by sending another being (the fourth man) into the midst of the furnace (Dan 3:25). This inspires the King to enact a law forbidding people from speaking against their God (Dan 3:29). In this way, Shadrach, Meshach, and Abed-Nego demonstrate faithfulness to God that is rooted in the Spirit. Moreover, they render the transcendent God immanent and tangible. In this sense, they fit as sacraments of a personal encounter with the Spirit of God's faithfulness.

The Faithful Daniel and the Relational Spirit

Daniel is another individual who bore the fruit of faithfulness. It is noteworthy that his colleagues decide to plot against him. Indeed, his colleagues testified to his faithfulness both in his spiritual (religious) and professional life: "But they could find no grounds for complaint or any corruption because he was faithful, and no negligence or corruption could be found in him" (Dan 6:4). His colleagues persuade King Darius to enact a law prohibiting anyone from praying to anyone except the king for thirty days (Dan 6:7).

The violators are threatened with death by being thrown into the den of lions. Daniel continues to worship the God of Israel until he is found (Dan 6:11). In other words, Daniel chooses to remain faithful to his God. Consequently, Daniel is thrown into the den of hungry lions, but God delivers him (Dan 6:22). Notably, King Darius issues a decree wherein everyone in his kingdom should worship Daniel's God (Dan 6:26).

Seen in this light, Daniel demonstrates the fruit of faithfulness even in the face of death. By so doing, Daniel rendered God's empowering presence to be visible to all, including King Darius. This is because everyone, including King Darius, knows that only divine action can rescue one in the manner Daniel experienced.

As the author of Hebrews reports, Christ was faithful to the one who appointed him (Heb 3:1–2). Drawing from the Old Testament, Keener adds that faithfulness means that "one shows trust in God by cleaving to him in obedience based on a relationship with him."[14] Seen in this light, Christ is the faithful Man *par excellence*. This is because Christ was faithful to the Father in the face of hostility (Heb 12:3). Thus, the faithful believers reflect Christ's character and render God visible by the Spirit. In this way, the faithful believers are sacraments of a personal encounter with the faithful Christ by the Spirit.

Since living out a faithful Christian life demands Spirit empowerment, a manifestation of faithfulness as the fruit of the Spirit in a believer suggests an invisible encounter in grace with God. Thus, living faithfully is a manifestation or a sign of an invisible encounter with God's presence in Christ by the Spirit. Notably, this ability to live faithfully is occasioned by the Spirit.

---

14. Keener, *Gift & Giver*, 81.

The Relational Spirit and Gentle Believers

Gentleness is the fruit of the Spirit, sometimes referred to as meekness. God demonstrates a gentle character in his dealings with humankind (Job 15:11; Jer 10: 24; Hos 11:4). As a fruit of the Spirit, gentleness finds its fullest manifestation in and through the life of Christ (Matt 11:29; 2 Cor 10:1; 1 Pet 3:16). In fact, gentleness, or meekness, as a character of Christ features heavily in the Pauline corpus (1 Cor 4:21; Gal 5:23; 6:1; Col 3:12; Eph 4:2; 1 Tim 6:11; 2 Tim 2:25; Tit 3:2).

Though God in human flesh, Christ does not show a condescending attitude toward others. Christ manifests the gentlest character of God in his self-giving death on the Cross (Matt 11:29; 12: 19–20; 21:5; Mark 11: 15–16; Phil 2:8). Similarly, the believers who demonstrate gentleness toward others are signs of the grace of personally encountering the presence of God by the Spirit of gentleness (Eph 4:2; 1 Tim 3:3; Titus 3:2; Jas 3:17; 1 Pet 3:4, 16). Such demonstrations make God's gentleness visible. It implies that gentle believers are sacraments of God's relational grace by the Spirit. Notably, they are like Jesus Christ the gentle Man *par excellence*.

The Relational Spirit and Self-Controlled Believers

The fruit of self-control refers to self-discipline or temperance. As a relational character of God, self-control shows how God deals with humankind (Gen 18:23–32; 2 Tim 1:7; Titus 2:11–12; 2 Pet 1:6). God's relational character of self-control finds full manifestation in Christ. His self-control peaked when he was arrested and led to the Cross of his crucifixion (Matt 26:51; John 18:8; 19:9). Precisely, Christ manifested the fruit of self-control by restraining himself from calling the twelve legions of angels to intervene in his arrest which was the most humanly pressing situation (Matt 26:53).

The Spirit empowered Christ to exercise self-control. Notably, Christ is the primordial sacrament of God's presence of self-control. Similarly, self-controlled believers are sacraments of the relational Spirit (1Thess 2:7; 1 Tim 3:3; 2 Tim 2:24; Titus 3:2; Jas 3:17; 1 Pet 2:18; 3:4). By exercising self-control, believers reflect Christ by the Spirit. In this way, they make the Spirit of Christ visible to others. Therefore, the self-controlled are sacraments of a personal encounter with God's relational presence by the Spirit of Christ as the self-controlled Man *par excellence*.

The Relational Spirit and Humble Believers

Humility is a character of God in his dealings with humanity. In some ways, humility speaks of not wanting to exalt oneself. This thinking reflects the biblical claim that God is against the proud but exalts or gives grace to the humble (Ps 147:6; Prov. 3:34; 29:23; Ezek 21:26; Jas 4:6, 10; 1 Pet 5:5–6). God's character of humility finds full manifestation in and through the humanity of Christ. Though God, Christ took upon himself the form of a servant and human flesh to identify with sinful humanity (John 1:14; 1 Tim 2:5; Phil 2:6–8). In his dealings with the disciples and others, Christ displays utmost humility by the Spirit. Seen in this light, Christ is the primordial sign of the grace of God's relational character of humility by the Spirit. More adequately, he is the primordial sacrament of encountering the relational Spirit of humility.

Next, we also encounter Old Testament believers who demonstrate the fruit of humility. For example, God describes Moses as a very humble man (Num 12:3). Though the Spirit did not indwell believers in the Old Testament, Moses shows humility in his dealings with others to the point of attracting God's attention. As the Spirit enables Moses to be humble, it is theologically plausible to call him the most concrete sign of humility in the Old Testament.

As the humblest in the Old Testament, Moses manifests God's relational character. As such he points others to the reality of God's presence at work in and through him. Accordingly, Moses is a sacrament of an encounter with God's Spirit. Likewise, humble believers make God's relational Spirit visible or tangible to both fellow believers and also unbelievers. Believers show humility in dealing with others (Rom 12:16). The character of humility issues in God hence the humble are signs of grace. More pointedly, the humble believers are sacraments of a personal encounter with God's relational presence by the Spirit of Christ the humble Man *par excellence.*

The Relational Spirit and Forgiving Believers

Forgiveness is central to the Christian faith; thus, Christianity is inconceivable without it. Forgiveness is a relational character of God toward humanity. This fruit of forgiveness finds its full manifestation in and through Christ; hence he is the forgiving Man *par excellence.* Christ is the embodiment of God's grace of forgiveness by the Spirit. At the Cross, he perfectly reveals this forgiving character when he asks the Father to forgive those that crucified him (Luke 23:34).

In the same way, believers who forgive others manifest the Spirit of Christ's forgiveness. In this way, forgiving believers can point others to the reality of God's grace of forgiveness. For example, inspired by Christ, Stephen forgives those who stone him to death (Acts 7:59–60). Stephen points others to the reality of the grace of God's forgiveness. This is because there is no human ability that can provide a human being with this level or capacity of forgiveness except by the Spirit. Thus, the forgiving Stephen renders tangible the grace of God's relational presence.

The Relational Spirit and Hospitable or Hosted Believers

> I was a stranger, and you did not welcome me, naked and you did not give me clothing, sick and in prison, and you did not visit me.
>
> (MATT 25:43)

That the disciples in the early church practiced hospitality is difficult to miss in Acts. For example, some in the early church practiced hospitality toward missionaries (Acts 16:15; 17:5; 18:2–3, 7; 21:16). Hospitality is as ancient as humanity itself. Hospitality holds a privileged place in Judaism and in the New Testament.[15] Paul also employed the principle of hospitality when he rallied believers in the churches of Achaia to help believers in the churches of Judea due to famine (2 Cor 8:14–15).

To be sure, hospitality can be seen in the garden of Eden, where God welcomes Adam into the Garden (Gen 2:8). Essentially, Adam was a stranger in the garden and thus his host (God). Certainly, God as the host of Adam would come to him in the cool of the day to attend to him (Gen 3:8). Significantly, God ensured that Adam and Even had access to all resources necessary for their livelihood (Gen 2:8–14).

Similarly, Adam is the first human to practice hospitality as he welcomes Eve into the Garden, replicating what God did to him (Gen 2:23). As host, God briefs Adam about the rules meant to enhance and not impair his wellbeing. As a responsible host, God does not hide from his guests, Adam and Eve, his intention and desire to improve their lives (Gen 1:22, 28). Unfortunately, as can happen to any host-guest relationship,

---

15. See Koenig, *New Testament Hospitality*.

things do not turn out as expected. In this case, it is because of the guest that the host-guest relationship is fractured.

Adam and Eve's act of disobedience forces God to evict them from the garden (Gen 3:23). Notwithstanding this, God provides for Adam and Eve's clothing made of animal skin, which shows that hospitality is ontological to his being (Gen 3:21). Thus, God and hospitality are inextricably linked. Later, God extends his invitation to host Israel's children by entering into a covenant with Abraham (Gen 15:18). To be sure, God already planned to extend this host-guest relationship to include non-Israelites (Rom 4:16; Gal 3:6–9, 14, 29). This host-guest relationship between God and Israelites would experience constant setbacks until the birth of Jesus Christ, the hospitable Man *par excellence* (John 1:14; Gal 4:4) and the hosted Man par excellence who didn't have a place of his own to lay his head (Matt 8:20; Luke 9:58).

In and through Christ, all humanity would once again be the guests of God following the host-guest fractured relationship between God and Adam and Eve. When the Spirit descends upon Christ, it manifests the restoration of the host-guest relationship in the Garden of Eden. This is partly why God the Father expresses delight in the Son (Matt 3:17; Mark 1:11; Luke 3:22; cf. John 1:27, 33).

God expects the believers to be hospitable to the suffering thereby reflecting Him as the primordial host of both human creation and non-human creation (Acts 17:28). Believers who care for their environment as God's guests in this world, render the Creator Spirit visible hence are signs and sacraments of the Spirit (Gen 1:2; 2:5, 8). Upon conversion, believers become temples of the Spirit (1 Cor 6:19). Thus, the Spirit is the prime guest and host of believers from the point of conversion. Like in the words of Christ to his disciples, it is expected of them to be hospitable to strangers, the prisoners, the hungry, the naked, the poor, or merely the vulnerable among us (Matt 25:43). This sense of hospitality is extended to the weak and vulnerable, whether they are believers or not.

Interestingly, Christ defines hospitality to the vulnerable as to himself (Matt 25:45). The hospitable are concrete signs of God's hospitable presence. It is noteworthy that Christ himself played host to the vulnerable in many instances. Christ stressed the significance of hospitality when he talked about extending an invitation to a banquet to the underserving (Matt 22:8). In fact, Christ likens the invitation to the kingdom of heaven to an invitation to a banquet. In other words, the way Jesus welcomed strangers or outcasts in society is quite challenging for believers. Christ recognized that even the strangers are at the center of God's heart.

Certainly, some people followed Christ, not because of his miracles, signs, or wonders, as crucial as these are, but because of his hospitality (John 6:26). Instead, the way that Christ was hospitable to strangers was a polemic against the religious establishment of the day. The Pharisees, Sadducees, and Scribes were mostly concerned about occupying places of honor in synagogues and society (Mark 12:39; Luke 14:7; 20:46). In contrast, Christ gave pride of place to meeting others' needs.

In fact, Christ privileged hospitality to the most vulnerable. Certainly, most miracles that Jesus performed engendered an attitude of hospitality. Christ was not merely interested in demonstrating God's empowering presence by the Spirit through miracles, signs, and wonders. Christ was interested in being hospitable to the vulnerable or strangers that were hopeless and almost at a breaking point in life. Interestingly, Christ makes his interest in being hospitable to strangers or the vulnerable as he reads from Isaiah chapter 61 (Luke 4:18).

Hospitality and Sacramentality

To be sure, there is a risk involved in being hospitable to the vulnerable or strangers. For example, Jesus risked his reputation when he acted hospitably toward the Samaritan woman at the well (John 4:27), or when he dined with Zacchaeus, a well-known sinner in society (Matt 9:9–17; 11:19; Mark 2:15–22; Luke 5:29–39; 7:34; 19:7), and healed the sick on a Sabbath (Matt 12:10; Mark 3:2; John 9:14–16). The Spirit enabled Christ to act hospitably toward the strangers, the needy, the outcasts, the sinners, etc. Similarly, the Spirit enables the believers to exercise hospitality toward the needy other in the same sense as the hospitable Jesus Christ.

Notwithstanding this, many saw the Spirit tangibly present in and through such acts motivated by hospitality. This also connects to the notion that believers are given spiritual abilities like spiritual gifts so they can freely give to the needy (Matt 10:8; cf. 1 Cor 4:7). In this sense, the hospitable are sacraments of God's presence as they reach out to the vulnerable or strangers. After his ascension, the hospitable disciples continue to manifest the presence of God in Christ through their acts of hospitality by the Spirit. For example, the hospitable Christ fed multitudes of strangers (Matt 14:21; Mark 6:44; Luke 9:14; John 6:10–13).

This miracle prompts people to conclude that he is the prophet who was to come (John 6:14). This hospitable act leads others to recognize him as the Spirit-bearing Man *par excellence*. Notably, hospitality is a sacramental character that reveals God's presence. The hospitable reveal God's relational presence because in him believers live, move and have their being (Acts 17:28).

Hospitality in Christian tradition traces back to Christ and the early church. It is by making room for the vulnerable that believers render the Spirit tangibly or visibly present to others. In other words, the hospitable believers point to the reality of the Spirit as the guest-indwelling believers. Of course, there are diverse ways that believers can go about being hospitable to the vulnerable. For example, some churches or individual believers organize food pantries for the poor in communities.

Similarly, other believers engage in ministry to prisoners, distribute clothes, offer financial assistance or sponsorship to the needy, offer home care services to the elderly or those with a disability, or serve in church parking lots. While such activities may not be classified as spiritual, they manifest God's presence as the primary guest. In other words, hospitality to corporeal guests is hospitality to the incorporeal guest (the Spirit). This suggests that not only do hospitable believers signify the reality of the Spirit, but they make the Spirit as the primary guest, tangible or visible. Hospitality is a common calling to all believers. In church history, the role of hospitality in advancing the Great Commission has been unequally emphasized in churches.

It seems fair to suggest that mainline church traditions like the Roman Catholic Church and Protestants or Evangelicals have privileged the role of hospitality in the Great Commission. For example, these mainline churches established hospitals, schools, home care homes, etc., even in developing countries. In fact, these forms of delivering services to the vulnerable have played a role in bringing others to the saving knowledge of Christ. Of course, others point out that some of these initiatives by mainline churches are not primarily meant for hospitality to the vulnerable but rather for profit. For example, it is mostly the well-off in developing countries who can afford to pay for the "hospitality" services these mainline churches offer.

Hospitality services offered by mainline churches generally cost less than those offered by for-profit organizations. Notwithstanding this, the poverty level in developing countries still makes it difficult for the most vulnerable to access these services. In contrast, Pentecostals have historically not given hospitality pride of place. Typically, Pentecostals emphasize encounters with the Spirit, albeit not in social contexts. Admittedly, Pentecostals have stepped up their efforts to offer hospitality services in their communities.

Indeed, hospitality ministries now play a prominent role in many Pentecostal churches, as in mainline churches. To be sure, there is not a normative approach to hospitality so that different churches, parachurch groups, or individual and collective believers can undertake hospitality ministry at different scales depending on their resources. It seems that when Christ talked about being hospitable to the vulnerable, he did not make a necessary appeal for organizations but for individuals to play their role.

Believers ought to be hospitable to the vulnerable they come across to the extent that their resources allow. In this way, hospitable believers fulfill Christ's teaching and enable the indwelling Spirit as the supreme stranger or guest within to be tangibly or visibly present. By so doing, hospitable individuals are sacraments of an encounter with God's relational presence. It is in this sense that the hospitable individuals help alleviate others' suffering. Thus, Paul appeals to the believers to do good, especially to the households of faith or the fellow believers (Gal 6:10).

Paul does not mean that he privileges the hospitality of believers to unbelievers. If this were the case, Paul would contradict Christ, which he would not want to do. It is instead to emphasize that hospitality flows from sacred spaces to secular spaces. Paul realizes that it is in one's household of faith that one learns about the hospitable Christ. Seen in this light, it may be difficult for believers to be hospitable to strangers if they cannot be hospitable to their own biological household or their worshiping community.

As a parallel to the above, Christ points out that doing good to those who do you good and loving those who love you does not distinguish from unbelievers or sinners (Matt 5:43–48; Luke 6:27–36). It is in doing good, loving those who do not deserve that the Spirit of Christ finds concrete expression. Jesus points out that by doing good and loving the undeserving stranger, believers reveal God's hospitable character (Matt 5:45, 48; Luke 6:35–36).

The sacramentality of hospitable believers has ecumenical import. All Christian churches, denominations, or theological traditions do not oppose helping the vulnerable or weak. It is undeniable that hospitality to the vulnerable opens space for manifesting the Spirit of God's relational presence. The hospitable believers are not limited to any particular denomination, church, or theological tradition. Roman Catholics, Eastern Orthodox, Methodists, Presbyterians, Anglicans, Lutherans, Pentecostals, and Charismatics who provide concrete manifestation to God's relational presence via hospitable acts are signs of grace. These render Christ tangible.

Notably, they are sacraments of an encounter with the Spirit's relational presence. The Spirit of hospitality within the Trinity empowers believers to be hospitable toward others. By welcoming the needy into their homes, believers function as sacraments of the Spirit of Christ. But, the hosted or guests can also serve as channels for manifesting God's relational presence.

The Relational Spirit and Guests or Hosted Believers

> Jesus said to them, "They need not go away;
> you give them something to eat."
>
> (MATT 14:16)

It is not only the hospitable who manifest God's presence but also guests. When the Spirit overshadowed Mary for Christ to descend into her womb (Luke 1:35), she became a human host of the presence of God. As a corporeal human being, Mary became a concrete site or a sign of the grace of the presence of God by the Spirit. Notably, Mary became a concrete sign of grace that pointed to the reality of God's presence by the Spirit. More adequately, Mary enabled God to be tangibly or visibly present by the Spirit. Seen in this light, Mary is the first human to be a host and indeed indwelled by the presence of God. Drawing from this, the hospitable Mary functions as a sacrament of a personal encounter with God's relational presence through the Spirit.

On the other hand, Christ became the guest of Mary. As the God-Man, this suggests that Christ (the guest) also serves as the primordial sacrament of the encounter with the Spirit. Specifically, Christ became the sign *par excellence* inasmuch as he pointed to the reality of God's presence by the Spirit. In fact, Christ not only pointed to the reality of God's presence but enabled him (God) to be present in and through Mary's humanity. This suggests that in Mary, one finds the double sacramentality of host-guest and guest-host relation, or indeed vice versa.

Nonetheless, after Christ was born into the world, the presence of God in him became most tangible. More relevantly, taking on human flesh (incarnation) created space for believers to be both hosts and guests of the presence of God by the Spirit. John alludes to this double sacramentality when he writes, "On that day you will know that I am in my Father, and you in me, and I in you" (John 14:20; cf. 15:4; 17:21). It implies that hosts are not always superior to guests. But Christ is still superior in any host-guest or guest-host relation to humans or believers.

In keeping with this, Zacchaeus was the host of Jesus (Luke 19:5). Put another way, Christ hosts and thereby manifests the Spirit to Zacchaeus. Likewise, believers who host strangers are vulnerable and concretely manifest the Spirit. Indeed, strangers like Zacchaeus play a role in rendering the Spirit tangibly present (Matt 25:40, 45). In the case of Jesus (hosted) and Zacchaeus (host), they both fit as sacraments of encountering the Spirit of God's presence.

Drawing from the above discussion, it shows that there is always a transposition between the host and the guest in hospitality events. Precisely, the roles of host and guest frequently switch as they share with one another, especially when realizing God's presence in the other. This demands humility on the part of hosts of the vulnerable or strangers as the latter seem to be at the former's mercy.

A classic example is when Abraham welcomes or hosts three angels, at which point God tells him that Sarah will give birth (Gen 18:2, 4–8, 10, 14). This is significant as it shows that hospitality and sacramentality are inextricably linked. Put differently, the host and the hosted are always connected to the sacramental presence of God. In other words, an event of hospitality is also an event of sacramentality.

In Abraham and Sarah's case, God takes the initiative to self-disclose his presence, to which Abraham and Sarah respond (Gen 18:1). This is important as an example of the hospitable serving as a sacrament of an encounter with the presence of God. Abraham and Sarah welcome and host these angels with great humility. It is also true that there is a transposition of the roles of host and guest between the angels and Abraham and Sarah. The two are willing to be hosts and guests as they interact with the three angels. To be sure, Abraham and Sarah are not aware that they are dealing with angels. Although they are strangers, they are God's sacramental presence. In short, it is not the case that strangers (guests) are always vulnerable to their hosts.

In contrast, strangers as guests may even enrich or enhance their host. This is the case with Abraham and Sarah (hosts), blessed by their guests (angels) with an exceptional promise of being parents in their old age against all odds. The hosts' hospitality creates space for their guests to enrich or enhance them. The magnitude of blessing that Abraham and Sarah experience for being hospitable to the strangers cannot be overemphasized. This is profoundly motivating for believers to be hospitable to strangers or the vulnerable. In fact, believers are not encouraged or inspired by potential blessings they might experience by engaging in hospitable acts.

Instead, they are primarily motivated, or at least they ought to be motivated, toward being hospitable, knowing that in strangers or the vulnerable sits God's sacramental presence. In other words, authentic hospitality engenders or issues in valuing God's sacramental presence in strangers or the vulnerable, regardless of one's needs. It is the authentically hospitable who are concrete signs of God's sacramental presence. The authentic hosts provide tangible manifestation or expression to the intangible Spirit of God's relational presence fully revealed via Jesus Christ.

It is also interesting to note that while Peter is in prison, he welcomes or hosts an angel who sets him free (Acts 12:7–11). To be sure, one could also say that an angel hosts Peter. Importantly, there is a transposition of roles of host and guest between the two. On the one hand, the angel waits on Peter, who is host by being in the prison space before the angel. However, Peter is also a guest of the angel (host) inasmuch as he oversees the rescue operation. It is the angel who, as host, gives Peter (guest) instructions and leads him out of prison.

Like Abraham and Sarah, Peter shows humility and surrenders being a host and allows the stranger he does not know to assume the role of a host (Acts 12:11). Peter acts secondarily to God's primary action in and through the angel. By so doing, Peter has an encounter with the presence of God and is rescued. Humility and openness of believers as they serve strangers or the vulnerable create space for manifesting God's presence. The practice of communing with other believers plays a role in discovering and meeting other people's needs.

CHAPTER 5

Manifesting the Communing Spirit
Communicant Believers

> For where two or three are gathered in my name, I am there among them.
>
> (MATT 18:20)

THIS CHAPTER CLAIMS THAT communicant believers are sacraments of a personal encounter with the communing Spirit. Believers imitate Jesus who fellowshipped especially with his twelve disciples. The Spirit inspires incarnational fellowship among believers. The communing Spirit who concretely manifested in and through the humanity of Jesus manifests concretely in and through believers. I use the terms "fellowship" and "communion" interchangeably to mean divine intimacy. I also use the term communicant broadly to refer to any believer who participates in a corporate worship activities including the Lord's Supper, preaching or teaching the Scripture, giving offering, fellowship, etc.

The communing Spirit inspires vertical fellowship or communion between the Trinity and believers, as well as horizontal fellowship or communion among the believers. A believer cannot genuinely fellowship or commune with God without fellowshipping or communing with believers. The vertical fellowship shapes and informs the horizontal fellowship. Christ is the fellowshipping Man *par excellence* and the standard for assessing fellowship. The incarnation is hermeneutical lens for clarifying the nature and the depth of vertical and horizontal fellowship.

The vertical fellowship with the Godhead finds authentication in incarnational fellowship with other believers. Both vertical and horizontal fellowship peak during corporate worship or in ecclesial contexts of worship. The vertical fellowship with the Godhead has a dual orientation. It occurs between an individual believer within a community of believers and the Godhead as well as between the believers, communally, and the Godhead. It flows from this that the sacramentality of worshiping believers is not a solo experience of the Godhead. Instead, it is fundamentally a communal and an incarnational experience of God's presence in and through the other believers.

Even when a believer worships by himself or herself, he or she engages in a communal experience of the Three Persons of the Godhead. Seen in this light, when the Samaritan woman met with Christ at Jacob's Well (John 4:6), she essentially encountered the Godhead (John 4:21, 23). When the Godhead encounters a person, it is often for the benefit of others as well. In that case, the Godhead expects the encountered person to testify to others about the encounter. This is what the Samaritan Woman did at Jacob's Well (John 4:29, 30) when she encountered Christ, or when Christ encountered her. Her experience inspired others in her village to encounter and fellowship with the Godhead in Christ (John 4:42). The Samaritan woman's incarnational fellowship with Christ was a means of grace for the others to encounter and to worship the Triune God in spirit and truth (John 4:24).

In corporate worship, the believers encounter and fellowship with the Godhead and other believers so that they can testify to sinners in need of salvific encounter with God. The corporate worship enables the believers to make God's communing grace visible. The effects of believers' encounter with God's communing presence manifest both within and outside church contexts.

The word church, the ecclesia or *ekklesia* in Greek, refers to those called out to worship. It is reminiscent of God's call to the Pharaoh through Moses to let the Israelites free so that they worship him in the wilderness (Exod 5:1; 7:16; 8:1,20; 9:1,13; 10:3). In this light, a church is where believers gather together to worship God in Christ by the Spirit (Matt 18:20). The Spirit of God's presence graces the community of worshiping believers. Although the Holy Spirit indwells each believer, the corporate body or community of believers itself is also indwelled by the

Holy Spirit (1 Cor 3:16–17; 6:19). The Spirit ensures intimate communion or fellowship both between God and believers and among fellow believers. The fellowship or communion within the Trinitarian community reflects in and through fellowship or communion within the community of believers.

The Greek term *Koinonia* captures this fellowship motif. Accordingly, the fellowship of believers is a manifestation of Trinitarian fellowship. More specifically, it manifests the Spirit as the bond of love within the Trinity. The activities of believers' corporate worship include but are not limited to praying, preaching/teaching, singing, giving, the Lord's Supper, and fellowship. The early church engaged in these following the outpouring of the communing Spirit (Acts 2:1).

It is not a coincidence that the 120 disciples encountered the communing Spirit within the Pentecostal communal context. The corporate worship context creates a space for worshipers to encounter and manifest the communing Spirit. Believers' communion with each other and with God reflects concretely via worship or liturgical activities.[1] Precisely, they reflect a deep sense of communion with God and fellow believers when they engage in corporate praying, preaching (call and response), sung worship, giving, the Lord's Supper, and fellowship. These activities set up the corporate worshipers as signs and means of the grace of God's communing presence by the Spirit. Such corporate-worshipers fit as sacraments of encountering the communing Spirit.

Different church traditions have different liturgical activities, with some viewed as "high" or as "low." In high liturgical churches, the corporate worshipers follow laid-down activities rigidly. In low liturgical churches, the activities are flexible, and thus the corporate worshipers may stress some but not others. Although liturgy is basically the work of the people, it facilitates encounters with God. Low liturgical churches like Pentecostals and neo-Pentecostals emphasize encounters and concrete manifestation of the Spirit of God's presence more than high liturgical churches.

Pentecostals and neo-Pentecostals encourage active participation in liturgical activities like Bible Study, corporate prayer or intercession, praise and worship, testimony, preaching, altar call, the Lord's Supper, offering or giving, foot-washing, and fellowship. They hold these as rites in

---

1. Cartledge, *Mediation of the Spirit*, 115.

the Spirit, as participating in such activities fosters concrete encounters with God's presence.[2]

By engaging in rites in the Spirit, corporate worshipers are sensitized to God's presence. Engagement in rites in the Spirit requires words (saying or uttering something) and deeds (doing something or undertaking an activity). As such, believers' liturgical words and deeds are points of conscious and intentional engagement with the Spirit. More pointedly, they are entry points into the spiritual realm. Granted the incorporeal nature of the Spirit, he delights in the concrete manifestation of his presence in and through corporate worshipers engaged in rites in the Spirit. Corporate worshiping is ideal for the Spirit's concrete expression as he is fellowship by nature.

As the Spirit was drawn to Christ for concrete manifestation due to Christ's proclivity for fellowship, believers in corporate worship contexts attract the Spirit. Manifestations of the Spirit intensify as believers engage, especially in liturgical activities that enhance fellowship with God and others. In worship, believers engage in deep communion with the Spirit of God in Christ.

It is in this sense that corporate worshipers are signs of the grace of God's communing presence. Different churches espouse distinct, albeit related, worship styles and theology. For example, Pentecostal and Neo-Pentecostal churches prefer a lively and active worship style that intensely engages the bodies of the worshipers, to a less bodily engaging or laid-back worship style. Different congregations therefore exhibit varying levels or degrees of sacramental intensity or divine manifestation during worship. Likewise, different worshipers within churches exhibit varying levels or degrees of sacramental intensity depending upon their spiritual disposition.

This does not imply that those who use a lively style of worship are more spiritual. Instead, it is to highlight that vibrant or freestyle worship powerfully engages the corporate-worshipers. That is to say, signs of encountering God's presence are more tangible or visible in the low liturgical churches of worship style that is lively and engages the worshipers' bodies.

Notwithstanding this, there are also varying degrees of sacramental intensity in lively worship. This depends on the level of individual worshipers' participation and openness to join fully in the various rites of the

---

2. See Albrecht, *Rites in the Spirit*.

Spirit. In keeping with this, Luke describes the 120 disciples as together in one place or one accord prior to the day of Pentecost (Acts 2:1). Worship creates a context for a Pentecostal experience if only a worshiping community desires to encounter and manifest the Spirit.

To the extent that the believers render the Spirit in worship tangible to others, they inspire others to seek Christ and therefore are means of grace. For this reason, the worshiping fit as sacraments of an encounter with the Spirit. In keeping with this, Jesus Christ participated in public worship by engaging in activities like praying; reading, preaching, and teaching Scripture; ministering to the needy, such as the marginalized, the sick, and the poor; foot-washing; and celebrating the Passover (Matt 26:14–39; Mark 1:21–28; 3:1–6; Luke 4:15–21; 31–37; 13:10–17; 22:7–23; 19–27; John 13:1–17). In his worship, Jesus manifested the Spirit with primordial sacramental intensity. Christ shapes and informs the theological conviction that a worshiping believer is a sacrament of an encounter with the Spirit. A worship service creates space for the worshipers to function as signs of grace.

Next, God is the one who invites believers to come into his presence and to worship him. In other words, the intimate communion with God that believers experience in worship is never possible without God's invitation in Christ and by the Spirit. Worship is a human response to God's primary act of invitation. Worshipers stand in God's presence by the grace of the Spirit of Christ (John 14:6; Rom 3:24; 5:2; Eph 2:5; 3:12; Heb 4:16). Corporate worshipers signify God's grace of communion; thus, they are sacraments of the communing Spirit of Christ.

In worship, the total person (soul, body, and spirit) is engaged (1 Thess 5:23). Because God is the Spirit, the soul and spirit enable the worshiping bodies to connect with God (John 4:23–24; 1 Cor 6:19). As worshipers engage in liturgical or worship activities, they point to or signify the Spirit. The heavenly and earthly realms interpenetrate during worship (Ps 22:3; 100:2; Zeph 3:17; Matt 18:20; Acts 13:2). Moreover, the corporate worshipers participate in and point others to the heavenly corporate worshipers (Isa 6:3; Rev 4:8). Worship takes place in the "here and now" and in the "not yet." The corporate worshipers render the transcendent God immanent.

Christ joined others in corporate worship of the Father. In this way, he revealed the Spirit of God's communing presence. Notably, Christ is the communing Man *par excellence* and the primordial sacrament of the personal encounter with the Spirit of God's communing presence. In worship, God's transcendent presence is immanent. As Jesus participated in corporate worship, he tangibly manifested God's immanent presence by the Spirit (Matt 26:17–30; Mark 1:21–28; 14:12–26; Luke 4:16–21, 31–37; 22:7–39). Jesus also manifested God's tangible presence by the Spirit outside communal worship contexts (Matt 17:2; Luke 7:11–17; 8:49–56; John 11:38–44).

In corporate worship, believers do not engage in empty or Spirit-less activities but in God himself. In worship, believers engage in rites in the Spirit since it is the Spirit who gives rise to such activities. Believers engage in worship or liturgical activities in response to God's self-disclosing presence by the Spirit. Liturgical activities are meaningless without the presence of God by the Spirit. Liturgical activities are not lifeless but engender partly or wholly in the Spirit of life. Liturgical activities partly reflect the acts of the Spirit in and through the corporate-worshiping believers.

Communal worship reflects the life and the unity of the Three Persons of the Trinity. It is partly in this sense that a worshiping community reflects the Trinitarian community. The Spirit who joins the Father and the Son in the Trinitarian community also joins believers in communal worship. By joining others in worship, believers enable the bonding Spirit to be palpably present. As the Son worshiped the Father and rendered him palpably present by the Spirit, the believers in communal worship are, in their persons, tangible expressions of God's presence in Christ. For example, praying for one another, encouraging each other, sharing the Word, and fellowshipping are human modes of manifesting the concrete presence of God. To engage in corporate worship is to engage the Three Persons of the Trinitarian community, concomitantly. Simply, it is vertical and horizontal communion between the Trinity and believers, and also between fellow believers.

The Spirit was poured out at Pentecost in an atmosphere of deep collective worship as Christ instructed the disciples (Luke 24:49). In collective or communal worship, believers signify and orient themselves for a fresh encounter with the Spirit. It is partly herein that we see the sacramental character of worshipers. The presence of God is visible in communal worship. The tangible rendering of the presence of God in Christ through worship engenders worshipers as sacraments. In communal worship, believers' relationships with God are enhanced as they experience more of his tangible presence.

Seen in this light, the disciples' relations to God in Christ were enhanced as they shared his concrete presence through the poured-out

Spirit. It is partly because of this tangible manifestation of God's presence that unbelievers were attracted to the disciples' worshiping community (Acts 2:12). The tangible rendering of God's presence underlies the sacramentality of believers in a worshiping community. To clarify this, let us reflect further on the Spirit's role in the worshiping community.

Christ is the worshiping Man *par excellence w*ho shapes and informs all the believers' approach to corporate or individual worship. The Spirit who inspired Jesus in his humanity to worship the Father is the same who also facilitates fellowship or communion, in the Trinity: God the Father; the Son; and the Spirit (John 14:16; 2 Cor 13:14; Phil 2:1). This does not suggest that the Trinity is susceptible to divisions, as God is one, yet manifested in Three Persons (Deut 6:4; Mark 12:29; 1 Cor 8:6; Gal 3:20). The fellowship or communion of corporate worshipers is ontological to the Triune God. In keeping with this, St. Augustine held the Spirit as the bond of love in the Trinity. Also, it is telling that Luke describes the disciples as in one accord as they waited for the Spirit (Acts 2:1). Luke highlights that the Spirit manifested tangibly in the early church beyond Pentecost (Acts 2:42).

This disposition of unity and fellowship that we encounter among the early disciples cannot be explained separately or distinctly from the Spirit poured out at Pentecost. It suggests that the Spirit always leads toward and not away from other believers. It is antithetical to the nature of the Spirit of Pentecost to promote individualism rather than fellowship. To clarify this, let us consider Saul's conversion as he met the risen Christ on his way to Damascus to arrest or murder those of the Way (Acts 9:1–10).

Although Saul encounters Jesus by the Spirit on the road to Damascus, he is nonetheless led to Ananias, who prays for him and baptizes him (Acts 9:4–6). This is significant as it shows that Saul was reborn and incorporated into a community of believers. Paul understands early that his growth into Christ-likeness was not a private adventure but would need other believers. This can be inferred from the fact that Ananias encountered the same Christ Saul met on his way to Damascus. This is what happens when believers engage in corporate worship: they encounter the same Spirit. This suggests that communal worshipers give concrete expression to the same Spirit of Christ, albeit with different intensity.

Notwithstanding this difference, every believer engaged in corporate worship contributes to the concrete manifestation of God's presence by the Spirit. It is no wonder that Paul stresses the role of corporate worship in the spiritual formation of believers (Rom 12:5; 1 Cor 10:17; 12:12–27).

This also clarifies why Paul and Barnabas sought counsel from apostles and elders in Jerusalem (Acts 15:1–2). Fellowship distinguished the early church community from others, as it centered upon Christ. In this way, the fellowshipping or worshiping early church community provided concrete expression to the Spirit at work in and through them (Acts 2:42).

Believers of distinct cultures, tribes, tongues, races, color, socioeconomic status, etc., reflect the work of the Spirit. The Spirit incorporates believers into new communities that transcend human categories. When this happens, one can conclude that it is the work of the Spirit. The new community of believers is most visible when believers come together in worship. Thus, they depict the character of the Trinitarian community. The three Persons of the Trinity, the Father, Son, and Spirit, commune primordially with each other. Seen in this light, Christ fits as the human site or sign of the grace of the Spirit of God's communing presence *par excellence*.

Next, one cannot be a believer without being in communion with other believers. One's salvific experience finds concrete expression in and through a community of believers. When believers commune with other believers, especially in worship, their personal relationship with God is proved or disproved. Communal worship concretely manifests the unity Jesus prayed for (John 17:11, 22). This concrete unity in church communities derives from the communing Spirit.

Drawing from this, I assert that believers who give concrete expression to the unity of the Trinity through communal worship are sacraments of an encounter with the Spirit. One liturgical aspect wherein believers manifest God's tangible presence is when they fellowship at the Lord's table via the Lord's Supper. Seen in this light, the Lord's Supper-participants or communicants are individually and communally, signs of the Spirit of God's communing grace in Christ. More adequately, corporate partakers of the Lord's Supper are sacraments of Trinitarian fellowship.

Christ instituted the Lord's Supper that the early church practiced (Acts 2:42, 46). The Lord's Supper is similar to the Passover during which Jews remember their deliverance from bondage in Egypt (Exod 12:11, 21, 27, 43, 48; Lev 23:5; Num 9:2–6, Deut 16:1–2, 5–6; Josh 5:10–11; 2 Kgs 23:21–23; 2 Chr 30:1–2, 5, 15; 35:6–19; Ezra 6:19–20; Ezek 45:21). The memorial motif is not meant to suggest that the Passover celebration is an esoteric event. The Passover celebration brings forth fresh memories of the Israelites' remarkable deliverance.

Precisely, the Passover brings forth, as it were, the very presence of God who delivered them to Egypt. In this way, the Passover allows the

Israelites to manifest the presence of the God who delivers from bondage. This is especially the case with the Israelites' second Passover celebration (Num 9:1–14). This Passover reminded the Israelites that the God who delivered them from Egypt was still in their midst. In this way, the Israelites' faith in God was strengthened, and they took concrete steps to renew their covenant with God.

Next, the blood of the lamb upon the doorposts was an efficacious sign that protected the Israelites (Exod 12:13–14). More adequately, the sign includes both the blood and the lambs that were slaughtered. Both are constitutive of this efficacious sign. However, it is also noteworthy that it is the Israelites who occasioned this sign. The absence of the blood upon the Egyptians' doorposts distinguished them from Israelites who had a covenant relationship with God. The blood on the Israelites' doorposts signified to the angel of death this covenant relation.

More robustly, the Israelites were themselves a sign of God's presence to the Egyptians. It implies that the blood and the lamb's sign manifested the Israelites themselves as signs of God's presence to the Egyptians (Exod 8:23; 9:4; 11:5; 11:7). The Passover meal, especially the sign of the blood upon their doorposts, bolsters the claim that the Israelites themselves are a sign of God's presence to the Egyptians. Therefore, Passover is an occasion wherein the Israelites are manifested as signs of encounters with God's presence. Whenever the Passover is celebrated, the Israelites make visible the God who delivered them from Egypt's bondage.

God is first prefigured at Mount Moriah, where Abraham slaughtered a lamb as a burnt offering to God instead of his son, Isaac (Gen 22:1–14). Isaac is a sign of the Old Covenant God made with Abraham (Gen 17:19, 21; Exod 2:24; Gal 4:28). Notice that this covenant occured well before the Israelites were enslaved in Egypt. To be sure, God reinforces this covenant relationship with the children of Israel when he calls and sends Moses on the redemptive mission to Egypt:

"I have observed the misery of my people who are in Egypt . . . and I have come down to deliver them from the Egyptians" (Exod 3:7–8). Notably, the children of Israel still served as a sign of God's presence amid their suffering. Again, this establishes that the Passover itself or the posted blood manifests the Israelites as a sign of God's presence to Egypt and other nations. Notably, this thinking finds strength in the biblical description that Jesus is the Lamb of God (Isa 53:7; John 1:29, 36; 1 Peter 1:18–19; Rev 13:8).

Manifesting the Communing Spirit

As a Jew, Jesus celebrated the Passover from his childhood until the end of his earthly ministry (Matt 26:2, 17–19; Mark 14:1, 12, 14, 16; Luke 2:41; 22:8, 11, 13; John 2:13; 23). The last Passover that Jesus celebrated is what Christians consider the Last Supper or the Lord's Supper. Jesus looked forward to celebrating his Passover with his disciples before his death on the Cross (Luke 22:11, 5). Interestingly, Jesus commanded his disciples to celebrate the Lord's Supper just as the Passover (Exod 12:14, 17, 24, 27:21; 28:43; 29:9, 28; 30:21; Num 27:11; 35:29; 1 Sam 30:25; Luke 22:19; 1 Cor 11:24–25). The blood of Christ is the prime sign the blood of the Passover anticipates. More importantly, Jesus Christ himself is the pre-eminent sign of the New Covenant in his blood (Luke 22:20; 1 Cor 11:25; Heb 8:6, 8; 9:15; 12:24).

Certainly, Christ has made the Old Covenant obsolete (Heb 8:13). He is now remembered and made present via the celebration of the Lord's Supper in the Spirit. As the Passover draws the Jews' or Israelites' attention to God who delivered them from Egyptian bondage, the Lord's Supper draws believers' attention to Jesus. He delivers them from the bondage of sin (John 1:29). Paul clarifies this when he writes: "For indeed Christ, our Passover, was sacrificed for us" (1 Cor 5:7, NKJV).

As the blood on doorposts of Israelites, the blood of Christ is posted on doorposts of the believers' hearts (Rev 3:20). Christ himself is the ultimate sign to which the sacramental rite of the Lord's Supper manifests or points. Put another way, Christ is the ultimate sign that precedes the sign of the Lord's Supper. More notably, Christ is the primordial sacrament of a personal encounter with God's presence and precedes the sacrament of the Lord's Supper itself.

This thinking also has vast implications on the theological conviction that believers, or, more precisely, communicants, are sacraments of a personal encounter with God's presence. Let's remember that Jesus already had a covenant relationship with his disciples before taking part in the Lord's Supper. It follows that the Lord's Supper bolstered Christ's relation to the disciples.

Furthermore, this Last Supper allowed the disciples to foretaste the new covenant relationship that Jesus would unveil through his death on the Cross (1 Cor 11:25; Heb 12:24). Thus, Jesus refers to the bread and the wine as his body and blood (Matt 26:26; Mark 14:22; Luke 22:19; 1 Cor 11:24). Thus, the Lord's Supper is a sign and sacrament that manifests Christ as the primordial sign and sacrament of God's presence by the Spirit. Drawing from this, celebrants of the Lord's Supper reveal deep communion with God in Christ through the Spirit.

The primacy of communicant believers as sacraments of a personal encounter with Christ by the Spirit arises in the assertion that the communicant Christ is the primordial sacrament of God's presence. It is essential here to understand that the primacy of the communicant Christ as the primordial sacrament of God's presence enhances rather than deflates the significance of the sacrament of the Lord's Supper itself. In fact, the meal is called the Lord's Supper because it prefigures the redemptive sacrifice of Christ via death on the Cross (Rom 3:25; Heb 9:22; 10:18). Precisely, the Lord's Supper is meaningless without Jews and Gentiles in the bondage of sin.

The Passover derives its meaning from the Israelites' deliverance from economic slavery in Egypt through the death of the Passover lambs, just as the Lord's Supper derives its meaning from the believers' (Jews and Gentiles) deliverance from the slavery of sin through the death of Christ as the perfect Passover Lamb (1 Cor 5:7). Therefore, from a New Testament perspective, there is neither Jew nor Gentile (Col 3:11; Gal 3:28). A real Jew is one whose heart is right with God (Rom 2:28–29). Many churches administer the Lord's Supper to those with a soteriological relation to God, or simply, believers.

Thus, I contend that communicants are sacraments of an encounter with God. The Lord's Supper celebration creates space for those who have personally encountered God by the Spirit to be identified. All the disciples had personally encountered Christ before participating in the Last Supper, including Judas, who would later betray Jesus (Matt 26:15, 21, 23; Mark 14:20; John 13:21). It follows that participating in the Lord's Supper does not in and of itself make a communicant believer invincible to sin. Therefore, Paul appeals to those seeking to participate in the Lord's Supper to examine themselves (1 Cor 11:28). This introspection allows them to discern the Lord's body, both the corporate worshipers and Christ's flogged, crucified, buried, resurrected, and ascended body.

It follows that communicants are, in their persons, concrete signs of intimate relation with the Triune God. The Lord's Supper transcends time and space, thus the heavenly hosts, including angels, departed saints, and believers on earth, participate in it until the *Parousia* (Heb 12:22). By implication, communicants make visible God's eschatological community. As such, they are sacraments of a personal encounter with the reality of the eschatological community they signify. As sacraments, communicants point others to the reality of eschatological communion with God.

At the Last Supper, Jesus pointed the twelve disciples to the reality of the eschatological communion. The Last Supper was a moment in which Jesus engaged in deep communion with his disciples (Matt 26:26–29; Mark 14:22–25; Luke 22:19; John 6:54–56; 1 Cor 11:24–25). Besides his disciples, he communed with heavenly hosts that cheered him on to complete the redemptive mission (Luke 22:43). The Last Supper reveals his communion with the Father and the Spirit.

Further, Christ as the communicant manifests vertical communion with the Father and the Spirit. Moreover, Christ as the communicant shows horizontal communion with his disciples. Notably, despite different theological conceptions about the Lord's Supper, the claim that the communicants are sacraments of personal encounters with the presence of God still holds. Here communicants are presumed to be those in good standing or in a salvific relationship with God.

The Corporate-Praying and the Communing Spirit

Corporate prayer and intercession play a critical role in communal worship. The Spirit and the Son are particularly involved in intercessory prayer (Rom 8:26, 27, 34). For Pentecostals, prayer and intercession are militaristic or aggressive. Pentecostals believe that the physical and spiritual realms interpenetrate; prayer and intercession enable believers to engage unseen forces. Given Pentecostals' acute awareness of unseen forces, it is not surprising that spiritual warfare is a center for Pentecostal theology.[3] Praying and interceding are therefore allocated more time in Pentecostal liturgy than most activities. For this book's purpose, it is worth pointing out that praying and interceding enable believers to encounter and manifest the Spirit.

At its basic level, prayer is communicating with the Spirit. Prayer played a considerable role in the earthly ministry of Jesus (Luke 6:12). Consequently, he challenged his disciples to pray without ceasing (Luke 18:1; cf. 1 Thess 5:17). The early church is also depicted as given to prayer and intercession (Acts 1:14; 2:42). More significantly, Jesus and the Spirit continue to pray and intercede for believers (Rom 8:26–27, 34). This

---

3. Onyinah, *Spiritual Warfare*.

shows that prayer or intercession is not human activity but a partnership with the Spirit and Christ.

Moreover, prayer and intercession enable believers to make visible the interceding Spirit and Christ. When praying and interceding, believers do not speak to mortal beings but the invisible God. In the same way, spiritual warfare enables believers to engage unseen forces of evil (2 Cor 10:4; Eph 6:12). Since it is impossible for believers, in and of themselves, to engage unseen forces of evil, partnering with Spirit and Christ in prayer and intercession is a necessity. By implication, the praying and interceding believers themselves become signs of spiritual conflict. Put simply, praying and interceding believers point to the reality of Jesus and the Spirit who lead them in spiritual warfare.

Although others only see the praying and interceding believers' actions, those actions merely reflect the Spirit and Christ's ongoing intercessions. Thus, Jesus rightly asks Peter, James, and John, "Could you not stay awake with me one hour?" (Matt 26:40). Praying and interceding believers manifest, mediate, and draw others into an encounter with God. Moses exemplifies partnership with God in prayer and intercession as per the biblical testimony that "whenever Moses held up his hand, Israel prevailed; and whenever he lowered his hand, Amalek prevailed" (Exod 17:11).

Nevertheless, the raised hands of Moses manifested God's extended hands, or God's involvement, hence yielding victory for Israel. On the other hand, Moses's lowered hands also manifested God's lowered hands or God's noninvolvement, and so Amalek prevailed. Thus, biblically-grounded postures of kneeling, crying, lifting hands, etc., during prayer and intercession have sacramental import inasmuch as they signify God's posture when believers pray and intercede. Notably, the postures of kneeling, crying, lifting hands, etc., when praying and interceding reveal believers' partnership with God.

Even in a prayer of adoration or thanksgiving, Scripture-based actions and words of believers signify God's involvement in the activity. They render God's presence tangible to the extent that believers' postures in prayer and intercession signify communion with God. The praying and interceding believers reveal, mediate, and draw others into an encounter with the Spirit. It is worthy accenting that such postures and affective words seem inevitable when believers pray and intercede in the face of life-threatening circumstances or situations.

In keeping with this, Luke reports that Jesus prayed earnestly with sweat coming down his face like many drops of blood (Luke 22:44). The context indicates that Jesus' prayer posture manifested deep communion with his Father in the face of betrayal and brutal death on the Cross (Luke 22:42). The Father acknowledged the Son's situation and sent an angel to strengthen him (Luke 22:43). Likewise, Jesus' disciples prayed earnestly when they faced death threats (Acts 4:29). As a result, the praying disciples encountered and were filled with the Spirit. The disciples manifested a concrete sign of this divine encounter by boldly speaking about Jesus (Acts 4:31).

Further, the praying disciples partnered with the interceding Spirit and Christ and were strengthened just like Christ was strengthened by an angel in the face of death. Also, Daniel prayed when faced with a life-threatening situation (Dan 6:10–11). Daniel's boldness in the face of such a life-threatening situation can only be attributed to his encounter with God in prayer. Daniel did not change his kneeling posture three times as he prayed with his house's windows open. Through his passionate prayer of deliverance from the hungry lions, Daniel manifested God's presence and inspired King Darius to acknowledge the God of Israel (Dan 6:26–27).

We can conclude that the praying Jesus, the disciples, and Daniel are signs of grace pointing to God's presence. More notably, the praying Jesus, the disciples, and Daniel are sacraments of an encounter with the Spirit. It should be pointed out that Jesus (Luke 3:21; John 11:41–42; 17:1–25), the disciples, and Daniel did not pray because they faced life-threatening circumstances. Instead, praying was their way of living and communing with God's presence.

When reading about the testimonies of Jesus, the disciples, Daniel, and others who encountered and manifested God's presence through prayer, believers can be drawn into an encounter with God's presence. It flows from this that praying and interceding believers—individually or communally—partner with, encounter, and manifest God's presence to others. The praying believers are signs of encountering God's communing presence and thus means of grace.

Next, praying is fellowshipping with the Spirit, whether it is individually or communally done. Of course, it is not uncommon for people to treat prayer as a way to receive things from God (Mark 11:24). However, prayer's primary purpose is for people to fellowship with God (Acts 2:42; 1 John 1:3, 7). The conception of prayer as fellowship with God inspires a lifestyle of prayer (Luke 18:1). Personal needs do not drive this prayer but a desire to fellowship with God in whom we live, move, and have our being (Acts 17:28). Fellowship with God through praying and fasting intensifies the manifestations of God's indwelling presence in and through believers.

The role of prayer and fasting in a believer's spiritual growth cannot be overemphasized. This thinking arises primarily in Christ. Christ devoted himself to prayer and fasting in his humanity, among other things that enhanced his sacramentality. Christ taught not only through logical and inspired discourse but by the example of the life he lived. That is to say, Christ taught by his words and his deeds. For example, Jesus taught his disciples to pray always (Luke 18:1–8), which he personally practiced (Mark 1:35; Luke 5:16). But he also valued communal prayer (Matt 26:38, 40; Mark 9:2; 14:32–34; Luke 9:28). Especially, Jesus practiced fasting (Matt 4:2; Luke 4:2; 10:21; John 4:31–32). While we do not have many explicit passages that Jesus fasted, one can infer from his teachings that he practiced fasting (Matt 6:16–18).

As mentioned earlier, Jesus never taught what he did not practice. Seen in this light, we can posit that the manifestations of God's presence by the Spirit in and through the life of Jesus are inseparably linked to his fellowship with the Father via prayer and fasting. In other words, fellowshipping with his Father through praying and fasting contributed to the intensity of God's tangible presence in and through Christ. Spiritual disciplines of praying and fasting engendered Christ as the concrete site or sign of God's communing grace *par excellence*. More adequately, Christ is the primordial sacrament of the personal encounter with God's communing presence.

Inspired by the lifestyle of Christ, the early disciples fellowshipped with God via prayer and fasting (Acts 13:2; 14:23; 1 Cor 7:5; 2 Cor 6:5; 11:27). This spiritual discipline contributed to the intensified manifestation of God's presence by the Spirit in and through the early disciples. In other words, the early disciples are concrete signs of the grace of God's presence partly due to their devotion to fellowship with God via prayer and fasting.

In the same way, believers who fellowship with God via prayer and fasting experience intensification of the manifest presence of God. Intensified manifestations of God's presence at work in and through believers engender them as concrete signs of grace. Notably, the believers who fellowship with God via prayer and fasting in Christ are sacraments of an encounter with God's presence. In particular, inspiring words and deeds flowing from a life of fellowshipping with God via prayer and fasting enable believers to provide tangible manifestation to the Spirit. It is partly in this sense that praying or fasting are spiritual disciplines that facilitate fellowship with the Spirit of God's presence. The activity of prayer reveals the sacramentality of believers.

To be sure, praying for other people's needs also opens up space for concrete manifesting of the Spirit. Precisely, intercessors or believers who stand in the gap of others provide concrete manifestation to the Spirit of God. Notably, the Spirit intercedes on behalf of believers; hence, interceding believers replicate the same by standing in the gap of others' needs. In keeping with this, Christ the interceding-praying Man *par excellence* provided concrete manifestation to the Spirit when he interceded for Peter, "but I have prayed for you that your own faith may not fail; and you, when once you have turned back, strengthen your brothers" (Luke 22:32).

The Corporate Sung-Worshiping and the Communing Spirit

Many biblical passages, especially the book of Revelation, hint that believers will join the other heavenly host in worshiping God. In particular, believers will sing songs of praise and of thanksgiving. For example, John writes, "And they sing the song of Moses, the servant of God, and the song of the Lamb: Great and amazing are your deeds, Lord God the Almighty! Just and true are your ways, King of the nations!" (Rev 15:3).

Drawing from this biblical apocalyptic text, believers who engage in worship by means of corporate singing foretaste the worship of God that awaits the coming kingdom of God. This corporate-singing worship of God takes place both in the "here and now" (the "already" or "realized") but is also yet to fully take place in the eschatological kingdom (the "not-yet" or "unrealized").

Further, corporate-singing worshipers join the ongoing worship of the triune God on the other side of the *eschaton*. The corporate singers both individually and communally signify personal encounters with the Spirit of God's presence. To be sure, inter-participation between corporate earthly singers and the corporate heavenly singers is a mystery. The human or natural faculties are inadequate for one to fully and adequately explicate the nature of this communion.

By implication, the corporate earthly singers are a lens for discerning the ongoing worship in the heavenly realms (Heb 12:22–25). Seen in this light, what goes on in corporate singing of believers in this present world provides concrete expression to the corporate singing that is ongoing on the other side of life. It follows that corporate-singing believers provide concrete expression to the reality of God as the object of worship. Indeed, the believers' physical and affective expressions in corporate-singing worship bolster the conviction that corporate-singing believers are sacraments of encounters with God.

Generally, the physical and affective expressions of corporate-singing believers suggest to others that the worshipers are engaged in an encounter with the supreme other. Moreover, physical and affective expressions of corporate-singing worshipers may also signify a sense of edification. In fact, corporate-singing worshipers not only signify personal edification but may also edify the others within their worshiping communities beset by diverse vicissitudes of life.

In corporate worship, especially within Pentecostal and Charismatic churches, worshipers may lift or clap hands, jump up and down, dance, etc., to signify their personal encounters with the Spirit. This does not mean that one cannot do these physical activities without being filled with the Spirit (Isa 29:13; Matt 15:8; Mark 7:6). Notwithstanding this, sincere sung worship that engages one's soul, body, and spirit, manifests the Spirit tangibly. Worship can be spontaneous or unrehearsed as led by the Spirit.

This is not to say that rehearsed sung worship does not open space for manifesting God's presence. Instead, it is to accent that worship is not about the worshiper but encountering God, the worship object. Interestingly, worshipers may flow with unrehearsed sung worship that shows the Spirit in concrete ways. Accompanying body movements during sung worship signify a deep communion with the Spirit. In fact, bodily expressions during sung worship sometimes reflect a believer's response to the Spirit's promptings. It is like God rejoicing or delighting over you (Isa 62:5; Zeph 3:17), since it is an act of obedience (Ps 95:2; 100:2; 150:6). The communing or the fellowshipping Spirit of God finds concrete expression in and through sung worshipers. Thus, corporate sung worship creates space for the worshipers to make visible God's joyful presence.

Corporate sung-worshipers are signs of the grace of God's communing presence. Inasmuch as the worshiping manifest, mediate, and draw others into an encounter with the Spirit, they function as sacraments. Even unbelievers in a worshiping community can be drawn into an encounter with God during corporate sung-worship when the Spirit moves. It does not make any difference whether the songs are contemporary praise and worship or traditional like hymns. The messages in the songs contribute to rendering the Spirit in and through worshiping believers. In this sense, sung-worshiping believers manifest the Spirit's reality and render him tangible.

It is not uncommon for Pentecostal worship leaders to say "the Spirit is here" when they observe tangible signs of his presence in and through the worshiping believers' activities. Indeed, Pentecostals maintain that the Spirit leads their worship. Therefore, in some Pentecostal worship services, a person who is not an official member of the "praise and worship" team on a stage can raise a song as he or she feels inspired by the Spirit and be joined by the worshiping team itself. As long as the Spirit truly orchestrates that, the congregation is edified.

Spontaneous corporate singing may manifest the Spirit of prophecy to meet an urgent need, like in a worshiping community. In this way, the worshiping believers individually and communally manifest the Spirit's communing presence. For this reason, the sung-worshiping believers function as sacraments of the communing Spirit. Another characteristic that enables the worshipers to concretely manifest God's communing presence is joyful corporate singing.

The Communing Spirit and Joyful Singing

Joyful corporate singing is synonymous with worship.[4] Several Psalms encourage believers to sing with joy; for example: "Make a joyful noise to the Lord, all the earth; break forth into joyous song and sing praises" (Ps 98:4). Joyful singing in worship engages the whole person, including the soul, body, and spirit of believers. More notably, the God-honoring body movements of joyful worshipers are a human response to the Spirit. Precisely, the believers who clap hands in worship do not merely engage in a physical or emotional activity.

The clapping of hands is an expression of joy which engenders in the Spirit (Neh 8:10; Ps 98:8; Rom 14:17; 15:13; Gal 5:22; 1 Thess 1:6). As such, believers who demonstrate joy in worship provide concrete expression to the Spirit himself (Ps 98:8). In fact, joyful sung worship signifies that the worshipers are in deep communion with God (Rom 14:17; 15:13; Gal 5:22; 1 Thess 1:6). In particular, they provide concrete expression to

4. Ingalls and Yong, *Spirit of Praise*.

the Spirit they commune with. It is also ministering to God individually and communally (Ps 146–50; Matt 4:10; Col 3:16).

Since joyful corporate singing is biblical, joyful-singing worshipers manifest God's communing presence (2 Tim 3:16; 2 Pet 1:21). Scripture-based corporate singing provokes the Spirit of God's communing presence to manifest in a worshiping community (Ps 22:3). This means that the joyful-singing believers point others to the tangible reality of the Spirit.

Hence, joyful-singing believers are characteristically sacraments of an encounter with the communing Spirit of God's presence in Christ. They participate and manifest divine joy within the Trinitarian community. For example, the Israelites broke forth into singing after they crossed over the Red Sea, signifying the Spirit's tangible presence (Exod 15:1–21). Note that they danced and sang with timbrels (Exod 15:20–21). This is not mere emotion but inspired corporate worship.

Through singing, dancing, and shouting to honor God's mighty deeds following the unprecedented crossing of the Red Sea, the Israelites render him concretely present in their midst. The acts of praising, singing, dancing, and shouting were the Israelites' response to God's primordial acts, not the other way around. Praising or singing, dancing, and shouting intensify God's manifest presence in and through the believers. As with the Israelites, believers are motivated to sing as they become more aware of God's presence at work in and through them. Believers who shout or make a joyful noise (Ps 47:1), dance as David did (2 Sam 6:16; 1 Chr 15:29; Ps 149:1–3), etc., do manifest concretely the Spirit of God's communing presence and inspire others in the process.

In keeping with this, Paul and Silas break into prayer and song despite being unjustly chained, as Luke writes: "About midnight Paul and Silas were praying and singing hymns to God, and the prisoners were listening to them" (Acts 16:25). After an earthquake shakes the prison's foundations, the prisoners' chains are broken, doors are open, yet none escape. It is clear that Paul's and Silas's acts of praying and singing hymns to God while in chains deeply inspired faith, hope, and love toward God in the other prisoners. The fact that they do not escape from the prison suggests that they have become aware of God's immanent presence. The biblical text confirms this as Paul ministers to the jailer and his household and baptizes them (Acts 25:30–34).

By praying and singing hymns, Paul and Silas enable the fellow prisoners to encounter the Spirit's concrete presence personally. No reason can explain why these prisoners did not take advantage of the open prison doors, except the manifest, concrete presence of the Spirit in and through Paul and Silas's acts of praying and singing. Seen in this light, the joyful-singing Paul and Silas are signs of the grace of the Spirit's communing presence. Notably, they fit as sacraments of an encounter with God's communing presence. Paul and Silas render the Spirit palpable or visible.

Similarly, believers who praise via singing, dancing, shouting, etc., are signs that point to the Spirit's reality. More significantly, they are sacraments that enable the Spirit to be palpably or tangibly present. To be sure, different church traditions or theological traditions understand or practice liturgical praise or singing in diverse ways. Few would disagree that music or singing is an essential liturgical activity in many church traditions. The liturgical segment, widely known in Pentecostal churches as praise and worship, is hugely participatory.

This segment engages bodies of believers via singing, dancing, shouting, etc. Bodily movements are concrete expressions of the Spirit's touch. Notably, the persons engaged in praise and worship signify deep communion with God. Put differently, such persons are themselves signs of encountering the Spirit. This is because they render the Spirit tangible or palpable.

Seen in this light, the praising or singing believers are sacraments of the Spirit of God's presence. Singing believers render tangible the reality of God's presence. Notably, the existence of God's presence that is signified in joyful singing is both immanent and transcendent, or realized and unrealized. Thus, the joyful singers do not merely encounter God's presence in a cerebral sense but in space and real time. The sung-worshiping signifies an encounter with God's presence.

The Communing Spirit and Testifying Believers

> I will tell of your name to my brothers and sisters; in
> the midst of the congregation I will praise you.
>
> (PS 22:22)

In Pentecostalism, believers testify to encountering God's presence. Early Pentecostals conceived testifying as normative.[5] Those with testimonies stand in the front of a congregation to share their stories of encountering God. More adequately, believers who testify to encounters with God

---

5. Wacker, *Heaven Below*, 58.

are themselves a testimony. The testifying individuals communicate facts about their encounter with God and render him tangible.

When testifying, believers make tangible what they have become following the encounter with God. Testifying is not just communicating facts about the encounter with God. By testifying and thus authenticating the divine encounter, one can inspire others to encounter God. The act of testifying serves like thinking in the Spirit,[6] thinking in tongues,[7] or speaking by the Spirit.[8] Thus, testifying can provoke or inspire fresh encounters with the divine. It is a Spirit-inspired act.

Conceived this way, testifying persons provide concrete manifestation to the Spirit. Testifying persons thus are signs of grace and can facilitate fresh encounters with God. When narrating their stories of encounters with God, testifying persons point others to Christ by the Spirit (John 15:26). Drawing from this, the testifying persons are sacraments as they reveal, mediate, and draw others into an encounter with God. It also justifies the claim that the testifying persons are means of grace. Let me illustrate how the testifying to healing are means of grace.

The Communing Spirit and the Testifying about Healing or Triumphant Experience

> One thing I do know, that though I was blind, now I see.
>
> (JOHN 9:25)

Pentecostals believe that Christ suffered on the Cross to take away sin and sickness (Isa 53:3–4; 1 Pet 2:24). In early Pentecostalism, testimonies of healing were given pride of place.[9] Unsurprisingly, healing testimonies are familiar in global Pentecostalism.[10] Pentecostals insist that the Spirit who worked healings in and through Jesus works in and through them. Often, they use testimonies of healing as a polemic against cessationism[11]

---

6. Jacobsen, *Thinking in the Spirit*.
7. Smith, *Thinking in Tongues*.
8. Richie, *Speaking by the Spirit*.
9. Alexander, *Pentecostal Healing*.
10. See Anderson, "Pentecostal Approaches."
11. See Ruthven, "On the Cessation of the Charismata."

as attested to by the aphorism that: "The person with an experience is never at the mercy of another person with a doctrine."[12]

Moreover, Pentecostals see themselves as people on a mission to continue the ministry of Jesus and the early church. This does not suggest that Pentecostals expect all sick people to be healed. In fact, some succumb to death despite holding on to faith for healing. This does not mean that Christ did not atone for sickness, but the will of God determines if one is healed or not. Notwithstanding this, when believers experience and testify to healing, they enable the Spirit's healing presence to be tangible to others in a Pentecostal community.

To illustrate how the testimony of healing renders God's presence tangible, let us consider the story of a blind person who encounters Jesus. The Pharisees do not necessarily dispute his healing experience but that Jesus is the one who has performed the miracle. Precisely, they tell him, "Give glory to God!" (John 9:24). The formerly blind man does not only have a testimony but is himself a "living testimony." The Pharisees acknowledge that the once-blind man supplied concrete manifestation to God's healing presence. It follows that those who testify of healing are themselves sacraments of encountering God. Those that testify to healing function as signs of the grace of God's therapeutic presence. By rendering God's presence tangible, they inspire others to encounter God. Thus, the testifying to encountering God's healing are means of grace of the therapeutic Spirit. The same could be said about testifying to tragic experiences.

The Communing Spirit and the Testifying about Suffering/Tragic Experience

It is noteworthy that prayers for healing do not always result in testimonies of healing in Pentecostal churches. Nonetheless, Pentecostals typically pray for the sick until they pass on to glory. Pentecostals hold in tension "God's will to heal and his will not to heal."[13] We must state that God's therapeutic presence also manifests in and through narratives of tragic experiences.

By testifying about tragic experiences, one can encounter the comforting presence of the Spirit. In other words, a community of believers manifests the Spirit's comforting presence through words of

---

12. Burgess and van der Maas, *New International Dictionary*, "Spirituality," 1097a.
13. Alexander, *Pentecostal Healing*, 113.

encouragement, prayer, and different concrete ways to a fellow believer that testifies about a tragic experience. Creating space for lament in an ecclesial worship context engenders "communities of disaster," which can cause a therapeutic experience.[14] Therefore, churches need to allow members to publicly testify to their tragic experiences in Christian life.

To be sure, scholars are beginning to challenge Pentecostals and Charismatics to do that.[15] This is important as the sacramentality of believers issues in both stories with good and bad endings. The practice of sharing stories of tragic experiences in corporate worshiping communities demystifies the false belief that depicts such experiences as divine punishment.

Biblically, the Spirit finds concrete manifestation in and through both testimonies of triumph and tragedy, for example, the story of Job. To be sure, Job lost his children and his property yet remained faithful to God. In this way, Job proved to his wife and friends that the Spirit was at work regardless (Job 1). Of course, this does not suggest that one takes delight in tragic experiences. Instead, one finds comfort that even biblical characters relatively close to God experience tragic losses in several ways and situations (2 Sam 12:14–31; Ps 22).

Drawing from this, church leaders who open up space for parishioners to share stories of tragic experiences can facilitate fresh encounters with God. This can happen when church leaders share personal, unpalatable experiences with their congregation. If leaders share testimonies of lament, they can enable those who feel let down by God despite their good relationship with him to be healed when they find out that even their leaders are not immune to tragedy. This justifies that those who share testimonies of lament are sacraments of encountering the Spirit Comforter.

The Communing Spirit and Preachers or Teachers

They devoted themselves to the apostles' teaching . . .

(ACTS 2:42)

Preaching aims at communicating objective information about doctrines and creating a context for encountering God's presence. For example, "much of Pentecostal/charismatic preaching and testimony-giving is

---

14. Turner, *Communitas*, 73–84.
15. Torr, *Dramatic Pentecostal/Charismatic Anti-Theodicy*.

meant to increase and strengthen faith, and consequently, to heighten expectation of miracles."[16] When seen in this light, Christ is the preaching Man *par excellence* as he preached with power and authority (Luke 4:22–32; cf. Matt 7:29). The Spirit manifested in and through Jesus' preaching (Isaiah 61:1; Luke 4:18; 5:17).

Notably, God's presence was tangible in and through the Spirit-inspired preaching of Jesus. It is not just the content of Jesus' preaching but his total person who is constitutive of his preaching itself. In other words, the preacher cannot be divorced from his or her preaching. Accordingly, it is more adequate to say that God's presence manifested in and through Jesus the preacher than in and through Jesus' preaching by itself (John 7:46). After all, preaching is not a disembodied activity. The Spirit speaks in and through the preachers armed with the biblical text.

God's presence is tangible in and through Spirit-inspired preachers, not just in and through the content of their preaching. The total person of a preacher is present when he or she preaches and contributes to rendering God's presence tangible. Precisely, the soul, the body, and the spirit of a preacher all actively take part in communing with God and with one's audience.

Accordingly, Spirit-inspired preachers themselves are means of grace inasmuch as through their preaching they provide concrete manifestation to the Spirit. It flows from this that during preaching, the Spirit-inspired preachers themselves are concrete signs. That is to say, they point others to the reality of God's presence by rendering the reality visible, palpable or tangible.

Next, Spirit-inspired preachers disclose God's mind when preaching and communicating the truth of Scripture. The Spirit enlightens preachers' understanding of Scripture's reality in preparing and delivering scriptural truth. Granted this characterization, preachers are conduits of truth, especially if they embody the same. Spiritual disciplines like studying and waiting upon God in fasting and praying enhance preachers' sacramental efficacy (Acts 13:2).

At Pentecost, for example, the preaching Peter fits as a sacrament of God's presence. This is partly because Peter's preaching revealed the presence of the eschatological Spirit that Joel prophesied about (Joel 2:28–29; Acts 2:16–17). Also, the preaching Peter enabled three thousand people to encounter the saving grace of God in the ascended Christ (Acts 2:41).

---

16. Ma et al., *Spirit and Spirituality*, 151.

The three thousand repented, received the gift of salvation, and manifested the Spirit's saving grace.

Thus, there is double sacramentality in a preaching event where both preachers and those who respond positively to the preached Word provide concrete expression to the Spirit. It means that both Peter and the three thousand individuals saved signify personal encounters with the Spirit. The Spirit who inspired Peter's preaching convicted the three thousand that were saved (John 16:8). Both Peter and the three thousand are sacraments of an encounter with the Spirit.

Paul describes his preaching as demonstrating the Spirit and power (1 Cor 2:4). In keeping with this, Pentecostal preachers typically communicate in ways that show others that the Spirit inspires them. Of course, this is not only related to style but to the substance of biblical truth. Preaching style does not make up for the absence of substance. Furthermore, preaching style may inspire an emotional response, which does not in and of itself signify the Spirit. Sermon content contributes to concrete expression of the Spirit, and thus to the sacramentality of the preachers.

While preaching content affects the sacramental intensity of a preacher, preaching context does not. This is so because the Spirit manifests wherever and whenever the truth of Scripture is preached. Preachers provide concrete expression to the Spirit in the Word and within themselves. To the extent that preachers manifest the Spirit to others in preaching, they facilitate fresh encounters with God. In this light, they fit as sites, signs, and means of grace, and indeed, sacraments of God's presence.

Phillip is a biblical example of a preacher as a sacrament of God's presence. The Spirit led Phillip to the Ethiopian eunuch in search of biblical truth (Acts 8:29–35). Inspired by Phillip's interpretation of the Word, the eunuch was baptized. By so doing, both Phillip and the eunuch provided concrete manifestation to the Spirit (Acts 8:28). Precisely, the eunuch's response does signify to Phillip that he encountered the Spirit in and through the preached truth. The joyful reaction of the eunuch shows that the Spirit deeply touched him (Acts 8:39).

In some ways, seminary professors, Bible college teachers, etc., are means of grace to the degree that they manifest the Spirit in and through their teaching. Such teachers draw students to encounter with the Spirit as they exegete the biblical text. The Spirit who manifests in and through preachers on the pulpit can and does manifest in and through seminary or Bible teachers.

The Communing Spirit and the Lord's Supper Celebrants

Another significant event in Christian worship is the celebration of the Lord's Supper. There is no universally agreed-upon frequency or mode of celebrating the Lord's Supper. For example, churches observe this rite daily, weekly, monthly, biannually, or annually. In addition, some churches have an open-table fellowship (anyone) while others practice a closed-table fellowship (either members or those baptized in water). Notwithstanding this, the Lord's Supper symbolizes communion with God and with believers. Not only this, but it also deepens or enhances communion with God and fellow believers. As such, communicants or participants render tangible God's fellowshipping presence in Christ through the Spirit.

Communicants are signs of grace that point to the reality of God's communing presence. Significantly, Christ is the center of the Lord's Supper celebration as the true bread that came down from heaven (John 6:32). Christ's presence is not contained in the Lord's Supper elements themselves but in the communicants or celebrants through the indwelling Spirit. The efficacy of the Lord's Supper issues in the Spirit, not the Lord's Supper elements in themselves.

Indeed, Christ refers to the bread as his body, (Matt 26:26; Mar 14:22; Luke 22:19; 1 Cor 11:24), and to the cup (the drink) as his blood (Matt 26:28; Mark 14:24; Luke 22:20; 1 Cor 11:25). The bread and wine or drink are nothing apart from the presence of God in Christ through the Spirit. In other words, the Lord's Supper is about communing with God and not just ingesting the elements of this rite. By extension, the Lord's Supper is also about followers of Christ being in communion with other believers.

Similarly, partaking of the Lord's Supper is reserved for believers or followers of Christ. Notably, one does not partake of the Lord's Supper to encounter God as such but to show others that he/she is in communion with the Spirit (2 Cor 1:22; 5:5). Partakers of the Lord's Supper are presumed to have had a salvific encounter with the Spirit. Elements of the Lord's Supper have no inherent grace of the Spirit. Consequently, the Lord's Supper is not a standalone rite. A worship service is a context for communion, and partakers of the Lord's Supper manifest this *koinonia*.

Next, the Lord's Supper is communal in nature; hence it creates space to manifest the Spirit's communing presence. Thus, partaking in the Lord's Supper encourages fellowship with God and believers. In fact, believers grow as they learn to commune with God and with others. This partly explains why the early disciples broke bread from house to house to encourage fellowship (Acts 2:46). Therefore, Paul is right to appeal to Corinthian brothers and sisters to wait for one another to partake of the Lord's Supper (1 Cor 11:33). The Lord's Supper creates space for believers to acknowledge their relationship with God and with each other publicly.

Certainly, the Lord's Supper creates space for self-reflection on one's relation to God and to each other in Christ (1 Cor 11:28). The Spirit guides communicants in this self-examining process (John 14:26; 16:7–13). It presupposes that the Lord's Supper is a context wherein believers come face to face with God. This is because it is the Spirit who convicts one of sin, acknowledges righteousness, and oversees judgment (John 16:8).

In addition, believers receive the gift of the Holy Spirit at the moment of conversion (Acts 2:38). Thus, participation in the Lord's Supper creates space for believers to manifest the Spirit's indwelling presence concretely. Paul rightly notes that the presence of God indwells believers (Rom 8:9, 11; 1 Cor 3:16; 6:19). The Spirit engenders believers as temples of God's presence. Precisely, communicants are the location of the grace of the Spirit's invisible presence. Partakers of the Lord's Supper point others to the reality of the Spirit.

To be sure, one cannot partake in the Lord's Supper only and neglect other liturgical activities and expect to grow in Christ-likeness. After all, the Bible encourages participation in the Lord's Supper (Luke 22:19; 1 Cor 11:24–25), prayer for one another (Jas 5:16), fellowship (Heb 10:25), and worship (John 4:23–24). In other words, preaching, singing, fellowshipping, praying, offering, etc., are vital as they enrich and enliven the celebration of the Lord's Supper.

As believers engage in worship activities, they give tangible expression to the presence of God. In this way, the communicants manifest the Spirit in Christ. Thus, the Spirit finds concrete manifestation in and through partakers in the Lord's Supper. One cannot meaningfully partake in the Lord's Supper and concomitantly fail to participate in fellowship with other believers.

True participants in the Lord's Supper are sacraments of an encounter with the Spirit. While participation in the Lord's Supper presupposes participation with God, it also inspires one to participate in the other. In this way, partakers in the Lord's Supper are signs of grace as they provide tangible expression to the Spirit. Similarly, submission to Water Baptism presupposes a relation to God and inspires a connection to the other members of one's ecclesial community.

The Communing Spirit and Foot-Washing Believers

Some scholars consider the rite of foot-washing as a sacrament.[17] In keeping with this, some churches practice foot-washing during worship service. Of course, this may not have to be performed every Sunday. This theological conviction is rooted in the example of Jesus when he washed his disciples' feet (John 13:14). A fundamental lesson is about serving others, not the activity of washing feet itself. Thus, we can postulate that a believer who washes others' feet reveals humility issuing in the Spirit.

Specifically, the act of washing others' feet itself creates space in a worship community to know those with a servanthood heart. Thus, though some regard foot-washing as a sacrament by itself, this seems inadequate. Instead, we should hold the person washing others' feet as a sacrament to the extent that this act arises in the Spirit of humility and therefore points to God in Christ. To conceive foot-washing as a sacrament is to concomitantly acknowledge the person who does the washing as sacrament too. This is because the total person (soul, body, and spirit) is involved in washing others' feet.

Though the hands appear to one as washing someone's feet, a person's totality is engaged in the exercise. You cannot bifurcate between the physical (body) and non-physical parts (soul, spirit) of a believer. To conceive a person who washes others' feet as a sacrament keeps together the physical and the non-physical aspects of the human body.

To clarify this thinking, let's consider the example of Christ, who manifested the Spirit of humility by washing his disciples' feet (John 13:17). Notice that Christ assumed the appropriate posture before washing the disciples' feet by, among other things, laying his garments aside, and took and girded himself with a towel and poured water into a basin. His mental faculty, or mind, was actively engaged in setting up the scene and also in the actual washing of the disciples' feet. Jesus' invisible and visible being actively participated in washing the disciples' feet. Jesus did not merely desire to wash his disciples' feet. He actually did it and demonstrated divine humility.

When Christ washed the disciples' feet, he manifested the grace of humility by the Spirit. Notably, washing the disciples' feet was an act of worship as it reflected the humble and servant attitude of God in Christ and thereby glorified his Father. Foot washing in a worship community allows believers to serve each other and to demonstrate the Spirit of

17. Thomas, *Footwashing*.

humility and servanthood. Understood as an act of worship, foot-washing believers are concrete signs of God's presence.

The Communing Spirit and Generous Believers

God's character as the author and giver of life reflects in believers' acts of giving to support ministry work (Acts 3:15; Rom 6:23). Genuine giving is borne out of the conviction of the Spirit. Precisely, believers are truly touched or moved by the Spirit when they respond by giving freely. It follows that believers, who give out of their substance in support of God's work, provide concrete manifestation to the Spirit at work in and through them. For example, in the early church, wealthy members sold their properties and brought the leaders' proceeds to support the poor, especially those in their midst (Acts 4:34–37).

Genuine giving is a divine-human act, as it reflects the Spirit who prompts the giver to give. This reflects the spirit of a freewill offering. For example, the poor widow gave out of her poverty as Jesus testified (Mark 12:42–44; Luke 21:1–4). Giving is an act of obedience to God to whom belongs all that anyone can give (Job 41:11; Rom 11:35–36). Seen in this light, givers acknowledge and demonstrate to others that God is their ultimate provider. In this way, givers signify or point to the Spirit's reality at work in and through their lives.

Since the act of giving cannot be isolated from the person who gives, we can say that the giving person is a sign of the Spirit. Moreover, giving believers not only point to but participate in the reality of God who provides. In churches, those who give toward God-honoring projects are sacraments of God's presence. These manifest the giving Spirit (Acts 2:38; 10:45; 1 Cor 12:4; Heb 2:4). The sacramentality of giving believers extends to helping the poor, orphans, widows, prisoners, refugees, etc. (Matt 25:44–45). Believers do not only give in corporate worship but they also engage in fellowship both with God and with one another.

The Communing Spirit and Fellowshipping Believers

In some churches, members fellowship together following the end of corporate worship. The act of fellowshipping creates space for believers to know each other more intimately than in a traditional worship service by allowing believers to open up to and bond with each other.

Notably, believers find small group fellowship contexts more comfortable to share testimonies of triumph or stories of lament than an entire congregation. Fellowship creates space for the Spirit to manifest concretely in and through believers in a community of worship. Such was fellowship in the early church (Acts 2:42). The fellowshipping believers reflect God's social character.

It is partly in this sense that fellowshipping believers are concrete signs of God's grace by the Spirit that point others to God. The Spirit who inspires fellowship within the Trinity is the same who inspires such in the worshiping community (2 Cor 13:14; Phil 2:1). To the extent that believers reflect Trinitarian fellowship, albeit not entirely, they render God's presence tangible to others. In this way, the fellowshipping believers reveal God's presence. We can infer from this that the fellowshipping believers function as means of divine grace of Trinitarian fellowship.

By manifesting the Spirit of fellowship, believers inspire and therefore draw others into an encounter with God in Christ. In this sense, fellowshipping believers are fitting as sacraments of an encounter with the Spirit of God's social presence. For example, by attending the wedding at Cana (John 2), Jesus manifested God's social or fellowshipping presence. The sacramentality of fellowshipping believers is most conspicuous in societies that are hostile toward Christianity.

The Communing Spirit and Corporate Worshipers in Hostile Society

Participation in public worship in locations or societies that forbid Christianity enhances the risk of torture, persecution, or death for Christians. The courage to confess Jesus as Lord in such environments can only be attributed to an encounter with the Spirit. For example, the early disciples were ordered not to teach in the name of Jesus or risk death (Acts 5:40; 16:23; 22:24; 2 Cor 11:23). But they continued to engage in corporate worship. By so doing, they rendered God's presence tangible. Fellowship also creates space for believers to share stories of suffering.

Chapter 6

Manifesting the Comforting Spirit

Suffering Believers

> The Lord gave, and the Lord has taken away;
> blessed be the name of the Lord.
>
> (JOB 1:21)

JOB'S STORY OF SUFFERING is one of the most touching in the Old and the New Testaments. Despite his righteous standing before God (Job 1:1), Job experiences enormous suffering arising in the death of his children (Job 1:18–19), in the death of his servants (Job 1:15–17), and in the loss of his property or wealth (Job 1:14–17). In response to these tragic events, Job tears his robe, shaves his head, falls to the ground and worships God, and says, "'The Lord gave, and the Lord has taken away; blessed be the name of the Lord.' In all this Job did not sin or charge God with wrongdoing" (Job 1:21–22).

This shows that Job maintains a faithful, hopeful, and loving posture toward God.

When Satan attacks him with painful boils (Job 2:7) and his wife wonders why he holds on to his integrity instead of cursing God, Job remains unmoved (Job 2:9–10). Even when his friends attack and accuse him of sin (Job 4; 5; 8; 11; 15; 18; 20), Job laments, but his trust in God does not wane (Job 3; 6; 9; 10; 13; 14; 19; 23; 26).

Without trivializing Job's pain, it seems reasonable to suggest that only God can provide inner strength to a person who undergoes such a tragic experience. In this light, Job signifies and renders tangible the grace of the Spirit of God's comforting presence at work in and through him. More adequately, Job is a sacrament of a personal encounter with God's comforting presence. In the New Testament, the Spirit's presence in believers does not render them immune to suffering. Believers who keep faith in God despite suffering shape others' responses to similar experiences.

Accordingly, they indirectly bestow on others grace of the Spirit of God's comforting presence. Peter states that believers should rejoice as they share in Christ's sufferings (1 Peter 4:13). This rejoicing in sharing Christ's sufferings does not necessarily mean that one must deny feelings of pain. It is to acknowledge one's suffering and redirect it to Christ in the form of a prayer of lament. This lament response is linked to Christ's own lament as he faced death on the Cross (Matt 27:46; Mark 15:34). By crying out to God because of unjust suffering, believers render him tangible. This is because such anguish signifies one's intimate relationship with God.

To be sure, Paul explains that believers are given the privilege not only of believing in Christ, but of suffering for him as well (Phil 1:29). Thus, believers are given the gift of the Person of the Spirit to comfort them in suffering. Though the Spirit is often linked to triumphant experiences in Christian life, his presence anticipates experiences of suffering. The Spirit's presence becomes concrete in and through believers' experiences of suffering as in triumphs. This chapter asserts that the suffering render the comforting Spirit tangible (2 Cor 4:17–18).

This tangible rendering of the Spirit of Christ depicts suffering believers as sacraments of God's presence. Through expressions of faith, hope, and love in suffering, believers serve as signs and means of grace of the Spirit's comforting presence. These expressions of faith, hope, and love imply that suffering believers do not set in opposition suffering against eschatological glory (Rom 8:18). Instead, they re-conceptualize their suffering through Christ's suffering. The Cross of Christ epitomizes human suffering, and therefore provides meaning to believers' suffering.

Believers who maintain faith in suffering reflect the suffering Christ (2 Cor 3:18). The Spirit of Christ enables believers to go through, not around, experiences of suffering. In suffering, there is an inter-participation between suffering believers and the suffering Christ. That is to say, in suffering, believers participate in the suffering of Christ and vice versa. This suffering at the center of this chapter can rightly be characterized as unjust suffering; it is considered unjust suffering precisely because believers are not a direct cause of the suffering.

Seen in this light, unjustly suffering believers are sacraments of an encounter with the comforting Spirit. As sacraments of God's comforting presence, suffering believers do not explain away their experiences but see them in and through the lens of the suffering Christ. Such believers experience God's comfort from deep within and hold on to faith in Christ. This does not mean that suffering believers do not lament. Instead, they draw supernatural strength from the suffering Christ by the Spirit's comforting presence. In suffering, believers come face-to-face with the suffering Christ, thereby rendering him visible to others.

The Spirit comforts suffering believers as he comforted the suffering Christ (Matt 4:1–11; Mark 1:12–13; Luke 4:1–13). The suffering believers reflect the suffering Christ (Phil 4:10; cf. Matt 16:24; Mark 8:34; Luke 9:23; 2 Cor 1:5; 1 Pet 4:13). Through suffering, believers reveal God's comforting presence at work in and through them. The Spirit comforted the early disciples in the face of persecution and continues to comfort believers presently subject to suffering.

As Mittelstadt rightly observes, suffering and the Spirit are inseparable in Luke and the Acts.[1] To the extent that the disciples in the early church endured persecution, they manifested the Spirit Comforter's presence. Keener also rightly notes that "partakers of Christ's sufferings might still experience the purging of his fiery trials in the form of suffering for his name; cf. Mark 10:39; 1 Pet 4:12."[2] Unjustly suffering individuals are signs of the grace of the Spirit of God's comforting presence fully visible in and through Christ the suffering Man *par excellence*.

Suffering believers draw inspiration from Christ, who suffered for doing good, not evil (1 Pet 3:17). By holding on to Christ despite unjust suffering, they render the Spirit Comforter concretely present. The unjustly suffering believers (1 Pet 3:14) are different from those who justly suffer for doing what is evil (1 Pet 4:15). Believers need not be ashamed of suffering for doing what is right or good. In this way, suffering believers identify with Christ (1 Pet 4:16).

To be sure, Christ forewarned his disciples about inevitable persecution (Luke 23:31; John 15:20). The sacramentality of suffering believers is linked to the Spirit Comforter's indwelling presence (John 14:16,

---

1. Mittelstadt, *Spirit and Suffering in Luke-Acts*.
2. Keener, *Spirit in the Gospels and Acts*, 193.

26; 15:26; 16:7). Notably, Jesus speaks of the Spirit as the Comforter and persecution in the same context. By so doing, Jesus enables his disciples to anticipate suffering and the sending of the Spirit. The same Spirit who comforted Christ during his sufferings leading up to the Cross would also provide comfort to the suffering disciples.

Like the suffering Christ, the suffering disciples provide a concrete manifestation of God's comforting presence by the Spirit. Significantly, the Spirit was poured out to empower and comfort the disciples. Seen in this light, Pentecost also symbolizes unjust suffering that believers experience on this side of life. It is relatively easy to overlook the relation of Pentecost to unjust suffering. Often, people relate the Pentecost event to God's empowering presence and neglect this dimension of suffering. Triumphs and sufferings are two sides of the Pentecost experience.

However, Pentecost as an encounter with God also implies suffering. For example, believers in the Asian countries of China, North Korea, Vietnam, Laos, Cambodia, Myanmar, Nepal, Bhutan, and Tibet provide concrete manifestation to the Spirit because "becoming a Christian in these countries is often a life-and-death decision which usually results in persecution."[3] To clarify this relation of Pentecost to believers' sacramentality, let us reflect on the following example of the sacramentality of a believer suffering from an incurable illness or condition.

In my pastoral role, I have had the privilege of ministering to church members suffering from incurable illnesses. In all cases, both the ill members and I expect God to answer our prayer offered in faith by healing them. However, a particular incident challenged me and gave me a fresh perspective about suffering believers. Precisely, when one of our church members was told that she had cancer, I was challenged by the member's response. The member said to me in a rather jovial mood that God had three options to deal with the situation: firstly, "God can miraculously heal me; secondly, God can use medical professionals to administer therapeutics to take care of the cancer; and thirdly, God can simply call me home. Either way, it is fine with me."

The suffering member's response inspired me and the other church leaders. One thing that I could deduce from this situation is that the Spirit was already comforting this member. In this light, this suffering member's response served as a lens that provided concrete manifestation

---

3. Ma, "Asian (Classical) Pentecostal Theology," 76.

to the comforting presence of God in Christ by the indwelling Spirit already at work from within.

This also implies that the prayer said over this suffering member simply enhanced the comfort that the Spirit was already administering to this person. In other words, our prayer and, indeed, our encouraging words only created space for the tangible manifestation of the comforting presence of God in Christ by the indwelling Spirit. It is not another Spirit coming from without this suffering member who brought about the comforting presence of God.

Drawing from this, suffering or ill believers signify the grace of God's comforting presence. This thinking takes Christ seriously as the unjust-suffering Man *par excellence*. But let us reflect deeply on the biblical motif of the Spirit Comforter. It is telling that the Bible describes God as one who comforts (Eccl 4:1; Lam 1:9, 16; Isa 52:9; Jer 8:18; Matt 5:4; John 14:16, 26; 15:26; 16:7; 2 Cor 1:3–5; 7:6; 13:11; Col 2:2).

This implies that all believers from all denominations or church traditions are not invincible to suffering. There is suffering that is common among human beings such as falling ill, whether one is religious or not. Such suffering pertains to this fallen world as distinct from the world to come. But, there is also suffering that one experiences by virtue of professing faith in Christ. Christianity does not entail living in bliss, as some assert. It also entails suffering.

To be sure, this suffering does not mean that one has sinned. Rather, it is undeserved. In fact, the biblical identity of the Third Person of the Trinity or the Godhead—the Spirit Comforter—anticipates believers' suffering. As God's indwelling presence, the Spirit Comforter enables the believers to endure unjust sufferings while they live in the body of the human flesh (2 Tim 2:3).

For this reason, suffering believers are concrete signs of the comforting presence of God. In other words, suffering believers make God's comforting presence tangible to both fellow believers and unbelievers. Suffering believers point to the reality of God's comforting presence. The unjustly suffering believers are sacraments of an encounter with the Spirit Comforter in Christ.

Unfortunately, some believers do not equate Christian life to suffering. Precisely, there is a tendency to emphasize triumphs over tragic experiences in Christian life. This mindset does not align with the experiences of the early church. For example, Pentecostals take the early church as a model, yet downplay sufferings in Christian life. This selective hermeneutics of emphasizing victory over suffering can lead to disappointments owing to unrealized expectations. In an extreme situation, it could jeopardize a believer's relationship with God.

In some sense, the underlying motif is that God's presence is tangible in experiences of victory but not in sufferings. If that is the case, one would have to say that God's presence is not tangible at the Cross, which is not true. At the Cross, the suffering Christ makes the comforting presence of God tangible. If Christ the anointed Man *par excellence* experienced sufferings, it is inevitable for believers to experience sufferings (Matt 13:21; Mark 4:17; John 16:33; Acts 8:1; 11:19; 13:50; Rom 8:35; 1 Thess 3:7; Heb 10:33; Rev 2:10). The Spirit is with believers both in triumphs and sufferings. The suffering believers render the Spirit's comforting presence tangible thus are signs of grace.

This chapter holds as sacraments of the comforting Spirit those believers who suffer unjustly. Believers who endure undeserved sufferings render the Spirit Comforter visible. Thus, they serve as signs of God's comforting grace. Among these believers are those who suffer from incurable or prolonged illnesses, persecution, poverty, marginalization or injustice, infertility, etc. The Spirit enables believers to endure unjust sufferings. Thus, believers identify with Christ, the suffering Man *par excellence*. Christ fully manifests God's comforting Spirit on the Cross.

Notably, he forgives those who crucified him though he did not commit sin (Luke 23:34; John 16:7). As he hangs on the Cross, the Spirit comforts and enables Christ to see joy ahead (Heb 12:2). To prepare his disciples for unjust sufferings they would face, Christ promises to send the Spirit Comforter (John 14:26; 15:26; 16:7). As Jesus predicted, the disciples experience unjust sufferings at the hands of religious and political leaders (Acts 5:40; 16:23; 22:24; 2 Cor 11:23). By enduring sufferings, the disciples signify the grace of God's comforting presence.

For example, Stephen asks God to forgive those who stone him to death (Acts 7:60). In this way, Stephen manifests the Spirit's comforting presence and inspires others to encounter God. Accordingly, Stephen is a sacrament of an encounter with the Spirit Comforter. Similarly, the believers who endure unjust sufferings are sacraments of encountering God's comforting presence. This is noteworthy that the sacramentality of believers depicts God's immanence and transcendence. The Spirit Comforter enables believers to endure sufferings of this present life as they await the *eschaton*. God gives the Spirit Comforter as a deposit (2 Cor

1:22; 5:5). Suffering and the Spirit's presence are inseparable from believers' lives individually and communally.

Moltmann notes that: "In the pains, slights and disablements, and in 'the sufferings of the Spirit,' God's suffering power is revealed."[4] I would add that the believers who endure unjust sufferings reveal God's immanence and transcendence. Likewise, Clarke observes an unbalanced emphasis upon triumphs concerning the anointing of the Spirit over and above suffering.[5] As a theological corrective, Clarke rightly says that "the anointing to endure suffering can be seen as eschatological in anticipation of God's future deliverance."[6] This means that the Spirit finds expression in and through believers' experiences of triumph and suffering. Believers who endure suffering manifest God's presence in the same sense as believers who exercise spiritual gifts.

The Suffering Christ and the Comforting Spirit

Jesus is the primordial sacrament of the encounter with God's comforting presence. From infancy to adulthood, Christ faced unprecedented, albeit predicted, sufferings. Indeed, Christ expected the sufferings through the scriptural testimony of the prophets. For example, Simeon, by the leading of the Spirit, prophesied about the opposition and the rejection that Jesus would experience (Luke 2:25–35). This is incredible in that it is about thirty years before Jesus would begin his ministry (Luke 3:23).

Right after Jesus is baptized and begins his ministry, the Spirit leads him on a forty-day journey into the wilderness, to be tempted by the devil (Matt 4:1; Mark 1:13; Luke 4:2). The sufferings of Christ reach the peak at the Cross (Matt 27:22–23; Mark 15:13–14; Luke 23:21; John 19:6, 10, 15). Because inspired prophets predicted these sufferings, opposition, rejection, and persecution of Christ, both in the Old and New Testaments, those familiar with these prophecies would see the Spirit at work in and through Jesus.

Also, the sufferings Jesus experienced are unjustified and beyond what any human being can ever bear. The endurance Jesus exhibits points to the reality of God's presence at work in and through him by the Spirit. One way to know the severity of the sufferings of Jesus is the fact that all

---

4. Moltmann, *Spirit of Life*, 357–61.
5. Clarke, *Pentecostalism*, 100.
6. Clarke, *Pentecostalism*, 100.

his disciples desert him (Matt 26:5). The disciples cannot imagine themselves undergoing this ordeal, at least not yet.

But after Pentecost, as the Spirit is poured out, the once-feeble apostles or disciples demonstrate remarkable boldness. The Spirit who enables Jesus Christ to endure opposition, persecution, rejection or simply suffering is now visibly present in and through the empowered apostles and the other disciples. In this sense, the suffering disciples are sacraments of the encounter with the Spirit Comforter. Likewise, believers with disabilities signify the grace of the Spirit.

The Comforting Spirit and Disabled Believers

> It was because of a physical infirmity that I
> first announced the gospel to you.
>
> (GAL 4:13)

Not all believers are healed from their disabilities. Thus, the Spirit Comforter plays a considerable role in comforting believers with disabilities. The Spirit comforts believers with disabilities despite their profession of faith in God through Christ. Believers who praise God despite their disabilities are signs of grace. This shows that God shares in the suffering of the believers with disabilities.

Seen in this light, believers with disabilities point to and render tangible the Spirit's comforting presence. Such inspire others toward faith, hope, and love in God. Like the suffering from sickness, not all believers with disabilities are healed despite their faith. Believers with disabilities manifest God's comforting presence when they demonstrate concrete faith in Christ by the Spirit despite their disabilities.

At the Beautiful Gate, Peter and John minister healing to a man born with a disability (Acts 3:1–12). In this way, the apostles provided a concrete manifestation of God's compassion for the disabled. It is evident in Scripture that God has compassion for people with disabilities even if he does not heal them of their physical condition but heals their soul. For example, one Zacchaeus, a tax collector, rich, and short in stature, was healed of his soul but not his physical condition (Luke 19:3). I should point out that this view links to a belief that Zacchaeus' shortness was a disability.[7] This granted, then his encounter with Jesus has enormous significance for the sacramentality of believers with disabilities.

In a turn of events, Zacchaeus experiences salvation and decides to give up to half of his wealth to the poor (Luke 19:8–10). The actions of Zacchaeus point to a deeper reality of God by the Spirit. Despite the shortness of his stature, the Spirit manifests visibly in Zacchaeus. Among other things, it shows that the Spirit of God delights in and, therefore, indwells and manifests his presence in and through disabled believers. Perhaps, the Spirit is more visible in and through believers with disabilities than believers without disabilities.

Despite the incredible miracle that God in Christ performs in and through the empowered Peter of the healing of a disabled forty-year-old man (Acts 3), there is reason to believe that there were members of this early church community who might have struggled with disabilities. Indeed, Paul is reported to have had a deformity linked to the thorn in the flesh (2 Cor 12:7). Even if this were not so, there have been many believers who, despite being filled with the Spirit, struggle with disabilities. Such disabled individuals point others to the Spirit at work in and through them.

Church leaders can provide comfort to members with disabilities by building churches with facilities that cater to their unique needs, such as providing realistic access to car parking and bathrooms, special audio-visual equipment, etc. In developing countries, the disabled lack facilities that could make their participation in corporate worship more manageable. Where believers with disabilities are accommodated, the church leaders are indeed seen as Spirit-filled.

Historically, Pentecostal churches did not privilege providing special-needs-accessible facilities partly due to their belief in divine healing. Of course, there are instances where some have expressed disappointment for not being healed, especially in mass-healing crusades. In keeping with this, the believers with disabilities like blindness, deafness, speech impediment, mental illness, Down syndrome, paralysis, stroke, etc., are sacraments of the Spirit Comforter.

---

7. Yong, *Bible, Disability, and the Church*, 67.

The Comforting Spirit and Impoverished Believers

Pentecostalism has a wide following among the poor and marginalized in society. The early church demonstrated compassion toward the poor in their midst (Acts 4:34–37). The Spirit poured out at Pentecost empowered the early church to care for those suffering. By so doing, the disciples reflected the life of Christ, who also prioritized or focused his ministry on suffering individuals, like the poor. In this way, the disciples provided a tangible manifestation to the Spirit of Comfort. The compassionate disciples manifested to others that the ascended Jesus was still at work in and through their generous acts by the Spirit.

Further, poor believers who hold onto their faith render the Spirit comforter tangibly present and hence are sacraments. That God cares for the poor can be seen in and through the life of Christ. Interestingly, Christianity is experiencing phenomenal growth in the global South, where many poor and developing countries are located. In fact, Pentecostal churches have attracted many poor people who find hope and meaning in their brand of Christianity that takes life's harsh realities seriously. Though there are reports that some needy members in Pentecostal and Charismatic churches and ministries experience economic improvement, the fact remains that the majority remain in abject poverty.

The significant part of the story is that those who remain poor do not seem to reject Christ. It is interesting to note that some poor believers in developing countries worship under trees or in buildings and environments generally deemed unthinkable by Western standards. Yet, some of these poor believers in developing countries exhibit such joy that surpasses that of the West's believers. One way to make sense of this is that these poor believers in developing countries are signs of God's comforting presence in Christ at work in and through them. In other words, they are signs that point to the Spirit Comforter and render him visible.

In this light, the poor and yet God-loving believers in the global South are sacraments. To be sure, Luke also reports about poor disciples in the early church that depended upon daily food distribution (Acts 4:35; 6:1). Yet, these poor disciples can be seen committed to the teachings of the apostles. Certainly, the Spirit is visibly present in these poor disciples as the rest or the rich. The Spirit of Pentecost does not necessarily resolve the economic conditions of poor disciples.

It is also interesting that Cornelius's generosity finds approval before God, resulting in his encounter with God (Acts 10). It implies that the

Spirit desires to manifest his presence in and through the poor. Elsewhere, Paul writes, "At present, however, I am going to Jerusalem in a ministry to the saints; for Macedonia and Achaia have been pleased to share their resources with the poor among the saints at Jerusalem" (Rom 15:25–26). The poor believers at Jerusalem gain sympathy from Gentiles who desire to minister to their material needs (Rom 15:27). Likewise, Paul notes that the apostles at Jerusalem expressed delight at his ministry work with the Gentiles and encouraged him to remember the poor (Gal 2:10).

The Comforting Spirit and Socioeconomically Marginalized Believers

The Old Testament describes God as defender of justice (Deut 10:18; 24:17; 27:19; 32:4; Isa 5:7; Jer 4:2; 7:5–6; 22:3–4; Ezek 18:5–9; Amos 5:24; Mic 6:8; Zech 7:9–10). The New Testament also supports this view of God as concerned about injustice (Matt 22:39; 25:40; Jas 1:27). In fact, God detests the leaders who stay mute in the face of socioeconomic injustice (Amos 2:6–7; 3:1–2; 4:1; Mic 3:9–12). Those who decry injustice in society function as signs and means of God's grace and sacraments of God's presence of justice.

Believers who speak truth to power render God's presence visible. By holding people accountable to the cause of justice, they become means of grace for those oppressed or deprived of justice. Believers who maintain faith in God despite suffering from injustice render the Spirit comforter tangibly present. In this way, such believers enable others to see the Spirit of justice at work and, thus, serve as sacraments.

The Spirit finds concrete expression in and through those who denounce socioeconomic injustices within society. Christ is the epitome of those who speak against injustice. Put another way, Christ is the primordial sacrament of an encounter with the Spirit of socioeconomic justice. To be sure, Christ expresses this concern in his maiden sermon by drawing from Isaiah (Isa 61: 1–8; Luke 4:16–21) and his teachings (Matt 22:39; 25:40).

Often, victims of socioeconomic injustice are minorities. The Spirit manifests in and through those who peacefully protest socioeconomic injustice and perform miracles, signs, and wonders. For example, Jesus ministers healing to Abraham's daughter, who suffers unjustly for eighteen years (Luke 13:16); and touches lepers as a polemic against social injustice for society holding them as outcasts (Matt 8:3–4; Mark 1:44; Luke 5:14).

In the same way, believers who comfort individuals' unjust suffering manifest the Spirit's compassionate presence in Christ. For example, the apostles intervene when the Hellenists feel discriminated against at the table (Acts 6:1–3). Likewise, Paul advocates for Gentiles' inclusion or recognition as equally belonging to the believers' community, just like Jews (Gal 3:28). Paul, who acts against his day's anti-Gentile culture, is a sign of the grace of God's egalitarian Spirit in Christ. By doing that, Paul risks his life and demonstrates self-denial for the sake of the gospel's truth.

The Comforting Spirit and Martyred Believers

"Martyr" is a Greek term translated as "witness" in English. From a biblical perspective, a witness attests to the resurrection of Jesus. Luke likely has this witness motif in mind when he quotes Jesus: "and you will be my witnesses . . ." (Acts 1:8). Precisely, John employs this term concerning someone who testifies about Christ as the Son of God (John 1:1; 1 John 1:1; cf. Matt 10:32). Aptly, the book of Revelation uses the term "martyr" to refer to one who gives his life for his or her witness, i.e., a blood-witness (Rev 17:6).

Martyrs differ from confessors in that the former die for their faith. In contrast, the latter are persecuted but not killed and are, thus, called "confessors." However, the witness motif also links to the belief that martyrs do not merely confess faith in Christ but encounter him in visions. Seen in this light, Christ is the martyr *par excellence* who shapes and informs all martyrdom. Jesus is the one who has seen the Father and given his life as a ransom via death on the Cross (Heb 12:2).

Next, martyrs are historically held as those with special grace to identify with Christ's sufferings. Precisely, martyrs are not people who do not have anything else to live for but choose Christ more than anything else, including their lives.[8] Jesus demonstrates this Spirit of martyrdom at the Cross when he gives up his life for the sake of his brethren. Similarly, Stephen is martyred due to his confession of Christ, whom he counts as more valuable than his life (Acts 7:55–56). Drawing from this, Jesus and Stephen are signs of grace for martyrdom (Luke 23:46; Acts 7:59).

---

8. Litfin, *Early Christian Martyr Stories*, 173.

Stephen's narrative is a lens to understand the disciples' attitude toward martyrdom. His boldness suggests the endowment of special grace to see beyond the immediate realm of life (Acts 7:54–60). James is another martyr and sacrament of God's presence in the early church (Acts 12:1–2). It is clear from reading Acts that Herod was behind his unjust death for professing faith in Christ. Like Stephen, James manifests the Spirit's comforting presence at work in and through him. In this way, James inspires other disciples, including Peter, whom Herod arrests (Acts 12:3). The unshakable faith of martyrs demonstrates that they have indeed encountered the Spirit in Christ. Martyrs in the history of the church draw inspiration from early church martyrs.

Eusebius discusses the martyrdom of Procopius in chapter 1 of *The Martyrs of Palestine*.[9] Eusebius describes Procopius as the first of the martyrs beheaded for refusing to pour libations to the four emperors. Procopius' courage to face martyrdom strengthened the faith of others. Notably, Procopius was a sign and means of grace of the Spirit's comforting presence in Christ.

In chapter 2, for example, Eusebius reports that Romanus had a cheerful countenance as he was led to his martyrdom. With his tongue cut out for not recanting faith in Christ, Romanus demonstrated that the Spirit was at work in and through him. These martyrs' bravery and fortitude inspired other persecuted believers and challenged pagans to consider their stand before God. In this light, Procopius and Romanus are sacraments of an encounter with the Spirit.

Next, the *Martyrdom of Polycarp* is reported in the letter from the church at Smyrna to the church at Philomelium in Phrygia. Although he is retired from the city to avoid death, Polycarp is captured and executed. He looked forward to receiving the reward in God's coming kingdom (Matt 5:12). Polycarp manifests the Spirit when he responds to the governor, who encourages him to renounce faith in Christ when "For eighty-six years I have served Christ and he has done me no wrong; how can I blaspheme against my King and Savior?"[10]

Seen in this light, Polycarp is a sacrament of an encounter with the Spirit's comforting presence through Christ. The *Letter of the Churches of Vienne and Lyons* reports of martyrs being beheaded or condemned to

---

9. Eusebius, *Martyrs*, 1–48.
10. Kleist, "Martyrdom of Polycarp," 9.3.

wild beasts.[11] Anyone who dies in such a manner likely draws strength from the indwelling Spirit.

Next, the *Acts of Justin and his Companions* records the circumstances under which Justin and his companion died, i.e., by beheading. Similarly, the *Acts of Saints Carpus, Papylus, and Agathonice* (Pergamene saints) reports of martyred women Agathonice and Charito. Many women were martyred just as men during ancient times when women were not valued, attesting that the Spirit is egalitarian.

In keeping with this, the martyr Perpetua came from an affluent background as a daughter of noble and wealthy parents. Her martyrdom in Carthage is detailed in *Passions of Perpetua and Felicitas*.[12] Among other things, Perpetua was flogged, torn apart by beasts, and beheaded as she publicly professed Christ. *Perpetua* rendered Christ tangible by the Spirit and thus fits as a sacrament of a personal encounter with God's comforting presence.

During the persecutions of the reign of Emperor Trajan, Ignatius wrote a letter to the Roman Church. Notably, he asked the church not to prevent his martyrdom so that he should be God's wheat to be ground to bread by the lion's mouth.[13] In the face of death, this attitude arises in the Spirit, who empowered Christ as he faced his own martyrdom upon Calvary's Cross. Ironically, the church experiences tremendous growth during persecution and martyrdom.[14] For example, the church historian Eusebius reports that prisons were so crowded with Christian leaders and their members that there was no room for criminals! Those who confessed faith in Christ were punished by losing property, being exiled or imprisoned, and execution either by the sword or wild beasts.[15]

Luke reports that the early church experienced tremendous growth in the face of persecution (Acts 5–7). This confirms the theological claim that martyrs render tangible the Spirit's comforting presence. By holding on to Christ in the face of death and pain, martyrs inspire others toward faith, hope, and love in God. This is because "dying without denying the faith was a confirmation of the passion of Christ."[16]

11. Eusebius, *Ecclesial History*, Book 5.
12. Kaatz, *Voices of Early Christianity*, 119–24.
13. Cairns, *Christianity*, 91.
14. Cairns, *Christianity*, 85.
15. Eusebius, *History*, 8.6.
16. Ferguson, *Church History*, 84.

Martyred believers are means of grace as they point others to Christ's eschatological kingdom (Rom 8:18). As they are martyred, believers allow others to see this present life join with eschatological life in time and space. For this reason, I postulate that martyrs are sacraments of an encounter with the eschatological Spirit.

The Comforting Spirit and Racially-Marginalized Believers

It is said that Sunday is the most segregated day in the United States. To be sure, things have changed compared to decades ago. For example, William Seymour Jr., of the famous Azusa Street revival, was racially segregated by his former mentor, Charles Parham. Yet, the Spirit manifested so powerfully in and through Seymour that he drew multitudes across races and cultures to encounter Christ. In this way, the racially-segregated Seymour signified grace of the Spirit comforter.

Indeed, White believers who associated with the ministry of Seymour were criticized. The White believers who fellowshipped with Seymour pointed others, especially their kind, to God's anti-racial presence in Christ. Seen in this light, it is fitting to identify these White believers as sacraments of encountering the Spirit's comforting presence in Christ.

Similarly, believers who endure racial discrimination, whether Black, Latino, Asian, even White, etc., are signs of the grace of the Spirit's comforting presence in Christ. The fact that they hold on to their faith in Christ in the face of racial discrimination from fellow believers is itself a testament to their encounter with God's comforting presence. Racial or tribal discrimination is not limited to the United States but occurs in many parts of the world at different intensity levels.

For example, sometimes, believers from minority tribal groups in Africa and the African diaspora also face marginalization. To the extent that they endure marginalization from believers of dominant tribal groups, they are signs of the grace of the Spirit's comforting presence in and through the marginalized Christ (Matt 1:20; Matt 26:56; John 8:41). It is worth remembering that the early church leaders were faced with a similar challenge (Acts 6).

The day of Pentecost attracted representatives from various parts of the known world, like Parthians, Medes, Elamites, and residents of Mesopotamia, Judea and Cappadocia, Pontus and Asia, Phrygia, Pamphylia, Egypt, Libya, Cyrene, and Rome, including Jews and proselytes, Cretans, and Arabs (Acts 2:9–11). Remarkably, they heard the disciples speak in the native languages of their homeland (Acts 2:4–7). We can infer from this experience that Pentecost is a polemic against racial, tribal, gender, socioeconomic discrimination, marginalization, etc.

To be sure, the Spirit was poured out upon both men and women despite the latter's marginalization in society (Acts 10:34–35). Similarly, the Spirit's descent upon Cornelius, a Gentile, and his household points to this anti-discrimination character of God (Acts 10:34–35). It follows that Cornelius and his household are sacraments of a personal encounter with the Spirit of God who embraces people from diverse races, cultures, ethnicities, nationalities, and languages, in the same sense as the Jews at Pentecost. People who preach the gospel across diverse races, cultures, ethnicities, nationalities, or languages are often vulnerable to all kinds of sufferings.

The Comforting Spirit and Suffering Preachers

The preaching of the gospel is essentially spiritual warfare. In fact, Jesus warned the disciples they would be persecuted (John 15:20). The early church disciples faced opposition as they shared the good news of salvation (Acts 4; 6; 7). As believers preach the gospel across national, tribal, or racial borders, they face diverse forms of challenges. Paul suffered as he preached the gospel to Gentiles (1 Cor 4:12; 2 Cor 4:9).

In this way, others conclude that Paul had indeed encountered the ascended Jesus by the Spirit (Acts 9:5; 22:8; 26:15). Unjust suffering for the gospel's sake occurs in different forms including, but not limited to, persecution, imprisonment, death, illness, rejection, etc. Thus, the unjustly suffering preachers manifest the Spirit of God's comforting presence through Christ.

The Comforting Spirit and Blacks Denied of Baptism

There is an abundance of literature documenting incidents of Black Christians to whom White religious leaders denied Water Baptism. As such, many slaves conceived Christianity as a religion of White people. Slave masters thought that baptizing their slaves would lead to their freedom. Seen through the lens of theological conviction that Water Baptism initiates one into the body of Christ, it implies that slaves denied of this rite were subjected to suffering.

Likewise, some slave owners struggled with the idea of baptizing Black believers. In fact, some refused to be immersed in the same baptismal waters as Black believers. As Water Baptism signifies freedom from the slavery of sin, Black believers were, in effect, subjected to the bondage of sin. It was humanly difficult for Black believers to reconcile this racial segregation, yet some held on to their faith in Christ. In this way, they signified to their masters that they had encountered God's grace of forgiveness by the Spirit. Put another way, they manifested the Spirit of God's forgiveness.

Drawing from this, Black believers who suffered via Water Baptism deprivation served as sacraments of an encounter with the Spirit. Through their endurance of racial segregation at baptismal waters, they rendered the Spirit of God tangibly present. The spirituality of slaves links to modern Pentecostalism in general and within Black Pentecostal liturgy in particular.[17] This shows that Black believers or slaves who were denied Water Baptism functioned as human signs of grace by the Spirit Comforter. It is noteworthy that Christ extends Water Baptism to believers of every race, tongue, and tribe (Matt 28:19–20).

According to Luke, the disciples were commanded to make disciples of all nations (Matt 28:19). Further, they were to baptize the newly reborn as a sign of initiation and incorporation into the body of believers, locally and universally. Implicit in the mandate to baptize all nations' converts is the anti-racist nature of God revealed in Christ by the Spirit. In other words, baptism provides concrete manifestation to the presence of God's anti-racist Spirit.

The Water Baptism of the Ethiopian eunuch is a polemic against racism (Acts 8). As Luke reports, Phillip was divinely instructed to go to a specific route or roadside to meet with the Ethiopian eunuch (Acts 8:26–27). The Spirit of God located the eunuch and specifically instructed Phillip to speak to him (Acts 8:26). This event has several implications, including the sacramentality of anti-racists. Phillip's obedience to the Spirit as he helped the eunuch understand what he read, and baptized him, suggests that he had an anti-racist attitude. To appreciate this, one needs to know how eunuchs were perceived.

There are several implications of the baptism of the Ethiopian eunuch. For example, Jews abhorred eunuchs because they were castrated.[18]

---

17. See Vondey, "The Making of a Black Liturgy."

18. *Josephus*, Apion 2.270–71.

Seen in this light, it is remarkable that the Spirit of God directed Phillip, a Jew, to minister to the Ethiopian eunuch. Also, one whose testicles were crushed or whose penis was removed was not to be admitted to the assembly of the Lord (Deut 23:1; cf. Lev 21:20). Although the eunuch was returning from Jerusalem, where he had gone to worship (Acts 8:27–28), it is clear that the Spirit had unfinished business with him.

Notably, God spoke of the future when he would welcome eunuchs into the assembly of his people (Is 56:4–5). We are not told how the Ethiopian became a eunuch. Some people are eunuchs by birth, men make others eunuchs, and some choose to be eunuchs to dedicate themselves to serving God (Matt 19:12). However, the eunuch was a high-ranking official of the queen of the Ethiopians in charge of the treasury (Acts 8:27). His openness to the gospel of Jesus preached by Phillip, and his submission to Water Baptism, show that the Spirit truly touched him. The baptism of the eunuch by Phillip shows that the latter was genuinely filled with the Spirit and was an anti-racist.

Hence, we can postulate that the anti-racist Phillip is a concrete site or an embodied sign of the anti-racist Spirit. More adequately, Phillip is a sacrament of a personal encounter with the Spirit of God in Christ. The baptism of the eunuch is a robust biblical polemic against racism in a community of believers. Another instance when God's anti-racist character is revealed is through believers' participation in the Lord's Supper.

The Comforting Spirit and the Blacks Denied of the Lord's Supper

To deny the believers participation in the Lord's table is to deny them incarnational participation in the body of Christ. In many church traditions, the Lord's Supper is reserved for those baptized in water. This is in keeping with the view of Water Baptism as an initiatory rite. In other words, Water Baptism is conceived as a rite of incorporation into the body of Christ and a local community of believers. Granted this, slaves or Black people whose White masters denied them Water Baptism could not be invited to the Lord's table.

To deny Black believers the privilege to commune with Christ at the table of the Lord's Supper is dehumanizing and subjects them to unfathomable suffering. Seen in this light, Black believers who endured segregation at the Lord's table and persisted in their faith, hope, and love in Christ signified to their masters and White church leaders that they genuinely encountered him. Thus, they served as signs of grace that rendered the Spirit of Christ tangible to their masters and White ecclesial leaders. In this sense, the suffering via deprivation at the Lord's Supper can be held as sacraments of an encounter with the Spirit of God's presence in Christ.

The Comforting Spirit and the Spirit-Baptized Believers

Unlike Water Baptism and the Lord's Supper, where human beings may be seen to control the administration of these ecclesial rites, the Spirit cannot be domesticated. To state the obvious, the Spirit has no color. Thus, it makes sense for Joel to prophesy that God will pour out the Spirit upon all flesh (Joel 2:28–29). Likewise, Paul states that the Spirit bestows gifts as he sovereignly wills (1 Cor 12:11).

At new birth, believers receive the gift of the Spirit (Acts 2:38). Water baptism and Spirit baptism belong together in that the Spirit underlines both. Drawing from this, White members of clergy who deprive Black people of Water Baptism and the Lord's Supper attempt to deny those individuals fellowship with the Spirit of God in Christ. In fact, Black people who were denied these ecclesial rites thought the Spirit did not indwell them. The thought of being denied the gift of the Spirit due to skin color is traumatizing.

Some slaves might have thought that White ecclesial leaders determined who received the Spirit. Those that endured such suffering and exhibited concrete signs of hope in words and deeds manifested God's grace. Accordingly, they can be held as sacraments of an encounter with the Spirit. God gives the Spirit to those who ask him regardless of race, tongue, and tribe (Luke 11:13; Acts 10:44–48).

Before he ascended to heaven, Jesus told his disciples they would receive power after the outpouring of the Spirit (Acts 1:8). Moreover, the Spirit would empower the disciples to be Christ's witnesses from Jerusalem, Judea, Samaria, and to the outermost parts of the world (Acts 1:8; cf. Matt 28:19). The same Spirit would empower people of different races. The Spirit poured out on the day of Pentecost was a polemic against racism, tribalism, and nationalism, etc. The Spirit baptism of Cornelius is a lens for understanding the anti-racist nature of God (Acts 10:44–48).

The Spirit poured out upon Jews on the day of Pentecost is the same as the one poured out upon Gentiles and, indeed, people of all races. It is against the Spirit's nature for believers baptized in the Spirit to exhibit a racist attitude. Among other things, the Spirit baptism of Cornelius and household, as Gentiles, signifies that God transcends racial, tribal, nationalistic, and gender barriers. Notably, the Spirit manifests his presence in and through believers from every tribe, tongue, culture, nationality, or race. Spirit-baptized individuals from diverse races serve as sites or signs of grace.

The Comforting Spirit and the Multiracial, Multicultural, Multiethnic, Multinational Worshipping Community

Being a victim of racial oppression does not give one the right to do the same toward others. In contrast, those who have been victims of racial oppression ought to be sympathetic toward others from different races. God reminded the Israelites not to maltreat foreigners in their midst since they themselves were once foreigners in Egypt (Exod 22:21). Believers who endure suffering from racial segregation concretely express the empowering Spirit of God's indwelling presence.

In the early church, Luke reports that the Hebrew-speaking Jews were favored during the distribution of food over the Greek-speaking Jews (Acts 6:1). To resolve this, the apostles appointed seven deacons to oversee this responsibility. Notably, the apostles stressed that those selected be full of the Spirit (Acts 6:3). In this way, those full of the Spirit of God would ensure that racism was dealt with accordingly. By so doing, these deacons enabled the Spirit, who is a Person without face and color, to manifest tangibly in and through their anti-racist attitudes.

In contrast, some believers take seriously Peter's discovery that God does not show favoritism but accepts people from diverse cultures, nations, colors, and tribes so long as they fear or acknowledge him (Acts 10:34–35). Interestingly, Peter makes this admission upon seeing Christ pour out the Spirit upon the Gentile Cornelius and his household (Acts 10:44–48). The Spirit poured out upon the Gentiles was a polemic against a seemingly racist mindset of some Jews that despised Gentiles. We can see from this pneumatic experience that God wanted Jewish believers to regard Gentile believers as equally sanctified in Christ by the Spirit (Acts 10:28).

Consequently, Paul says that in Christ, there is no longer Greek and Jew, circumcised and uncircumcised, barbarian, Scythian, slave and free (Col 3:11). It shows that the early apostles like Peter and Paul wrestled against racism. In this way, the Apostles Peter and Paul provided concrete manifestation to the presence of the Spirit without color. By so doing, Peter and Paul are signs of the grace of the Spirit of God's anti-racist character. More adequately, they are sacraments of a personal encounter with the colorless Spirit of Christ. Thus, the disciples stressed soteriological identity over cultural, linguistic, racial, or tribal identity. In other words, salvation through Jesus Christ and confirmed by the reception of the Holy Spirit is all that mattered.

In keeping with the above, racism remains a disturbing reality in churches, especially in the West. Generally, people of color are the most racially discriminated against in sacred spaces. A White American friend who loves the Lord Jesus told me that, "I know my people, it is difficult for them to worship with people of color, let alone submit to a leader who is of color," during our conversation about multicultural or multiracial churches, congregations, and ministries. This did not come as a surprise admission to me based on my personal experience. Notwithstanding this, White brothers and sisters who champion the cause against racism in their places of worship are sacraments of a personal encounter with the Spirit of God's presence. That is to say, they render God's presence tangible in and through their anti-racist words and deeds.

To be sure, there are also people of color who practice reverse racism toward White people in the West. The reverse racists or racist people of color are as guilty as their White counterparts. There is no biblical justification for people of color to engage in reverse racism toward their White brothers and sisters in Christ. The truth is that all believers are born of the same Spirit (John 3:6, 8), and are baptized into the same Christ in the same way the Israelites were baptized into Moses, ate the same spiritual food, and drank from the same spiritual rock, which is Christ (1 Cor 10:2–4).

Believers relate to others based on their relation to God in Christ by the Spirit. By taking concrete steps to deter racism in places of worship, believers serve as signs of the Spirit of God in Christ. Churches with diverse leadership that reflect representative races in their ecclesial community enable the Spirit of God in Christ to be tangibly or visibly present. The Spirit poured out upon all flesh finds concrete manifestation in and through multicultural, multiracial, or multi-ethnic churches or congregations. The believers in such churches or congregations function as signs of the Spirit of anti-racism.

Notably, anti-racial believers are sacraments of personal encounters with the Spirit of God in Christ, who is anti-racist by nature. As the apostles did in the early church, leaders in predominantly White congregations should intentionally seek to be sacraments of God's presence by the Spirit of anti-racism, taking all steps to accommodate minorities who feel excluded. This is important because sacraments are acts enacted by intention and guidance of the Spirit or the biblical text. Ecclesial sacraments or ecclesial rites or ordinances are practiced and directed in the Bible through the leading of the Spirit.

Likewise, Christ, the primordial sacrament, intentionally ministered to people from across cultures and thereby manifested God's concrete presence by the Spirit, who is anti-racist. There is also a subtle form of racism in immigrant churches in the West. One area that racist tendencies finds expression is in and through the use of the language of the dominant tribe or people-group in immigrant congregations. This is a common phenomenon especially among Asian immigrant churches, African immigrant churches, and Hispanic immigrant churches.

The majority are given pride of place in terms of being given the freedom to express themselves in their mother tongue. The minorities hardly have such opportunities. Sometimes, churches organize international days of worship, at which time minority members are given a chance to showcase something from their cultures of origin, e.g., singing, dressing, and foodstuffs. To be sure, such occasions mostly engender a superficial inclusion but do not address the fundamental feeling of discrimination.

Admittedly, leaders of immigrant churches that privilege the language or needs of members from the dominant cultures might have good reason to justify their actions. In fact, privileging, for example, the language of the dominant culture in their congregation, does not in and of itself suggest racist intentions on the part of ecclesial leaders.

After all, only God knows the deep secrets of human hearts to locate and identify those who harbor racist attitudes. Nonetheless, church leaders who intentionally fail to take steps to accommodate minority members in their worship services cannot be absolved of discrimination. In contrast, the leaders of multi-racial, multi-cultural, or multi-ethnic churches, individually and communally, provide tangible expression to God, who does not show partiality to the extent that they accommodate minority believers. (Acts 10:34–35).

It is interesting that tribalism, which is as unjust as racism, also manifests in churches even outside of the West, e.g., Asia, Africa, and Latin America. For example, South Africa is known to many people in and outside of Africa concerning its past struggles with racism. There are also instances where people of color in Asia and Latin American countries are subjected to discrimination in places of worship. African, Asian, and Latin American church leaders who help members to transcend tribal boundaries render the Spirit tangible. Notably, they are signs that point others to the colorless Spirit.

While suffering is often not linked to the Spirit, the early church disciples suffered despite their Pentecost experience. In this light, Luke explains the sufferings the early church faced (Acts 4–7; 12:1–5). For example, the early church disciples were often persecuted, arrested, beaten, or flogged. Yet the disciples grew firm in their commitment to Christ by the Spirit. To the extent that the disciples endured sufferings, they manifested the Spirit at work in and through them and inspired others' faith, hope, and love in Christ. To confirm this, the early church grew amid sufferings (Acts 5:14).

This implies that the suffering disciples are signs, means, and cause of grace by the Spirit as they inspired others to encounter God's salvific presence via Christ. Further, they are sacraments of an encounter with God's comforting presence. The Spirit comforted the disciples when they endured persecution. The Spirit's comfort is both a realized and an unrealized reality until the *eschaton*. We can infer that eschatological hope sustains the believers facing diverse sufferings.

CHAPTER 7

Manifesting the Eschatological Spirit

Hopeful Believers

> For through the Spirit, by faith, we eagerly
> wait for the hope of righteousness.
>
> (GAL 5:5)

BELIEVERS ARE HOPEFUL PEOPLE because of the indwelling eschatological Spirit. Their lives are thoroughly shaped and informed by a vision of God's coming kingdom. This is made real to them through the indwelling eschatological Spirit. As such, believers live with their end in sight. Believers are a lens for others to see the reality of the future in the present. They not only await the eschatological kingdom but proleptically experience the eschatological kingdom. The natural result of living this reality is that believers embody and express eschatological hope.

Hope is intrinsic to a sense of meaning in life. Notably, biblical hope is related to the eschatological kingdom of God. Eschatological hope insists that this life is temporary, whereas the life to come is eternal. This eschatological hope transcends present life's challenges and reaches for life's reality to come in Christ by the Spirit. Eschatological hope is not attainable except in and through one's relationship with God in Christ. The eschatological expectation is the foundation of Christian hope and engenders peace and joy in believers (Rom 15:13).

The anticipation of the eschatological kingdom relates to Christ's death (Rom 5:5–10), his resurrection (Rom 15:13), his ascension (Mark 16:19–20; Luke 24:50–53; Acts 1:9–10), the promised return of Christ (Acts 1:11), and the pouring out of the Spirit at Pentecost (Acts 2:1–4). This expectation is reserved for the saved (Eph 2:12; Col 1:27; 1 Tim 1:1), whose hope brings together the present and eschatological life (1 Thess 5:2). In other words, eschatological hope is not esoteric but finds concrete expression in believers' words and deeds. Such hope motivates believers to shun ungodliness or worldly passions and live godly as they await Christ's blessed hope (Titus 2:12–14). Thus, hopeful believers are concrete signs of grace for the eschatological kingdom.

Pentecostals, for example, interpret their entire existence as signs of the end[1] and have passion for the eschatological kingdom.[2] The Spirit poured out at Pentecost fulfilled Joel's prophecy that marked the beginning of the end times or the eschatological phase in the world's history. The sending of the Spirit at Pentecost signified to the disciples that Christ was seated at the right hand of God (Acts 2:33; 7:55–56). The early church was emboldened with eschatological hope in the face of immense suffering. The sending of the Spirit engenders believers as people who live in the eschatological tension between the "already" and the "not yet." The Spirit's sending serves as a deposit or guarantee of the coming end (2 Cor 1:22; 5:5).

In this light, hopeful believers are sacraments of encountering the eschatological Spirit. Hopeful believers provide concrete manifestation to the Spirit's immanent yet transcendent presence. Hope refers to an expected favorable outcome regarding a future event. In the Christian context, hope relates to the end of times tied to the return of Jesus. Therefore, it is only believers who have eschatological hope. Moreover, eschatological hope is grounded in the life, death, resurrection, ascension, and second coming of Christ.

Significantly, Christ is the eschatological hopeful Man *par excellence* as it is in and through him, one finds full manifestation of the hope linked to the eschatological kingdom. The hope Christ embodies engenders in the Spirit of God (Rom 5:5; 15:13; Gal 5:5). Put another way, the Spirit gives rise to Jesus as the hope of glory (Col 1:27). In his humanity, Christ

---

1. See Sisso, *Sign People*, 10–11; also McPherson, "Premilllenial Signal Towers," 32–37; also Vondey, "Pentecostal Ecclesiology," 227.

2. Land, *Pentecostal Spirituality*

looked forward to the fulfillment of the eschatological kingdom (Matt 24:36; Mark 13:32; Rom 8:24).

Likewise, believers who embody hope are sacraments of the eschatological Spirit. Eschatological hope is rooted in Christ's death, resurrection, ascension, and second coming. The Spirit enables believers to live between the "already" and the "not yet" eschatological tension. Precisely, the hopeful are signs that render tangible God's coming kingdom. This is particularly the case with believers who reflect Christ in words and deeds by the eschatological Spirit. One way that believers manifest eschatological hope is by submitting to the rite of Water Baptism.

The Eschatological Spirit and Water-Baptized Believers

The Water Baptism signifies a believer's death, burial, and resurrection with Jesus. The Spirit who raised Jesus from the dead will raise dead believers (Rom 8:11; 2 Cor 4:14; Gal 1:1). This means that Water Baptism has implications for the future. When believers emerge from waters of baptism, they symbolize newness of life in Christ. Notably, they foretaste their future bodily resurrection. To be sure, the eschatological Spirit will raise the dead (1 Thess 4:14).

Accordingly, water-baptized believers embody the hope of the resurrection. Seen in this light, they are human sites, locations, or signs of eschatological hope. Baptized believers make visible the reality of God's resurrection power. Water-baptized believers' visible rendering of the resurrection power justifies them as sacraments of encountering the eschatological Spirit.

Moreover, Water Baptism symbolizes that believers are washed or cleansed from sin. The feeling of being cleansed from sin engenders a sense of hope in those baptized. This is so because Christ himself commanded that his followers be baptized. The very fact that one obeys Christ's command regarding Water Baptism bolsters one's standing before Christ. For this reason, Christ insists that John baptize him to fulfill all righteousness (Matt 3:15). Jesus did not need to be baptized because in him is no sin.

To be baptized by John inspires hope in Jesus, who obeyed the Father's command and was publicly approved (Matt 3:17; Mark 1:11; Luke 3:22). Further, Christ's baptism legitimizes John's call to baptize people and inspires hope that they would not face God's wrath, which John warns about (Matt 3:7; Luke 3:7). The baptized individuals function as signs of hope for entering the eschatological kingdom of God (John 3:5).

Baptized believers enable others to see the hope of God's salvific grace in human flesh. In this way, they inspire others toward faith, hope, and love in God's grace of forgiveness of sin. One's decision to publicly acknowledge and identify with Jesus' death, burial, and resurrection in baptism, can inspire others toward the same, e.g., the three thousand baptized at Pentecost (Acts 2:41), and the various households, including those of Cornelius (Acts 11:13–14), Lydia (Acts 16:15), the Philippian jailor (Acts 16:33), Crispus (Acts 18:8), and Stephanas (1 Cor 1:16).

To the extent that believers who submit to baptism inspire others, they are means of grace. Believers inspire others toward hope for the eschatological kingdom of God through Water Baptism, wherein they depict their death, burial, and resurrection with Christ. Baptized believers thus function as means of grace and draw others to an encounter with Christ.

To be sure, the rite of Water Baptism itself is not a source of hope but the eschatological Spirit who indwells believers. The Spirit stirs hope in the heart of those seeking baptism, not in the waters of baptism. In other words, it is hope for the coming kingdom of God in Christ which drives believers to submit to Water Baptism. Thus, those who seek baptism respond to the primordial work of the Spirit who births hope through repentance and faith in Christ.

This partly justifies the theological view that Water Baptism is a post-conversion or a post-regeneration experience. The believers reflect this eschatological hope when partaking in the Lord's Supper as an eschatological meal, also known as the marriage supper of the Lamb (Rev 19:7, 9).

The Eschatological Spirit and Lord's Supper Celebrants

The Lord's Supper celebration creates space for believers to reflect on the fact that the bread and the wine represent the body and the blood of their Lord who is alive. When Jesus gave thanks over the bread and wine, he depicted his death and resurrection. Armed with the hope of this resurrection by the eschatological Spirit, he hopefully anticipated his death upon the Cross. This shows that the Lord's Supper is fundamentally a hope-inspiring meal. Participants in the Lord's Supper are reminded that their dead bodies will not remain in the ground but the Spirit will raise them up like Jesus. As such, participation in the Lord's Supper bolsters eschatological hope. Further, communicants point others to the reality of the Spirit of God's resurrecting power.

It is not a coincidence that Jesus celebrated the Last Supper with his disciples on the night he was arrested (1 Cor 11:23). The Last Supper was an eschatological meal that fostered hope for God's coming kingdom. It is from the Last Supper that the Lord's Supper draws its forward-looking motif. Specifically, the Lord's Supper is a meal in which believers are reminded of the day they will partake of the marriage supper of the Lamb in the eschatological kingdom upon the return of Jesus (1 Cor 11:26). Thus, believers who participate in this meal symbolize to others that they look forward to Jesus' return.

The eschatological nature of the Lord's Supper has implications for the sacramentality of believers. It is no coincidence that Luke mentions breaking of bread, which is another way to describe the Lord's Supper, in the same breath as the outpouring of the Spirit at Pentecost (Acts 2:42–46). The Lord's Supper orients believers toward the eschatological kingdom of God. This is what Jesus aims at when he tells his twelve disciples, "I will not eat it until it is fulfilled in the kingdom of God" (Luke 22:16). Christ links the Lord's Supper to an apocalyptic event that will take place in the coming kingdom of God.

John the Revelator echoes this when he writes, "Blessed are those who are invited to the marriage supper of the Lamb" (Rev 19:9). The Spirit enables John to discern this apocalyptic event (Rev 1:10; 4:2; 17:3). Likewise, the Spirit enables believers to discern the apocalyptic implication of the Lord's Supper. Precisely, it is an apocalyptic meal that points to the marriage supper of the Lamb in the eschatological kingdom.

Notably, the marriage supper is meaningless apart from the Lamb and his bride, just as the Lord's Supper is meaningless apart from Jesus and believers (communicants). As Christ and his disciples looked forward to the marriage supper while observing the Last Supper, believers also look forward to the marriage supper when they celebrate the Lord's Supper. This is what Jesus wants to impress upon his disciples when he says, "I will not eat it until it is fulfilled in the kingdom of God . . . from now on I will not drink of the fruit of the vine until the kingdom of God comes" (Luke 22:16-18 cf. Matt 26:29; Mark 14:25).

Consequently, the Lord's Supper facilitates remembrance of the future, i.e., the fulfillment of the marriage supper of the Lamb. Further, the Lord's Supper gives rise to believers as concrete signs of eschatological hope for God's kingdom. It implies that participation in the Lord's Supper bolsters hope by creating space for believers to reflect upon the coming kingdom. Precisely, the Lord's Supper enables believers to foretaste the marriage supper.

Drawing from this, we can posit that the Lord's Supper participants are sacraments of a personal encounter with the Spirit of God's eschatological presence by Christ. It is noteworthy that Jesus participated in the Last Supper just before his crucifixion. Moreover, Christ identified himself as the Lamb for Jews and Gentiles to post his blood on the doorposts of their heart to escape from eternal death. This is a new Exodus to their eternal home. It contrasts with the Israelites' escape from Egypt (Exod 12).

The Eschatological Spirit and Christ's Death

Christ's death opened the gate to eternal life confirmed by believers' reception of the Spirit as a deposit or guarantee (2 Cor 5:5). Notably, Christ's death ushered in the eschatological hope for once eternally alienated human beings (Eph 4:18; Col 1:21). Fear of death is common among human beings. However, Jesus' death and resurrection enable believers to face the threat of death through the lens of eschatological hope. Having a salvific relationship with Christ is a sure foundation of eschatological hope beyond this present life. Unbelievers have no hope beyond this life, which arises in rebirth through repentance and faith in Christ by the Spirit. Thus, Paul says, "I have been crucified with Christ; and it is no longer I who live, but it is Christ who lives in me" (Gal 2:19–20).

In fact, Paul concretely manifests this eschatological hope when he goes to Jerusalem despite the prophecy of Agabus that he will die (Acts 21:10–13). Elsewhere, Paul says that "my desire is to depart and be with Christ, for that is far better" (Phil 1:23). Paul's eschatological hope is rooted in the death and the resurrection of Christ by the Spirit.

The Eschatological Spirit and Christ's Resurrection

The resurrection of Jesus is the cornerstone of Christian hope (1 Cor 15:14). Notably, Jesus was in his humanity filled with hope beyond death. In fact, Jesus is the hope-filled Man *par excellence*. Jesus anticipated and looked forward to his death and resurrection (John 2:19; 12:27). For example, Christ manifests concrete hope when he decides to go to Jerusalem to face death by crucifixion on the Cross (Matt 16:21).

Even before his crucifixion, Jesus refers to himself as the resurrection (John 11:25). At Bethany, many people gather to mourn the death of Lazarus (John 11:19). Martha and Mary sent an urgent request for Christ to come and pray for Lazarus (John 11:3, 6, 21, 32). Understandably, Martha and Mary are disappointed because Jesus comes after Lazarus is dead (John 11:21, 32).

Notwithstanding this, Jesus tells them, "Your brother will rise again" (John 11:23). This seems humanly impossible, as Lazarus has been dead for four days (John 11:39). But Jesus raises Lazarus from the dead and manifests the powers of the age to come (John 11:41–44). Thus, Jesus demonstrates to the mourners that he is the hope of glory. Thus, many believe him and encounter God's salvific grace which engenders concrete hope (John 11:45). Christ thus fits as the primordial sacrament of the encounter with Spirit of God's eschatological presence.

The expected resurrection motivated Jesus to face death on the Cross (Matt 20:19; Mark 8:31; 10:34; Luke 18:33; 24:7; John 5:29) although his disciples did not grasp this (John 14:1–4; 20:29). Later, Peter interprets the resurrection of Christ as the source of living hope (1 Peter 1:3–6). That is to say, the resurrection of Jesus births eschatological hope, which affects in concrete ways the lives of his followers. Thus, Paul admonishes believers not to grieve as others without hope (1 Thess 4:13) because of the Spirit of eschatological hope in them (Rom 15:13). Through signs of hope in word and deed, believers render tangible the Spirit's coming kingdom in Christ.

Seen in this light, the hopeful believers are sacraments of encountering the eschatological Spirit. The resurrection of Jesus assures believers of their bodily resurrection. Believers are the firstfruits of the resurrection (Rom 8:23). This suggests that believers foretaste the Spirit who will raise their dead bodies at Christ' return. In this way, the eschatological hopeful point others to the reality of the resurrection and the coming end and is tied to Jesus' ascension (Acts 1:9–11).

The Eschatological Spirit and Christ's Ascension

The same power of the Spirit who raised Jesus from the dead also thrusted him into heaven (Acts 1:9). Luke uses the cloud as a metaphor for the Spirit of God's presence (cf. Exod 14:19, 20). This ascension likely inspired eschatological hope in the witnessing disciples (Acts 1:10). It is noteworthy that Elijah's ascension in the Old Testament parallels in some ways that of Jesus.

The ascensions of Elijah and Jesus set up Elisha (2 Kgs 2:11) and the disciples (Acts 1:9–11) as sacraments of encounter with the eschatological Spirit. Precisely, Elijah and Jesus served as human locations, sites, or signs of hope by the Spirit. Elijah's ascension and that of Jesus left their followers in a state of hopelessness, given the miracles, signs, and wonders they performed to benefit the needy. But, the descent of the Spirit on Elisha, Elijah's disciple, and on Jesus' disciples, restored hope attested to by the many miracles, signs, and wonders that they performed more than Elijah and Jesus, respectively (2 Kgs 2:9-15; John 14:12). It is noteworthy that the Spirit rested upon select individuals until Pentecost just ten days after the ascension of Jesus.

Others, too, regarded Elijah and Jesus as threats. For example, King Ahab held Elijah as the troubler of Israel (1 Kgs 18:17), while the Pharisees, the Scribes, and the Sadducees misrepresented Jesus' anti-Mosaic Law (Matt 23:1–39; Mark 12:35–40; Luke 11:37–54; 20:45–47). Jesus' ascension paved the way for sacramentality of the eschatological hopeful. Similarly, Elijah's ascension set up Elisha as a sacrament of eschatological hope. Elijah's ascension pointed to Jesus' ascension and opens space for conceiving believers as sacraments of eschatological hope.

To clarify the significance of the ascension to the sacramentality of believers, let us recall that Elisha's encounter with the Spirit depended upon the ascension of Elijah (2 Kgs 2:1) just as the disciples' encounter with the Spirit at Pentecost depended upon the ascension of Jesus (John 16:7). The Spirit upon Elijah manifested concretely in and through Elisha, just as the Spirit upon Jesus manifested in and through the disciples. Jesus' ascension links to the sacramentality of the disciples and, by extension, to the believers due to the eschatological Spirit of hope poured out.

The Eschatological Spirit and Spirit-Baptized Believers

In both the Old and New Testaments, the Spirit is linked to the eschatological kingdom of God (Isa 32:14–16; Zech 14:8–9; Mark 13:11; 2 Cor 3:7–18). The Spirit's descent upon Christ at Jordan gave hope to the Spirit's descent upon repentant humanity. The descent of the Spirit links to the Jewish expectation of the Messiah, which signals the beginning of the end time. This engendered expectation that the return of the Messiah would bring about the bodily resurrection of believers. This means that the resurrection of Jesus marked the "already" and the "not yet" periods. Another key eschatological event is the outpouring of the Spirit which links to Joel's prophecy (Joel 2:28–29). Peter tells us that this prophecy was fulfilled at Pentecost when the Spirit was poured out upon the disciples (Acts 2:16–18).

Luke's linking of the Spirit to the end times echoes Paul's characterization. Specifically, Paul holds the sending of the Spirit as the dawn of the Messianic Age and as a mark that the believers belong to God (1 Cor 15:20, 23; 2 Cor 1:21–22; 5:5; Eph 1:13; 4:30). The Spirit is the firstfruit and down payment toward God's grand plan (Rom 8:23).

Thus, Paul says, "you were marked with a seal for the day of redemption" (Eph 4:30). The Spirit motivates believers to anticipate Christ's return and the eschatological kingdom. This anticipation reflects concrete changes in the lifestyles of believers. In this way, believers who live in anticipation of Christ's return function as visible, tangible, or signs of the grace of the Spirit of hope by the eschatological kingdom of God.

Next, Jesus told his disciples to look forward to the promise of the eschatological Spirit (Luke 24:49; Act 1:8). The sending of the Spirit upon men and women, poor and rich, young and old, Jews and Gentiles, Black and White, literate and illiterate, is ground for eschatological hope. It signifies that something extraordinary has happened and is also yet to happen. Therefore, Peter was surprised that the Spirit came upon Gentiles in the same way as Jews (Acts 10:45; 14:27; 15:3). A church of people from different races, tribes, and cultures signifies eschatological hope (Rev 5:9).

Moreover, the poured-out Spirit empowers believers to perform signs and wonders that inspire faith, hope, and love. For example, Peter inspired faith, hope, and love by healing the sick laid along the streets as he passed (Acts 5:15). Thus, Peter manifested the Spirit of the healing power that points to the presence of the eschatological kingdom of Christ where illness does not exist. It follows that Peter is a sign of grace that renders tangible God's healing presence. Thus, Peter fits the theological conviction of a sacrament of encountering the Spirit of hope for God's eschatological kingdom to be fully realized through the second coming or the return of Christ.

The Second Coming of Christ and the Eschatological Spirit

The same power of the Spirit that lifted Jesus into heaven will one day bring him back (Dan 7:13; Matt 24:30; 26:64; Mark 14:62). As Jesus ascends into heaven, two men appear in white apparel, who say: "This Jesus, who has been taken up from you into heaven, will come in the same way as you saw him go into heaven" (Acts 1:11). This promise engendered hope in the early church, especially in the face of persecution.

Further, the expectation of Christ's return motivated the disciples to live holy lives as they awaited his return (Matt 25:6–7; 2 Pet 3:11; 1 John 3:3). By so doing, they functioned as signs of the grace of hope for the eschatological kingdom amid ungodliness. For example, Paul commends the believers at Thessalonica for turning from worshiping idols to serving God and waiting for the return of his Son from heaven (1 Thess 1:9–10). The belief in Jesus' imminent return influenced the Thessalonian believers to turn from idols to Christ. We can thus posit that these Thessalonians manifested eschatological hope, which rendered the Spirit tangibly present.

Next, Paul writes to the Corinthians "that you are not lacking in any spiritual gift as you wait for the revealing of our Lord Jesus Christ" (1 Cor 1:7). Paul shows the certainty about the second coming of Christ that makes believers eagerly look forward to this eschatological event. The anticipation of the second coming of Christ orients believers to live in a way that is pleasing in God's sight. This orientation reflects concretely in and through hope-filled lifestyles of believers as they await to be rewarded by Jesus, their Lord and Savior (1 Tim 6:14; 2 Tim 4:1, 8; Titus 2:12–13).

The eschatological Spirit who indwells believers enables them to wait for the return of Christ patiently. This patient waiting for the return of Christ is motivated by the promise of rewards in the eschatological kingdom (2 Tim 4:8). It is quite telling that Paul calls Christ the blessed hope, referring to Jesus' return in his glorified body (Titus 2:13).

Christ himself looked forward to the fulfillment of his glorious return (John 14:3). In this sense, Christ is the sign of hope for the eschatological kingdom *par excellence*. Jesus shapes and informs the view that the hopeful believers are signs of grace for the eschatological kingdom.

The Eschatological Spirit and Fellowshipping Believers

The fellowship of believers reflects the eschatological tension of the "already" and the "not yet." Precisely, *koinonia* points others toward the end of history while at the same time accenting that the kingdom of God is already underway. Fellowship among believers demonstrates that they currently partake in the Godhead's eternal life and look forward to *koinonia's* fullness in the *eschaton*. The believers experience eschatological hope as the "already" and the "not yet" reality.

It is noteworthy that the hospitality that the early church practiced relates to hope for the eschatological kingdom. Precisely, the early church disciples did not allow material possessions to be their reference point or determine their status in God. Instead, the disciples derived joy in hospitality in anticipation of being hosted by God in the coming kingdom. The believers who practice hospitality are signs and means of eschatological hope. To be sure, hospitality has a deeper meaning when practiced toward others from distinct cultures, nations, races, or ethnicity.

Multicultural/Multinational/Multiethnic Congregations and the Eschatological Spirit

The Bible teaches that representatives from all peoples would gather before the Lord in the end time (Isa 60:3–16; Zech 14:16–19; Rev 7:9). The Pentecost event inaugurated the church as the ethnically-reconciled community of believers. Admittedly, however, the Jewish disciples in the early church struggled to accommodate the Gentile disciples into their fold, but this changed over time (Acts 8:29; 10:19–20; 11:12–18). Accordingly, the ethnically-reconciled disciples are in their individual and corporate selves, signs of eschatological hope. More adequately, they are sacraments of a personal encounter with the Spirit of God's eschatological presence by Christ as the race-transcending, nationality-transcending, ethnicity-transcending, and culture-transcending Man *par excellence*. Christ is the bridge between the once ethnically-divided Jews and Gentiles.

The unbelievers of the day likely concluded that this ethnic reconciliation was of divine origin. To the extent that this happened, the early church functioned as a means of grace of eschatological hope. In this way, they inspired and drew others to an encounter with the Spirit, for example, Cornelius and his household (Acts 10:44). In keeping with this, churches that attract members from different ethnic groups, cultures, races, etc., are signs of eschatological hope that point others to God's egalitarian character. Pentecostals are egalitarian and culturally flexible.[3]

---

3. Anderson, *To the Ends of the Earth*, 250–51; Bergunder et al., *Studying Global*

Drawing from this, we can say that Pentecostals are largely sacraments of the Spirit of God's presence as they reflect eschatological hope. To be sure, some non-Pentecostal churches are multi-ethnic, multiracial, multicultural, multilingual, and multinational. As such, they signify hope and are a foretaste of the multiethnic, multiracial, multicultural, multilingual, multinational outlook of God's eschatological community in Christ.

The Eschatological Spirit and Witnessing Believers

The Spirit poured out at Pentecost empowered the disciples as effective witnesses to God's redemptive mission in Christ. This witnessing mission of the church is tied to Christ's return. Jesus tells his disciples to wait for the promise of the Spirit (Luke 24:49), so they can be witnesses from Jerusalem, Judea, Samaria, and to the ends of the earth (Acts 1:8). By preaching the gospel, they manifest the Spirit. Churches and parachurches engage in witnessing programs. Unlike in previous decades, churches in the global South now send missionaries to the West.[4]

Migration, in many ways, funds this reverse mission to the West. The witnessing believers are concrete signs of the grace of eschatological hope considering the impending judgment following the second coming of Christ. It is in this sense that they are sacraments of an encounter with the eschatological Spirit of hope.

Driven by the promised return of Christ, believers take the missional or the evangelistic functions of the church at individual and corporate levels seriously. For example, Pentecostals hold the world as their parish.[5] Those who witness to the redemptive mission of Christ around the nations of the world do justice to the Great Commission (Matt 28:18–20; Acts 1:8).[6]

The early Pentecostals stepped out in faith to unknown parts of the world to preach the gospel of the kingdom of God in Christ before his imminent return.[7] Through their witness, believers enable unbelievers to see the reality of the eschatological kingdom. The believers

---

Pentecostalism, 159–63; 69, 72; Kay, *Pentecostalism*, 305.

4. Kwiyani, *Sent Forth*; Ludwig and Asamoah-Gyadu, *African Christian Presence in the West*.

5. Martin, *Pentecostalism*.

6. Anderson, *To the Ends of the Earth*.

7. Anderson, *Spreading Fires*; Hunter and Robeck, *Azusa Street Revival*.

with a special grace manifest the Spirit of God's eschatological presence through martyrdom.

The Eschatological Spirit and Martyrs

Martyrdom is the highest form of persecution. Martyrs are driven by hope in Christ through God's Spirit of the eschatological kingdom. Jesus told his disciples, "Blessed are those who are persecuted for righteousness' sake, for theirs is the kingdom of heaven" (Matt 5:10). Drawing from this, the Spirit fills martyrs with hope by granting them visions about the eschatological kingdom's reality. In this way, they are strengthened or comforted. This Spirit-inspired hope for the eschatological kingdom inspires others toward God. It is noteworthy that some believe that martyrs enter directly into God's eschatological presence in heaven and enjoy special privileges.[8] But even before martyrdom, they manifest signs of eschatological hope.

In fact, this hope enables martyred individuals to see the present life differently and, importantly, as inferior to the life to come. The life of martyrs is characterized by signs of hope that point to life beyond the present. The hope for the eschatological kingdom of God in Christ peaks in an event of martyrdom. For example, although Stephen showed signs of hope for the eschatological kingdom before he was martyred, his hope peaked at his martyrdom (Acts 7:55–60). Thus, martyrs are signs of the grace of the Spirit of hope for the eschatological kingdom.

Next, it is noteworthy that persecution does not always lead to martyrdom. That is to say, one may be persecuted for confessing Christ without being killed. Such believers give concrete expression to the Spirit of hope for the coming kingdom of God in Christ. As indicated earlier, martyrdom demonstrates that one is consumed by the Spirit of hope for the coming kingdom.

It implies that the believers persecuted for the sake of righteousness in light of the eschatological kingdom are sacraments. Through persecution or martyrdom, believers render the Spirit tangible. Martyrs' desire for eschatological life inspire faith, hope, and love toward God. Martyrdom is not the conclusion of life but the beginning of eschatological life with God. To be sure, the martyred believers are the true ambassadors of Christ the martyred Man *par excellence*.

---

8. Ferguson, *Church History*, 84.

Conclusion

The Spirit and Sacramentality of All Believers

> So we are ambassadors for Christ, since God
> is making his appeal through us.
>
> (2 COR:5:20)

ADMITTEDLY, THE SUBJECT OF sacraments engenders intense debate among scholars. Drawing from the view that Christ is the primordial sacrament of the encounter with God's presence, this book suggests that all believers are, both individually and communally, sacraments of a personal encounter with the Spirit of God's presence through Christ. This is partly so because all believers are microcosmic (individually) and macrocosmic (communally) temples of God's presence.

To be sure, all believers make God's presence visible in word and deed by the Spirit of Christ. Jesus' ascension bolsters the believers' sacramental role until his return (Acts 1:11). At Jesus' return, there will be no need for sacraments as all will see him and believers will be like him (1 John 3:2). Believers' sacramental role relates to their ambassadorship. God's reality will be visible to all when Jesus returns thus there will be no need for sacraments or ambassadors.

Paul alludes to this when he tells the Corinthians that they are ambassadors of Christ (2 Cor 5:20). Notably, he clarifies that this ambassadorship relates to all the believers. God gives Christ's ambassadors the Spirit as a guarantee or promise (2 Cor 5:5). This promised or ordained presence of the Spirit with the believers offers a robust foundation for the

Conclusion: The Spirit and Sacramentality of All Believers

claim that all believers are sacraments of God's presence. Believers are ambassadors both individually and communally.

Thus, Paul self-identifies as an ambassador in chains (Eph 6:20; cf. Prov 13:17; Jer 49:14) and also identifies himself with the Corinthians as ambassadors (2 Cor 5:20). Conversion is the first step towards becoming Christ's ambassadors and sacraments (John 1:12; 2 Cor 5:17; 2 Tim 2:19). Conversion engenders believers as ambassadors, like political ambassadors (2 Chr 32:31; Ezek 17:15). The description of believers as ambassadors is a hermeneutical window to conceive believers as sacraments. To clarify this relation of believers to ambassadors and ambassadors to sacraments, let us first reflect briefly on the *modus operandi* of political ambassadorship.

Political ambassadors do not work incognito but represent their sending authority openly. This is because they act on behalf of their sending authority. In fact, political ambassadorship is ineffective without this sense of open representation and visibility. Political ambassadors render their sending authority visible to others. Their actions reflect their sending authority's actions. When political ambassadors discharge their duties, they act *de facto* as their sending authority. To be sure, political ambassadors are presumed to act in the interest of their sending authority.

At commissioning, political ambassadors are given a seal of the sending authority. In this way, they are empowered to represent the sending authority. Political ambassadors present letters of their appointment with the seal of the sending authority to their duly designated jurisdiction. Interestingly, the sending authority commits political ambassadors to act in certain ways. But, it is also true that political ambassadors commit their sending authority to act in certain ways.

This commitment between political ambassadors and their sending authority mirrors the commitment between believers and God's Spirit in Christ. More precisely, God self-commits to act and to manifest his presence in and through believers via the Spirit of Christ. Sacramentality speaks to this. Commissioning of political ambassadors relates to the disciples' commissioning and to the sacramental view of believers (Matt 28:16–20; John 20:19–23; Acts 1:4–14).

The disciples' commissioning involves the sealing of the Spirit. Notably, Christ commissions the disciples and gives them the Spirit as a seal (John 20:22). Some scholars regard this as John's Pentecost to contrast with Luke's Pentecost (Acts 2:1–4). This aligns with the Pauline idea that believers are given the Spirit as a seal (2 Cor 5:5). Further, the Father sends the seal of the Spirit upon Jesus (Matt 3:16; Mark 1:10; Luke 3:22;

John 1:32). This way, the Father inaugurates Jesus as the primordial ambassador and sacrament of God's presence (John 6:27; Col 2:9). Jesus' Pentecost is characterized by tangible phenomena, i.e. the Father's audible words and the dove.

At Luke's Pentecost, Jesus sends the seal of the Spirit upon the disciples and inaugurates them as ambassadors and sacraments of God's presence. Notably, tangible phenomena, i.e. wind, sound, fire, and tongues speech, which are visible and audible, characterize the Lukan Pentecost (Acts 2:1–4). Luke's Pentecost resonates with John's Pentecost, where Jesus breathes upon the disciples to impart the Spirit (John 20:22). This Spirit-sealing motif is critical for believers.

As ambassadors of Christ, believers render their sending authority visible by the Spirit. The Spirit empowers the disciples to act on their sending authority's behalf, openly and boldly. This is why they witness about Christ openly and boldly in the face of death threats (Acts 5:25, 40, 42; 16:23, 25). In this way, the disciples render the ascended Christ visible (Acts 4:13). More pointedly, the disciples render visible the Triune God working in and through them by the Spirit.

As political ambassadors symbolize and render their sending authority visible, believers symbolize and render their sending authority visible through the Spirit of God's presence. Peter ministers to the lame man at the Beautiful Gate conscious of the sending authority of the Triune God (Acts 3:6, 12). Peter exemplifies believers as ambassadors and as sacraments of a personal encounter with the Triune God's presence. Believers are conscious of their sending authority and act fittingly. Believers express this consciousness of their sending authority in words and deeds.

Believers manifest the Spirit via Christ-like words and deeds. These words and deeds are shaped and informed by the life of Christ through revelation of Scripture. In this sense, believers' words and deeds reveal the state of their relation to Christ (Matt 7:16, 20). To be sure, Christ's words and deeds also reveal the state of his relation to the Father (John 10:38). But, the Spirit is the seal and force behind all divine manifestations in and through Jesus Christ and the believers.

Jesus' incarnation is the foundation for conceiving believers as sacraments of the Spirit. A sacramental view of believers is a polemic against abstract theological propositions detached from real life experiences of both triumph and tragedy. Believers are not immune to sufferings and hence manifest the Spirit tangibly in and through triumphant and tragic experiences. The view that believers are sacraments of the Spirit does not

Conclusion: *The Spirit and Sacramentality of All Believers*   183

bifurcate between reflected and lived faith. In fact, it decries cerebral theologizing which has no concrete effects on real life situations.

Thus, Jesus calls his disciples the salt of the earth and the light of the world (Matt 5:13, 14). For Peter, the disciples are a chosen race, a royal priesthood, a holy nation, and God's own people called out of darkness into his marvelous light (1 Pet 2:9). They stress the disciples or believers' divinely-ordained role to host or be hosted by the Spirit and to manifest his presence.

The basic way for believers to render God's presence tangible is to reflect Christ's life. It is the Christ-like believers who are the light of the world, the salt of the earth, a royal priesthood, a holy nation, and God's own people. This suggests that Christ-like believers are signs or means of God's grace. Thus, they are God's gifts to the world as they render him visible and thereby inspire others' faith, hope, and love towards Christ.

At a primary level, believers show concrete signs of grace of the Spirit's presence when they respond to the altar call of salvation. This typically happens upon hearing the gospel. The experiences of Water Baptism, the Lord's Supper, Spirit baptism, worship, gifts and fruit of the spirit, sufferings, eschatological hope etc., allow believers to manifest God's presence. Both clergy and laity contribute to rendering God's presence tangible in diverse ways. The claim that believers are sacraments of the Spirit has theological, practical, and ecumenical implications.

Theological Implications

The debate about sacraments mostly focuses on ecclesial rites, especially Water Baptism and the Lord's Supper. Briefly, some churches hold the Water Baptism and the Lord's Supper as sacraments. That is to say, these rites are in and of themselves means of grace of an encounter with God in Christ by the Spirit. Other churches insist that these rites are ordinances. In other words, these rites enable the believers to remember God's redemptive acts in Christ by the Spirit.

The term "sacrament" is not defined primarily by any rites, including Water Baptism and the Lord's Supper. Instead, Christ shapes and informs the meaning of sacrament. Christ renders God fully visible and inspires all humankind to encounter his presence by the Spirit. Significantly, Christ is the primordial sacrament who shapes and informs all sacramental thought and practice.

A sacramental view of believers herein proposed is not contingent upon whether or not one accepts Water Baptism and the Lord's Supper as sacraments or as ordinances. Instead, it is rooted in the biblical motif that God ordained or promised to dwell and manifest his presence in and through believers (John 14:17). Thus, believers are God's preferred locations of his presence.

In keeping with this, I have posited that the Spirit of God's presence encounters human beings without the media of the Water Baptism and the Lord's Supper, as was the case with Saul (Acts 9:5). Similarly, believers can encounter the Spirit of God's presence without the media of Water Baptism and the Lord's Supper or any rites (Acts 5:15; 19:12). The rites like Water Baptism and the Lord's Supper, etc., allow believers to make visible their prior encounter with the Spirit.

Furthermore, I posited that Spirit baptism enhances the sacramental intensity of believers. The Pentecostal experience of Spirit baptism empowers believers to witness effectively to Christ. Spirit empowerment enables believers to speak and act in ways that reflect Christ. Accordingly, the empowered inspire others' faith, hope, and love towards Christ. In this way, the empowered reflect Christ who went about doing good and healing all whom the devil oppressed (Acts 10:38).

Practical Implications

The view of believers as sacraments of the Spirit has practical implications. For example, it challenges church leaders to open space for the Spirit to manifest in and through all members. This is not to suggest that one should do away with order in a worship service. Instead, it is a call for church leaders to recognize God's desire to reveal his presence in and through all believers as he wills (1 Cor 12:11). Leaders cannot domesticate the Spirit to the altar or pulpit. The Spirit can manifest his presence concretely in and through any members seated in pews. But, leaders should test claims of Spirit manifestation to see if they advance unity or edify the church (1 Cor 12:7).

Consequently, leaders could consider flexible liturgies that allow for surprises of the Spirit. Of course, Spirit manifestations in worship communities are not without tensions. For example, members may exercise spiritual gifts spontaneously which may appear as out of order. This may likely happen when members feel that they are not given opportunities to exercise their gifts. Others who feel deprived of opportunities to exercise their gifts may also resort to schisms.

To counter this, leaders could let members pray for each other while in their pews. By so doing, they will create more space for members to serve others through their gifts (1 Pet 4:10). In addition, this could disabuse misconception that only church officials or clergy bestow grace of the Spirit's presence or that a church altar is inherent with God's presence. The altar symbolizes God's open invitation to encounter his people. It does not domesticate God's presence. Further, God is not bound by physical space and church officials are not the sole repositories of his presence.

Encouraging believers to pray for each other increases space for concrete manifestation of God's presence. After all, both clergy and laity contribute to concrete expression of God's presence. Inviting members to the altar for prayer should be reserved for special occasions, like ordination services. Church leaders can also increase space for members to manifest the Spirit concretely by organizing events outside of worship services, e.g., serving food to the homeless, visiting prisoners or the sick in hospitals or nursing homes, cleaning the environment, helping the elderly people. Believers who undertake such activities are sacraments of God's presence. That is to say, they render God's presence visible in the same sense as in communal worship contexts. Believers' manifestations of the Spirit outside worship contexts have ecumenical implications.

Ecumenical Implications

Since all churches hold that believers are Spirit-indwelled, the view that believers are sacraments has ecumenical import and should minimize tension between sacramental and non-sacramental churches. In part, the *sacramentality of all believers* insists that no church tradition has monopoly over the Spirit. Christ sends all believers to manifest him visibly as he manifested the father (John 20:21). Thus, the Great Commission mirrors *the sacramentality of all believers*.

The Great Commission and Sacramentality of All Believers

Drawing from the discussion above, it seems reasonable to suggest that viewing believers as sacraments resonates with the Great Commission's imperatives (Matt 28:19; John 20:19–23; Acts 1:8; Acts 2:38). Christ commissioned his disciples to be witnesses of God's redemptive mission. The Great Commission extends to all subsequent believers. It transcends theological, denominational, and ecclesial traditions or boarders. Conceiving of believers as sacraments inspires believers to participate in the Great Commission by making Jesus visible in words and deeds by the Spirit. In other words, the idea of believers as sacraments stresses that every believer has the responsibility to make Christ visible by the Spirit in character and charisms, and in sacred and secular settings.

The *sacramentality of all believers* re-frames the sacramental debate centered upon the rites of Water Baptism and the Lord's Supper. Precisely, it calls us to rethink the chasm between sacramental and non-sacramental churches by re-focusing the sacramental discourse on Christ as the primordial sacrament instead of ecclesial rites. Of course, to conceive believers as sacraments does not impede but encourages submitting to Water Baptism and partaking in the Lord's Supper. This is so because Jesus was baptized in water and observed the Last Supper with his disciples.

Thus, true witnesses of Jesus submit to Water Baptism and partake in the Lord's Supper. This way, the believers imitate Jesus and make him visible as the Water Baptized-Man and the Last Supper-Participating Man or Communicant Man *par excellence*. Accordingly, I suggest that the dual theological categories of sacramental and non-sacramental churches are secondary to the theological category of believers as sacraments of the Spirit of God's presence through Christ.

Till He comes, make him visible!

Bibliography

Albrecht, Daniel E. *Rites in the Spirit: A Ritual Approach to Pentecostal/Charismatic Spirituality.* Sheffield, UK: Sheffield Academic, 1999.
Alexander, Estrelda, and Amos Yong. *Philip's Daughters: Women in Pentecostal-Charismatic Leadership.* Eugene, OR: Pickwick, 2009.
Alexander, Kimberly Ervin. *Pentecostal Healing: Models in Theology and Practice.* Blandford Forum, UK: Deo, 2006.
Anderson, Allan. *African Reformation: African Initiated Christianity in the 20th Century.* Trenton, NJ: Africa World, 2001.
———. *An Introduction to Pentecostalism: Global Charismatic Christianity.* New York: Cambridge University Press, 2004.
———. "Pentecostal Approaches to Faith and Healing." *International Review of Mission* 91.363 (2002) 523–34.
———. *Spreading Fires: The Missionary Nature of Early Pentecostalism.* Maryknoll, NY: Orbis, 2007.
———. *To the Ends of the Earth: Pentecostalism and the Transformation of World Christianity.* New York: Oxford University Press, 2013.
Anderson, Allan, and Edmond Tang. *Asian and Pentecostal: The Charismatic Face of Christianity in Asia.* Oxford, UK: Regnum, 2005.
Arrington, French L. *Encountering the Holy Spirit: Paths of Christian Growth and Service.* Cleveland, TN: Pathway, 2003.
Asamoah-Gyadu, J. Kwabena J *Contemporary Pentecostal Christianity: Interpretations from an African Context.* Eugene, OR: Wipf and Stock, 2013.
———. "Learning to Prosper by Wrestling and by Negotiation: Jacob and Esau in Contemporary African Pentecostal Hermeneutics." *Journal of Pentecostal Theology* 21.1 (2012) 64–86.
———. *Sighs and Signs of the Spirit: Ghanaian Perspective on Pentecostalism and Renewal in Africa.* Oxford, UK: Regnum, 2015.
Atkinson, William. *Baptism in the Spirit: Luke-Acts and the Dunn Debate.* Eugene, OR: Pickwick, 2011.
Aune, David Edward. *Prophecy in Early Christianity and the Ancient Mediterranean World.* Grand Rapids, MI: Eerdmans, 1983.
Banks, Robert J. *Paul's Idea of Community: The Early House Churches in Their Historical Setting.* Grand Rapids, MI: Eerdmans, 1980.
Bartleman, Frank. *Azusa Street.* Plainfield, NJ: Logos International, 1980.

Bergunder, Michael, A. F. Droogers, Cornelis van der Laan, Cecil M. Robeck, and Allan Anderson. *Studying Global Pentecostalism: Theories and Methods. The Anthropology of Christianity.* Berkeley, CA: University of California Press, 2010.

Boddy, Alex A. "The Anointing with Oil." *Confidence*, April–June 1992.

Boersma, Hans. *Heavenly Participation: The Weaving of a Sacramental Tapestry.* Grand Rapids, MI: Eerdmans, 2011.

———. *Scripture as Real Presence: Sacramental Exegesis in the Early Church.* Grand Rapids, MI: Baker Academic, 2017.

Boff, Leonardo. *Liberating Grace.* Maryknoll, NY: Orbis, 1979.

Brand, Chad, et al. *Perspectives on Spirit Baptism.* Nashville, TN: Broadman & Holman, 2004.

Bruner, Frederick Dale. *A Theology of the Holy Spirit: The Pentecostal Experience and the New Testament Witness.* Grand Rapids, MI: Eerdmans, 1970.

Burgess, Stanley M., and Ed M. van der Maas. *The New International Dictionary of Pentecostal and Charismatic Movements.* Grand Rapids, MI: Zondervan, 2002.

Cairns, Earle E. *Christianity Through the Centuries: A History of the Christian Church.* Grand Rapids, MI: Zondervan, 1996.

Cartledge, Mark J. *The Mediation of the Spirit: Interventions in Practical Theology.* Grand Rapids, MI: Eerdmans, 2015.

Clarke, Clifton. *Pentecostalism: Insights from Africa and the African Diaspora.* Eugene, OR: Cascade, 2018.

Coffey, David. *Grace: The Gift of the Holy Spirit.* Marquette Studies in Theology. Milwaukee, WI: Marquette University Press, 2011.

Congar, Yves. *I Believe in the Holy Spirit.* New York: Seabury, 1983.

Courey, David. *What Has Wittenberg to Do With Azusa?: Luther's Theology of the Cross and Pentecostal Triumphalism.* New York: Bloomsbury, T. & T. Clark, 2015.

Cross, Terry L. *The People of God's Presence: An Introduction to Ecclesiology.* Grand Rapids, MI: Baker Academic, 2019.

de Lubac, Henri. *Catholicism: Christ and the Common Destiny of Man.* San Francisco, CA: Ignatius, 1988.

Depoortere, Kristiaan. "From Sacramentality to Sacraments and Vice-Versa." *Questions Liturgiques/Studies in Liturgy* 82.1 (January 2001) 46–57.

du Plessis, David. *The Spirit Bade Me Go.* Plainfield NJ: Logos, 1970.

Dunn, James D. G. *Jesus and the Spirit: A Study of the Religious and Charismatic Experience of Jesus and the First Christians as Reflected in the New Testament.* London: SCM, 1975.

Eusebius. *Ecclesial History, Books 1–5.* Translated by Roy J. Deferrari. The Fathers of the Church: A New Translation. Washington, DC: Catholic University of America Press, 2005.

———. *History of Martyrs in Palestine.* Syriac Studies Library 39. Edited and translated by William Cureton. Piscataway, NJ: Gorgias, 2017.

Fee, Gordon D. *God's Empowering Presence: The Holy Spirit in the Letters of Paul.* Grand Rapids, MI: Baker Academic, 1994.

———. *Paul, the Spirit, and the People of God.* Peadbody, MA: Hendrickson, 1996.

Ferguson, Everett. *Church History: The Rise and Growth of the Church in Its Cultural, Intellectual, and Political Context.* Grand Rapids, MI: Zondervan, 2005.

Fransen, Piet F. *The New Life of Grace.* Tournai, Belgium: Desclée, 1969.

Gause, R. H. *Living in the Spirit: The Way of Salvation.* Cleveland, TN: Pathway, 1980.

Green, Chris E. W. *Pentecostal Ecclesiology: A Reader*. Boston, MA: Brill, 2016.
Heidegger, Martin. *Being and Time*. New York: Harper, 1962.
Hemphill, Ken. *The Antioch Effect: 8 Characteristics of Highly Effective Churches*. Nashville, TN: Broadman & Holman, 1994.
Hicks, John Mark, Johnny Melton, and Bobby Valentine. *A Gathered People: Revisioning the Assembly as Transforming Encounter*. Abilene, TX: Leafwood, 2007.
Hocken, Peter. "Jesus Christ and the Gifts of the Spirit." *Pneuma* 5.1 (1983) 1–16.
Hollenweger, Walter J. *The Pentecostals: The Charismatic Movement in the Churches*. Minneapolis, MN: Augsburg, 1972.
Horton, Harold. *The Gifts of the Holy Spirit*. Springfield, MO: Gospel, 1975.
Horton, Stanley M. *What the Bible Says about the Holy Spirit*. Springfield, MO: Gospel, 1976.
Hughes, Graham, and Steffen Lösel. *Reformed Sacramentality*. Collegeville, MN: Liturgical, 2017.
Hunter, Harold D. *Spirit-Baptism: A Pentecostal Alternative*. Eugene, OR: Wipf & Stock, 2009.
Hunter, Harold D., and Cecil M. Robeck. *The Azusa Street Revival and Its Legacy*. Cleveland, TN: Pathway, 2006.
Ingalls, Monique Marie, and Amos Yong. *The Spirit of Praise: Music and Worship in Global Pentecostal-Charismatic Christianity*. University Park, PA: Pennsylvania State University Press, 2015.
Irenaeus. "Against Heresies." In *The Apostolic Fathers: Justin Martyr and Irenaeus*. Ante-Nicene Fathers, Vol. 1, edited by Alexander Roberts and James Donaldson. Translated by A. Cleveland Cox. Peabody, MA: Hendrickson, 1994.
Jacobsen, Douglas G. *Thinking in the Spirit: Theologies of the Early Pentecostal Movement*. Bloomington, IN: Indiana University Press, 2003.
James, Shelton B. *Mighty in Word and Deed: The Role of the Holy Spirit in Luke-Acts*. Eugene, OR: Wipf and Stock, 2000.
Kaatz, Kevin W., ed. *Voices of Early Christianity: Documents from the Origins of Christianity*. Voices of an Era. Westport, CT: Greenwood, 2013
Kalu, Ogbu. *African Pentecostalism: An Introduction*. New York: Oxford University Press, 2008.
Kay, William K. *Pentecostalism*. London: SCM, 2009.
Kay, William K., and Anne E. Dyer. *Pentecostal and Charismatic Studies: A Reader*. London: SCM, 2004.
Kärkkäinen, Veli-Matti. *The Spirit in the World: Emerging Pentecostal Theologies in Global Contexts*. Grand Rapids, MI: Eerdmans, 2009.
Keener, Craig S. *Gift & Giver: The Holy Spirit for Today*. Grand Rapids, MI: Baker Academic, 2001.
———. *The Spirit in the Gospels and Acts: Divine Purity and Power*. Peabody, MA: Hendrickson, 1997.
Kleist, James A., trans. *The Didache; The Epistle of Barnabas; The Epistles and the Martyrdom of St. Polycarp; The Fragments of Papias; The Epistle to Diognetus*. Ancient Christian Writers 6. Westminster, MD: Newman, 1948.
Koenig, John. *New Testament Hospitality: Partnership with Strangers as Promise and Mission*. Overtures to Biblical Theology. Philadelphia, PA: Fortress, 1985.
Kwiyani, Harvey C. *Sent Forth: African Missionary Work in the West*. Maryknoll: Orbis, 2014.

Land, Steven Jack. *Pentecostal Spirituality: A Passion for the Kingdom.* Cleveland, TN: CPT, 2010.
Larson-Miller, Lizette. *Sacramentality Renewed: Contemporary Conversations in Sacramental Theology.* Collegeville, MN: Liturgical, 2016.
Litfin, Bryan M. *Early Christian Martyr Stories: An Evangelical Introduction with New Translations.* Grand Rapids, MI: Baker Academic, 2014.
Lombard, Peter, and Collegium S. Bonaventurae. *Petri Lombardi Libri IV Sentaiarum.* 2nd ed. Florence, Italy: Ex Typographia Collegii S. Bonaventurae, 1916.
Ludwig, Frieder, and Kwabena J. Asamoah-Gyadu. *African Christian Presence in the West: New Immigrant Congregations and Transnational Networks in North America and Europe.* Trenton, NJ: Africa World, 2011.
Ma, Wonsuk. "Asian (Classical) Pentecostal Theology in Context." In *Asian and Pentecostal: The Charismatic Face of Christianity in Asia*, edited by Allan Anderson and Edmond Tang. Oxford: Regnum, 2005. 46–72.
Ma, Wonsuk, Robert P. Menzies, and Russell P. Spittler. *The Spirit and Spirituality: Essays in Honour of Russell P. Spittler.* London and New York: T. & T. Clark International, 2004.
Macchia, Frank D. *Baptized in the Spirit: A Global Pentecostal Theology.* Grand Rapids, MI: Zondervan, 2006.
———. "Tongues as a Sign: Towards a Sacramental Understanding of Pentecostal Experience." *Pneuma* 15.1 (1993) 61–76.
Martin, David. *Pentecostalism: The World Their Parish. Religion and Modernity.* Malden, MA: Blackwell, 2002.
McPherson, Aimee Semple. "Premillenial Signal Towers." In *Pentecostal and Charismatic Studies: A Reader*, edited by William K. Kay and Anne E. Dyer. London: SCM, 2004. 32–37.
Menzies, Robert P. *Speaking in Tongues: Jesus and the Apostolic Church as Models for the Church Today.* Cleveland, TN: CPT, 2016.
Menzies, William W., and Stanley M. Horton. *Bible Doctrines: A Pentecostal Perspective.* Springfield, MO: Logion, 2020.
Menzies, William W., and Robert P. Menzies. *Spirit and Power: Foundation of Pentecostal Experience: A Call to Evangelical Dialogue.* Grand Rapids, MI: Zondervan., 2000.
Mittelstadt, Martin William. *Reading Luke-Acts in the Pentecostal Tradition.* Cleveland, TN: CPT, 2010.
———. *The Spirit and Suffering in Luke-Acts: Implications for a Pentecostal Pneumatology.* New York: T. & T. Clark International, 2004.
Moltmann, Jürgen. "The Blessing of Hope: The Theology of Hope and the Full Gospel of Life." *Journal of Pentecostal Theology* 13.2 (April 2005) 147–61.
———. *The Church in the Power of the Spirit: A Contribution of Messianic Ecclesiology.* London: SCM., 1977.
———. *The Spirit of Life: A Universal Affirmation.* Minneapolis, MN: Fortress, 2001.
———. *Theology of Hope: On the Ground and the Implications of a Christian Eschatology.* Minneapolis, MN: Fortress, 1993.
Neumann, Peter D. *Pentecostal Experience: An Ecumenical Encounter.* Eugene, OR: Pickwick, 2012.
Onyinah, Opoku. *Spiritual Warfare: A Centre for Pentecostal Theology Short Introduction.* Cleveland, TN: CPT, 2011.

Osborne, Kenan B. *Christian Sacraments in a Postmodern World: A Theology for the Third Millennium*. New York: Paulist, 1999.

———. *Sacramental Theology: A General Introduction*. New York: Paulist, 1988.

Perry, Sam C. "There Are Other Things as Well." *Church of God Evangel*, May 11, 1918.

Rahner, Karl. *The Church and the Sacraments*. Quaestiones Disputatae. Freiburg, Germany: Herder, 1963.

———. *Theological Investigations*. New York: Crossroad, 1974.

Richie, Tony. *Speaking by the Spirit: A Pentecostal Model for Interreligious Dialogue*. Lexington, KY: Emeth, 2011.

Ruthven, Jon. "On the Cessation of the Charismata: The Protestant Polemic of Benjamin B Warfield." *Pneuma* 12.1 (1990) 14–31.

Saliers, Don E. *Worship as Theology: Foretaste of Glory Divine*. Nashville, TN: Abingdon, 1994.

Schatzmann, Siegfried S. *A Pauline Theology of Charismata*. Peabody, MA: Hendrickson, 1987.

Schillebeeckx, Edward. *Christ, the Sacrament of the Encounter with God*. New York: Sheed and Ward, 1963.

———. *Christ, the Sacrament of the Encounter of God*. London: T. & T. Clark, 2012.

Semmelroth, Otto. *Church and Sacrament*. Notre Dame, IN: Fides Publishers, 1965.

Seymour, W. J. "Beginning of World Wide Revival." *The Apostolic Faith*, January 1907.

Sisso, Elizabeth. *A Sign People*. Springfield, MO: Gospel, 1918.

Smail, Thomas A. *The Giving Gift: The Holy Spirit in Person*. Lima: OH: Academic Renewal, 2002.

Smail, Thomas. *The Giving Gift: The Holy Spirit in Person*. Eugene, OR: Wipf and Stock, 1994.

Smith, James K. A. *Thinking in Tongues: Pentecostal Contributions to Christian Philosophy*. Pentecostal Manifestos. Grand Rapids, MI: Eerdmans, 2010.

Stronstad, Roger. *The Prophethood of All Believers : A Study in Luke's Charismatic Theology*. Cleveland, Tenn.: CPT Press, 2010.

Sullivan, Francis A. *Charisms and Charismatic Renewal: A Biblical and Theological Study*. Ann Arbor, MI: Servant, 1982.

Tertullian. *Apology. De Spectaculis. Minucius Felix: Octavius*. Loeb Classical Library 250. Translated by T. R. Glover and Gerald H. Rendall. Cambridge, MA: Harvard University Press, 1931.

———. *The Writings of Quitus Sept. Flor. Tertullianus*. Ante-Nicene Christian Library, Vol. XI, XV, XVII. Translated by Sydney Thelwall, Peter Holmes, and Robert Ernest Wallis. Edinburgh: T. & T. Clark, 1880.

Thomas, John Christopher. *Footwashing in John 13 and the Johannine Community*. Sheffield, UK: JSOT, 1991.

Tillich, Paul. *Systematic Theology*. Chicago, IL: The University of Chicago Press, 1963.

Tomberlin, Daniel. *Pentecostal Sacraments: Encountering God at the Altar*. Cleveland, TN: Center for Pentecostal Leadership and Care, Pentecostal Theological Seminary, 2015.

Torr, Stephen C. *A Dramatic Pentecostal/Charismatic Anti-Theodicy: Improvising on a Divine Performance of Lament*. Eugene, OR: Pickwick, 2013.

Turner, Edith L. B. *Communitas: The Anthropology of Collective Joy*. Contemporary Anthropology of Religion. New York: Palgrave Macmillan, 2012.

Turner, Max. *The Holy Spirit and Spiritual Gifts: In the New Testament Church and Today*. Grand Rapids, MI: Baker Academic, 2012.

Vondey, Wolfgang. "The Making of a Black Liturgy: Pentecostal Worship and Spirituality from African Slave Narratives to American Cityscapes." *Black Theology* 10 (2012) 147–168.

———. "Pentecostal Ecclesiology and Eucharistic Hospitality: Toward a Systematic and Ecumenical Account of the Church." *Pneuma* 32 (2010) 41–55.

———. *Pentecostal Theology: Living the Full Gospel*. New York: Bloomsbury, 2017.

Vorgrimler, Herbert. *Sacramental Theology*. Collegeville, MN: Liturgical, 1992.

Wacker, Grant. *Heaven Below: Early Pentecostals and American Culture*. Cambridge, MA: Harvard University Press, 2001.

Warrington, Keith. *Pentecostal Theology: A Theology of Encounter*. London and New York: T. & T. Clark, 2008.

Williams, J. Rodman. *Renewal Theology*. Grand Rapids, MI: Academie, 1990.

Wolfgang, Vondey, and Chris W. Green. "Between This and That: Reality and Sacramentality in the Pentecostal Worldview." *Journal of Pentecostal Theology* 19.2 (2010): 243–64.

Yong, Amos. *The Bible, Disability, and the Church: A New Vision of the People of God*. Grand Rapids, MI: Eerdmans, 2011.

———. *The Spirit Poured Out on All Flesh: Pentecostalism and the Possibility of Global Theology*. Grand Rapids, MI: Baker Academic, 2005.

———. "The Spirit, the Body, and the Sacraments: Pentecostal-Catholic Dialogue and the 'Pneumatological-Sacramental' Imagination." In *Renewal History & Theology: Essays in Honor of H. Vinson Synan*, edited by S. David Moore and James M. Henderson. Cleveland, TN: CPT Press, 2014. 263.

Subject Index

Abed-Nego, 102
Abraham, 107, 112, 122
Abraham's daughter, Jesus healing, 154
Achan, punishment of, 89
act of grace, sanctification as, 54
Adam, 31, 35, 106
"adoption," as a biblical term, 55
Agathonice, martyrdom of, 157
King Ahab, 174
all believers, as sacraments, 180, 181
"already" and "not yet" eschatological tension, 169
"already" and the "not yet" periods, 175
the "already" and the "not yet" reality, 177
altar, 28, 30, 35, 185
altar call of salvation, responding to, 27, 30, 46, 183
ambassadors, of Christ, 180
Ananias, Saul of Tarsus and, 37, 41, 120
Ananias and Sapphira, Peter exposing, 75, 89
angel, hosting Peter, 113
anointing oil, sacramental view about, 83
anointing the sick, requiring faith, 85
anti-Christian communities, the baptized in, 59
anti-discrimination character, of God, 159
Antioch disciples, as signs of transforming grace, 44
anti-racial believers, as sacraments, 165
anti-racist attitudes, deacons dealing with, 163
apocalyptic meal, Lord's Supper as, 171

apostles, 91. *See also* disciples
appearance, 17, 18
Aquinas, on Christ as the *mysterium Dei*, 12
Arrington, French L., 85–86
ascension, of Jesus Christ, 174, 180
Augustine, 8, 12, 120
Azusa Street revival, 81, 158

baptism, 53, 59, 161
baptism in or with the Spirit, definition of, 64
baptismal waters, 50
baptized believers
    in anti-Christian faith communities, 59
    bonding with the resurrection of Jesus, 47
    as concrete signs of a covenant relationship, 52
    embodying God's sanctification, 53
    functioning as signs of hope, 170
    incorporated into God's family, 55
    incorporated into the new community of believers, 48
    as primary with the rite of baptism as secondary, 51
    sanctified into the family of God, 58
baptized Christ, as the primordial sacrament, 50
Barnabas, 40, 44, 91, 121
believers
    actions as secondary, 8, 76
    anointed with oil (the Holy Spirit) after cleansing, 64

believers (cont.)
- as both salt and light, xiii
- called to offices, 92
- causing or mediating grace, 24
- causing Spirit manifestations indirectly, 9
- comforting individuals' unjust suffering, 155
- coming to Christ to be baptized, 65
- in communion with other believers, 121
- as conduits or channels for the tangible expression of grace, 17
- confessing and repenting their sins, 39
- with disabilities, 151, 152
- divinely-ordained role, 183
- empowering Spirit and, 64–66
- encountering God by the Spirit's indwelling presence, 5
- encouraging to pray for each other, 185
- exercising the gift of knowledge, 75
- expected to show kindness to others, 99
- fellowshipping with God, 128
- foretasting the eschatological encounter, 15
- given spiritual abilities to freely give to the needy, 108
- as God's preferred locations of his presence, 184
- as hopeful, 167
- hosting strangers, 112
- as human channels of God's grace, xiii
- incarnational fellowship among, 114
- inspiring others toward hope, 170
- keeping faith in God despite suffering, 145
- in the knowledge and the likeness of Christ, 58
- laying hands upon the sick, xiv, 25, 84
- manifesting fruit, 94
- manifesting God's presence, 1, 14
- manifesting the Spirit, xi, xii, 7, 9
- as means of grace (the Spirit), 24–26
- ministering healing to the sick, 81
- as mobile temples of the Spirit, 7
- motivated to sing, 132
- not immune to sufferings, 182
- not invincible to suffering, 148
- participating in the Great Commission, 186
- pointing others to God's reality, 1
- receiving the Spirit at conversion, 33
- reconciling with each other, 40
- reflecting Christ in experiences, 12–13
- reflecting *imago Dei*, or God's image, 31
- reflecting Trinitarian fellowship, 143
- rendering God's clothing presence visible, 23
- sacramental view of, 184
- as sacraments, ix–xvii, 3, 19, 21–24, 74, 133, 154, 169, 179
- serving others rendering the Spirit tangible, 91
- serving strangers or the vulnerable, 113
- sharing in Christ's suffering, 145
- as signs and means of grace, 10, 76
- as signs of the grace of the Spirit, xiv
- as sites, signs, or symbols of the Trinity, 23
- speaking in tongues, 67
- speaking truth to power, 154
- the Spirit indwelling them, 34
- struggling with disabilities, 152
- submitting to Water Baptism and partaking in the Lord's Supper, 22
- sufferings of, 149
- symbolizing and rendering sending authority visible, 182
- as temples of the Spirit, xiii, 16
- testifying to encounters with God, 133–34
- uttering words of wisdom, 74

Bible, 23, 33, 148
biblical characters, experiencing tragic losses, 136
biblical hope, related to the eschatological kingdom of God, 167

Black believers, 159, 160, 161
Black Pentecostal liturgy, 160
blind man, as himself a "living
    testimony," 135
blood of Christ, 123
blood of the lamb, upon doorposts, 122
Boddy, Alex A., 83
body movements, 130, 131, 133
body of Christ, 7, 20, 92
Boff, Leonardo, 95

cessationism, 78, 134
character, of believers, 11, 17
charisma, manifesting God's presence
    through, 11
charismata, 60, 69
charismatic believers, 60, 63
Charismatics, xii
Charito, martyrdom of, 157
Christ. *See also* Jesus Christ
    as the advocate for sinners, 39
    on all humanity needing cleansing,
        57
    asking the Father to send the Spirit,
        23
    baptizing with the Spirit, 12
    commissioned his disciples to
        preach, 48
    as the communing Man, 118
    death of opened the gate to eternal
        life, 172
    deciding to go to Jerusalem to face
        death, 173
    demonstrating God's kindness, 98
    devoted himself to prayer and
        fasting, 128
    displaying utmost humility, 105
    drew multitudes into an encounter
        with God, 83
    enabled others to encounter the
        Spirit of God's presence, 16
    as the eschatological hopeful Man,
        168
    expectation of his return, 176
    faithful to the one who appointed
        him, 103
    fed multitudes of strangers, 108–9
    as the fellowshipping Man, 114–15
    as the flogged Man, 101
    as the forgiving Man, 105
    forgiving those that crucified him,
        106
    forgiving those who crucified him,
        106, 149
    as the fruit-manifesting Man, 94
    as the guest of Mary, 111
    hospitality to the most vulnerable,
        108
    insisting that John baptize him, 169
    as the interceding-praying Man, 129
    joined in corporate worship of the
        Father, 118
    kindness of, 98–99
    as the Lamb for Jews and Gentiles,
        172
    Lord's Supper and, 121, 139
    manifested the empowering Spirit, 60
    manifested the grace of humility,
        141–42
    manifested the host-guest
        relationship, 107
    manifested vertical and horizontal
        communion, 125
    as the martyr, 155
    ministered to people from across
        cultures, 165
    not showing a condescending
        attitude, 104
    as the peace-manifesting Man, 96
    as the preaching Man, 137
    as the preeminent sacrament, 39
    as the preeminent sign of God's
        faithfulness, 100
    as the primordial sacrament, 8,
        11–13, 95, 99, 100, 183, 186
    referred to the bread as his body and
        to the cup as his blood, 139
    related patiently, 97
    rendered God tangible, 94
    replaced circumcision of the flesh
        with spiritual circumcision, 52
    revealing the Triune God's presence,
        22
    self-giving death on the Cross for
        others, 100

Subject Index

Christ (cont.)
  shaping and informing the meaning of sacrament, 183
  shaping the sacramentality of patience-bearing believers, 97
  as the sign of hope for the eschatological kingdom, 176
  strengthened by an angel in the face of death, 127
  stressing being born of the Spirit, 56
  sufferings of, 149, 150
  taking on human flesh (incarnation), 112
  taught by his words and his deeds, 128
  as the temple of God's presence, 33
  as the ultimate sign, 123
  as the unjust-suffering Man, 148
  washing the disciples' feet, 141
Christian life, 39, 148
Christianity, entailing suffering, 148
Christians
  in Antioch, 43
  in hostile countries, 147
Christ-like believers, as the light of the world, 183
Christ-like individuals, rendering God's presence visible, xvi
church (ecclesia or *ekklesia* in Greek), 115
church leaders, 136, 152, 184
church traditions, practicing liturgical praise or singing in diverse ways, 133
churches, organizing international days of worship, 165
circumcision, confirmed the covenant relationship, 51–52
clapping of hands, as an expression of joy, 131
Clarke, Clifton, 150
cleansing, of sinners by grace, 53
clergy, acting in *persona Christi* or on Christ's behalf, 36–37
closed-table fellowship, for the Lord's Supper, 139
clothed with power, as being endued with the Spirit, 66
clothing presence, of the Spirit, 23
comforting Spirit
  Blacks denied of baptism and, 159–61
  Blacks denied of the Lord's Supper and, 161–62
  disabled believers and, 151–52
  impoverished believers and, 153–54
  manifesting, 144–66
  martyred believers and, 155–58
  multiracial, multicultural, multiethnic, multinational worshipping community and, 163–66
  racially-marginalized believers and, 158–59
  socioeconomically marginalized believers and, 154–55
  Spirit-baptized believers and, 162–63
  suffering Christ and, 150–51
  suffering preachers and, 159
commissioning, of disciples, 181
commitment, between political ambassadors and their sending authority, 181
communal worship, manifesting unity, 121
communicant believers, as sacraments, 114, 124
communicant Christ, primacy of, 124
communicants, 123, 124, 125
communing Spirit
  fellowshipping believers and, 142–43
  foot-washing believers and, 141–42
  generous believers and, 142
  inspiring vertical fellowship or communion, 114
  joyful singing and, 131–33
  Lord's Supper celebrants and, 139–40
  manifesting, 114–43
  preachers or teachers and, 136–38
  testifying believers and, 133–36
"communion," meaning divine intimacy, 114
"communities of disaster," engendering, 136

Subject Index

confession, of Jesus as Lord and Savior, 34
confessors, differing from martyrs, 155
continuationism, Pentecostals favoring, 78
conversion
    allowing believers to host the Spirit, 58
    enabling individuals to receive the Spirit, 57
    as an inward encounter with God, 57
    as a life-giving event of the Spirit, 28
    as reconciliation with God, 36
    relation of Water Baptism to, 55
    restoring one as *imago Dei* or image of God, 31
    standard for authenticating claims of, 31
    as the step towards becoming Christ's ambassadors and sacraments, 181
    turning humans into signs of the grace of the Spirit, 33
converts
    commiting to live a life that is pleasing in God's sight, 44
    growth of, 32
    holding the world as their parish, 45
    incorporated into the body of Christ, 54
    justified before God, 34
    public response to the altar of salvation, 28
    reflecting God's image, 29
    as sacraments, 30–33, 49
    as signs, 27, 29
    transformed into agents of reconciliation with God, 38
conviction of sin, 35, 58
Cornelius, 21, 71, 153, 162
Cornelius and his household
    Christ pouring out the Spirit upon, 163
    encountering the Spirit, 177
    inspired by Peter, 8
    as sacraments, 159
    speaking in tongues, 68, 71
    Spirit baptism of as Gentiles, 163

corporate earthly singers, discerning ongoing worship in the heavenly realms, 129–30
corporate prayer and intercession, role in communal worship, 125
corporate singing, spontaneous, 131
corporate worship, 115, 116, 119
corporate worshipers, as sacraments, 118
corporate-singing believers, as sacraments, 130
corporate-singing worship, of God, 129
corporeal other, 17
council of Trent, on the number of sacraments, 2–3
Cross of Christ, 145, 150

Daniel, 103, 127
King Darius, 103
David, x, 40, 100
de Lubac, 12
deacons, 91
death to sin, Water Baptism and, 44, 45
demon-possessed individuals, 88
derivative cause of grace, Moses as, 25
descent, of the Spirit signaling the beginning of the end time, 174–75
devil, tempting Jesus, 150
disabled believers, comforting Spirit and, 151–52
discerning believers, as sacraments, 88–89
discernment, gift of, 88
disciples
    acting on their sending authority's behalf, 182
    at Antioch as the first to be called Christians, 44
    demonstrating boldness after Pentecost, 151
    disposition of unity and fellowship among, 120
    divinely-ordained role, 183
    empowering Spirit and, 66–68
    experiencing unjust sufferings, 149
    fellowshipping with God via prayer and fasting, 128
    manifesting the Spirit of Christ, 15

disciples (cont.)
    prayed earnestly when facing death threats, 127
    reflecting or embodying the life or values of the person being followed, 43
    rendering visible the Triune God, 182
    as sacramental, 127
    as sacraments, 43–44, 174
    speaking in tongues, 14, 69
    startled at Saul's testimony of conversion, 41–42
    stress soteriological identity, 164
    witnessing individually and communally, 7
disease, incapable of revealing itself directly, 18
disobedience, Adam and Eve's act of, 107
disposition of faith, role of, 84
diverse tongues, gift of, 90
divine action, 24, 49
Divine Person, without a face, 81
divine-human cooperation, fruit of patience-bearing Paul signifying, 97
divine-human encounters, biblical stories of, ix
divinity, of Jesus Christ, 9, 12
Dorcas, serving others, 91
du Plessis, David, 67
Dunn, James D. G., 62, 75, 76

early church, 153, 163, 166, 168
early disciples, corporate worship by, 143
early Pentecostals, preaching the Gospel, 178
earthquake, shaking prison foundations for Paul and Silas, 132
ecclesial rites, sacraments as, 183
ecstatic manifestations, 82
ecumenical implications, of believers as sacraments of the Spirit, 185
egalitarian nature, of the Pentecost event, 20
Elijah
    ascension of, 174
    challenging the prophets of Baal, 87–88
    God's presence working in and through, 85
    as a sacrament, 76, 88
    splitting the Jordan River and crossing over, x
Elisha, x, 77, 174
empowered believers, as sacraments of the Spirit, 61
empowered to heal, 79
empowering Spirit
    anointed with oil and, 84–85
    charismatic Cornelius and, 71
    charismatic Pentecost disciples and, 70
    charismatic Samaritans and, 71
    discerning believers and, 88–89
    discerning Paul and, 89
    discerning Peter and, 89
    disciples and, 66–68
    diverse tongues-interpreting believers and, 90
    diverse tongues-speaking believers and, 89–90
    faith-manifesting believers and, 75–76
    faith-manifesting Elijah and, 76
    gifted believers and, 72–73
    healing anointing and, 81–84
    healing believers and, 76–77
    healing Elisha and, 77
    healing Pentecostal-Charismatic believers and, 80–81
    healing Pentecostals-Charismatics and, 78–80
    healing Peter and, 77
    knowledge-manifesting believers and, 74–75
    knowledge-manifesting Peter and, 75
    manifesting, 60–92
    ministering and, 91–92
    miracle-working Paul and, 86
    miracle-working Peter and, 86
    miracle-working-believers and, 85–86
    prophesying believers and, 87–88
    prophesying Elijah and, 87–88
    prophesying Paul and, 88
    servanthood and, 91

Subject Index

tongues-speaking believers and, 68–70
wisdom-manifesting believers and, 73–74
empowerment motif, baptism in the Spirit and, 65
Ephesians, Spirit-baptized speaking in tongues and prophesying, 72
eschatological communion, believers foretasting, 17
eschatological expectation, as the foundation of Christian hope, 167
eschatological hope, 166, 167, 168, 173, 179
eschatological kingdom, 167, 168, 174
eschatological Spirit
  Christ's ascension and, 173–74
  Christ's death and, 172
  Christ's promise to his disciples about, 20
  Christ's resurrection and, 172–73
  enabling believers to wait for the return of Christ patiently, 176
  fellowshipping believers and, 176–77
  Lord's Supper celebrants and, 170–72
  manifesting, 167–79
  martyrs and, 179
  multicultural/multinational/multiethnic congregations and, 177–78
  second coming of Christ and, 176
  Spirit-baptized believers and, 174–75
  water-baptized believers and, 169–70
  witnessing believers and, 178–79
eschaton, 19
Ethiopian eunuch, 57, 138, 160
ethnically-reconciled disciples, 177
eunuchs, 161
Eusebius, 156, 157
evangelist, Jesus as, 91
Eve, welcomed by Adam, 106
evil Spirit, recognizing Paul and Silas as servants of God, 89

ex opere operantis, 11, 84, 85
ex opere operato, 84
experiences, Spirit linked to, 13

face, of Moses, 18
faith, 50, 75, 145
faithful believers, 100–103
faithful Daniel, relational Spirit and, 103
faithful disciples, 101
faithful Stephen, relational Spirit and, 101–2
faithfulness, 100, 101
fasting, Jesus practiced, 128
Father, sending the Spirit upon the Son at the Jordan, 63
fear of death, 172
Fee, Gordon D., 23, 73, 76, 96, 98
fellowship
  of believers, 116, 176
  creating space for believers to sharing stories of suffering, 143
  distinguished the early church community, 121
  with God, prayer as, 127–28
fellowshipping, of believers, 142–43
fellowshipping Spirit of God, in and through sung worshipers, 130
fig tree, cursed by Jesus, 87
fire, characterizing God's presence in the Upper Room, 14
firstfruits of the resurrection, believers as, 173
Five Books against Marcion (Tertullian), 2
five-fold ministers, as God's gifts to the church, 91
foot-washing, practicing during worship service, 141
forgiving believers, relational Spirit and, 105–6
freewill offering, spirit of a, 142
friends, of Job attacking and accusing him of sin, 144
fruit of the Spirit, 94–95, 98
fruit-bearing believers, as sacraments, 93–94
fullness of God, revealed in and through Christ, 19

furnace, Shadrach, Meshach, and Abed-Nego thrown into, 102
future in the present, believers experiencing, 23

garden of Eden, hospitality in, 106
generosity, as fruit of the Spirit, 99
generous act, of God of his self-giving of Christ, 100
generous believers, relational Spirit and, 99–100
Gentile Pentecost, breaking cultural borders, 71
Gentiles, 68, 163
gentleness, as the fruit of the Spirit, 104
gift of faith, exercising, 75
gifted believers, 73, 90
gifts, Spirit bestowing for the common good, 72
gifts-exercising believers, 70
giving, 142
global South, 78, 153, 178
God
    actions of as primary, 8
    anointed Jesus of Nazareth with the Holy Spirit, 83
    anti-racist nature of, 160
    believers as sacraments of the dynamic presence of, 24
    believers confessing sin to directly, 37
    calling to Pharaoh through Moses, 115
    causing Moses to act, 25
    clothed Adam and Eve with animal skin, 54, 107
    dwelling in temples of human flesh, 5
    encountering and manifesting his presence in and through human beings, ix–x
    encountering and worshipping in spirit and in truth, 16
    exalting or giving grace to the humble, 105
    generous act of, 100
    grace of forgiveness of, 46
    as the host of Adam, 106
    hosting Israel's children, 107
    indwelling believers, 1, 12, 23
    not bound by physical space, 185
    options to deal with cancer, 147
    pouring out his Spirit upon all flesh, 5
    praying and interceding speaking to, 126
    presence of, rendering visible, x
    promise to encounter the Israelites visibly and tangibly, 4
    as the repairer of broken human beings, 39
    self-committing to act and to manifest his presence in and through believers, 181
    self-disclosing his presence to Abraham and Sarah, 112
    sending rain upon both the just (believers) and unjust (unbelievers), 99
    sharing in the suffering of believers with disabilities, 151
    vision of the coming kingdom of, 167
    wanting Jewish believers to regard Gentile believers as equally sanctified, 163
Godhead, 4, 115
Goliath, x
grace, 9, 10
Great Commission
    advancing, 109
    doing justice to, 178
    making disciples of Christ, 43–44
    mirroring the sacramentality of all believers and, 185–86
    Spirit driving through baptized disciples of Christ, 48
guests, relational Spirit and, 111–13

handkerchiefs, blest and returned to the sick, 81
handkerchiefs or aprons from Paul, people healed by, 86
hands, raising at the altar of salvation, 29
Harris, Wade, of Liberia, 82
healed believers, as means of healing, 79
healed individuals, 77, 78, 80
healers, as means of grace, 80

Subject Index

healing, 78, 108, 134, 135
healing gifts, 77, 78
healing grace, 84
healing power, Peter manifested, 175
heart, inward circumcision of, 52
heavenly realm and the earthly realm, coming together, x
Heidegger, Martin, 17–20
Hellenists, feeling discriminated against, 155
Hemphill, Ken, 62
Herod, behind the death of James, 156
high liturgical churches, corporate worshipers in, 116
Hocken, Peter, 73
Hollenweger, Walter J., xiv
Holy Spirit. *See also* Spirit
    characterized by tangible phenomena, 61
    constituted Jonah as a sign, 10
    as God's personal presence in believers, 13
    reminding the reborn to stay on the path of righteousness, 32
hope, 167, 168, 179
hopeful believers, as sacraments, 168, 173
hope-inspiring meal, Lord's Supper as, 170
horizontal reconciliation, 40
Horton, Stanley M., 67, 74
hospitable believers
    being hospitable to the vulnerable, 109
    fulfilling Christ's teaching, 110
    making the Spirit as the primary guest, 109
    not limited to any particular denomination, 111
    as sacraments, 108, 111, 112
hospitable disciples, 108
hospitality, 106, 107, 108–11, 112, 113, 177
hosted believers, relational Spirit and, 111–13
host-guest relationship, 107
hostile societies, corporate worshipers in, 143
hosts, 112, 113

human actions, of Christ reflecting divine actions, 9
human beings
    all born in need of reconciliation, 35
    encountering God's presence, 21
    lost the *imago Dei* because of the fall of Adam, 31
human body, allowing believers to manifest God's presence, 7
human faculties, Spirit using, 74
human intermediary, prophecy communicated through, 87
human response
    as secondary, 24
    as submission to Water Baptism, 49
humanity of Christ, 9, 24, 33
humble believers, as sacraments, 105
humility, 105, 141

Ignatius, 157
imago Dei, 31
immersion, 49–50, 51
immigrant churches, privileging the dominant culture, 165
impoverished believers, comforting Spirit and, 153–54
incarnation, of Jesus, 182
incarnational fellowship, 115
the incorporated, as sacraments of the Spirit, 54–59
incorporeal nature, of the Spirit, 15
individualism, Spirit of Pentecost not promoting, 120
indwelling Spirit, 36
infant baptism, 55
injustice, God concerned about, 154
intercessory prayer, Spirit and the Son involved in, 125
interpreting tongues, gift of, 90
invisible grace, seven external signs of, 2
invitation, worship as a human response to God's, 118
inward circumcision, of the heart, 52
Irenaeus, xi
Isaac, 122
Israelites
    covenant relationship with God, 122
    Red Sea crossing by, 53

Israelites (cont.)
    reminded by God not to maltreat foreigners, 163
    as a sign of God's presence to the Egyptians, 122
    singing after they crossed over the Red Sea, 132
    on synagogues as special places to encounter God's presence, 16
    as visible signs of encounter with God's presence to other nations, 4

James, 83, 85, 126, 156
Jesus Christ. *See also* Christ
    ascension linking to the sacramentality of the disciples, 174
    on believers as bearers of the Spirit, xii
    calling apostles, prophets, evangelists, pastors, or teachers, 92
    celebrated the Last Supper with his disciples, 171
    celebrated the Passover from his childhood, 123
    challenged his disciples to pray without ceasing, 125
    commanded his disciples to celebrate the Lord's Supper, 123
    confessing as Lord and Savior, 29–30, 32
    cursed a fig tree, 87
    demonstrated the Spirit of martyrdom at the Cross, 155
    disciples of, 43
    divine-human encounters through, ix
    on doing good and loving the stranger, 110
    enabling his disciples to anticipate suffering, 147
    as fully God and fully human, 12
    gave thanks over the bread and wine, 170
    on the greatest commandment, 93
    healed the person whose ear was cut off, 98
    as the hope of glory, 168
    as the hope-filled Man, 172
    as the hospitable Man, 107
    looking forward to the promise of the eschatological Spirit, 175
    making visible as the Water Baptized-Man and the Last Supper-Participating Man or Communicant Man, 186
    manifested God's social or fellowshipping presence, 143
    manifested God's tangible presence outside communal worship contexts, 119
    mission of requiring the Spirit's manifestation, xv
    multitudes sought to touch for therapeutic purpose, xiv
    mystērion referring to, 2
    obeyed the Father's command, 169
    participated in public worship, 118
    people sought to touch for healing, 80
    as the perfect sign of grace, xv
    pointed the twelve disciples to the reality of the eschatological communion, 125
    prayed earnestly with sweat coming down his face like many drops of blood, 127
    as the primordial ambassador and sacrament, 182
    as the primordial sacrament, xi, xv–xvi, 83
    provided the meaning of Water Baptism and the Lord's Supper, 22
    raised Lazarus from the dead, 173
    referring to the bread and the wine as his body and blood, 123
    on the second greatest commandment, 93
    sending the seal of the Spirit upon the disciples at Pentecost, 182
    shaping and informing all the divine-human encounters, xvi
    on the Spirit indwelling his disciples, xvi
    as Spirit-baptized, 64

Subject Index

as the standard for evaluating believers' manifestations of the Spirit, xi
submitted to John's baptism, 22
told the thief crucified alongside him that he would be with him in Paradise, 28
as the visible sign of God's invisible presence, 4
welcomed strangers or outcasts in society, 107–8
"and you will be my witnesses," 155
Jewish disciples, struggled to accommodate Gentile disciples, 177
Jews
    abhorred eunuchs, 160
    expected Spirit of God's return to usher in the messianic age, xvi
Job, 136, 144–45
Joel, prophecy of, 20, 56, 68, 162, 168, 175
Johannine Pentecost, xvi
John
    on the baptism of Jesus, 12
    on blessed are those invited to the marriage supper of the Lamb, 171
    describing God as love, 93
    Jesus asking to stay awake with him, 126
    ministered to a 40-year-old man born lame, 86
    on singing, 129
John the Baptist, 57
Jonah, 10–11
Joseph, 74
joy, finding full expression in Christ, 95
joyful believers, relational Spirit and, 95–96
joyful singing, communing Spirit and, 131–33
Judas, 124
justice, God as defender of, 154
justified, as sacraments of the Spirit, 34
Justin, martyrdom of, 157

Keener, Craig S., 95, 98, 103, 146

kind believers, 98, 99
kindness, Christ manifesting, 98–99
kingdom of God in Christ, hope for, 170
knowledge or insight communicated, originating from the Spirit, 75
koinonia, 116, 176–77

Lamb of God, Jesus as, 122
lame man, Peter commanding to rise and walk, 86
lament, 16, 136, 145
Larson-Miller, Lizette, 6
Last Adam, Jesus as, 35
last days, beginning of, 15
Last Supper, 22, 123, 171. *See also* Lord's Supper
laying on of hands, upon the sick, 81, 83
Lazarus, 173
Lekganyane, 82
lepers, Jesus touching, 154–55
Levi, abandoned his career, 43
life circumstances, joy defying adverse, 96
light, xii–xiii, 31
liturgical activities, 116, 119, 133, 140
liturgical celebration, *mystērion* referring to, 2
liturgical words and deeds, 117
liturgies, 184
living water, rivers out of the believer's heart, xiii
Lombard, Peter, 2
long-suffering, 97
the Lord's Spirit, manifesting, 1–26
Lord's Supper. *See* Last Supper
Lord's Supper
    as about communing with God, 139
    allowing believers to make visible their prior encounter with the Spirit, 184
    believers encountering God's presence indirectly, 21
    bolstering Christ's relation to the disciples, 123
    celebration of, 139, 170
    Christ established, 4
    as communal in nature, 139–40
    creating space for self-reflection, 140

Lord's Supper (cont.)
    deriving meaning through the death of Christ, 124
    drawing believers' attention to Jesus, 123
    enabling believers to foretaste the marriage supper, 172
    eschatological nature of, 171
    as not a standalone rite, 139
    as an ordinance or sacrament, x
    participants in as sacraments, 121, 140, 172
    reserved for those baptized in water in many church traditions, 161
    as the rite of sharing a meal, 2
    as a sign and sacrament manifesting Christ, 123–24
    as similar to the Passover, 121
    Tertullian on, 2
    transcending time and space, 124
love, characteristics of, 93
loving believers, 95
low liturgical churches, 116, 117
Luke, on instances of baptizing the reborn, 55

Macchia, Frank D., 61, 66–67, 68
mainline churches, delivering services to the vulnerable, 109
manifestations, 25, 95, 117
marginalization, believers facing, 158
marriage supper, believers looking forward to, 171
Martha and Mary, as disappointed, 173
"martyr," translated as "witness" in English, 155
martyrdom, 48, 179
martyrs, 155, 156, 157, 158
Mary, as a human host of the presence of God, 111
maturity, transformation increasing with, 42
means of grace, 24–26, 47
mediation, clarifying how believers cause grace, 25
meekness. *See* gentleness
Menzies, Robert P., 67, 68
Menzies, William W., 67
Meshach, 102

ministering, to members suffering from incurable illnesses, 147
ministry, as a call to serve others, 91
minority members, taking steps to accommodate, 165
miracles, God performing through ordinary people, 85
miracle-working Paul, serving as a sacrament, 86
missionaries, hospitality toward, 106
Mittelstadt, Martin William, 146
Moltmann, Jürgen, 150
moon, reflecting light the Sun produces, 9
Moses
    acting by God's Spirit, 25
    face shining when he descends Mt. Sinai, 18
    raised hands of manifested God's extended hands, 126
    revealing God's action, 24
    as a sacrament of an encounter with God's Spirit, 105
    stopping the waters of the Red Sea from flowing, x
    total being encountering God, 20
    as a very humble man, 105
    visible actions manifesting God's invisible actions, 25
Mother Theresa, as a sacrament, 92
Mount Moriah, God first prefigured at, 122
mysteries spoken in the Spirit, containing a message to people, 90
mystērion, or mystery, finite beings hosting the infinite Spirit of God's presence as, xiii
mysterium Dei, Christ as, 12
mystery
    of God's action in and through human flesh, x
    Greek word for, 2

Naaman, 77
natural human, kindness foreign to, 98
nature
    of believers as inferior to God, 10
    of Spirit manifestation, 13–15
King Nebuchadnezzar, 102

Subject Index

neo-Pentecostals, encouraging liturgical activities, 116–17
new birth, giving believers the right to participate in the Spirit, 26
new community of believers, visibility of, 121
New Testament believers, as signs and means of God's grace to other nations, 5
Nicodemus, 32, 56
Nineveh, 10
non-humans, Spirit manifestations in and through, 7
non-sacramental churches, on Water Baptism, 47

offices, in the church, 92
oil, 81, 84–85
Old Covenant, made obsolete by Christ, 123
Old Testament
believers as signs and means of God's grace to other nations, 5
believers demonstrating the fruit of humility, 105
believers manifesting God's presence, 1
on blood and oil symbolizing cleansing, 64
encounters with God preceding the building of altars, 28
God promised to manifest his presence in certain places, 4
sacramentality of select believers, xvi
120 disciples
each as a site or sign of the grace of the Spirit's empowering presence, 66
encountered the communing Spirit within the Pentecostal communal context, 116
encountering and manifesting God's presence at Pentecost, 20
endued with power at Pentecost, 61
exhibiting essential characteristics of sacraments, 30
as sacraments of the Spirit, 14

speaking in tongues manifesting God's presence, 70
open-table fellowship, for the Lord's Supper, 139
ordinances, 183
orthodoxy (right belief), in the theological triad, xvii
orthopathy (right affection), in the theological triad, xvii
orthopraxy (right practice), in the theological triad, xvii
outpouring of the Spirit, linking to Joel's prophecy, 175
outward circumcision, presupposing inward circumcision, 52

Parham, Charles, 158
Passover, 121–22, 124
pastor, Jesus as, 91
patience, 96–97
patient believers, as sacraments, 97
Paul. *See also* Saul of Tarsus
admonishing believers not to grieve without hope, 173
advocating for Gentiles' inclusion or recognition, 155
on "anyone who does not have the Spirit does not belong to him," 23
appealing to the believers to do good, 110
on bearing the fruit of patience, 97
on believers at Thessalonica turning from worshiping idols to serving God, 176
on believers given the privilege of suffering for Christ, 145
on Christ who lives in me, 172
clarifying baptism as sanctification, 53
on Corinthians as ambassadors of Christ, 180
describing the fruit of the Spirit, 93
employed the principle of hospitality, 106
encountering God afresh, 72
on fruit as light, 94
on the Godhead's fullness dwelling in Christ, 12

Paul (cont.)
  going to Jerusalem despite the prophecy of Agabus that he will die, 172
  having a deformity linked to a thorn in the flesh, 152
  healing a man who has never walked since his birth, 17
  on his desire is to depart and be with Christ, 172
  on his preaching as demonstrating the Spirit, 138
  on introspection before the Lord's Supper, 124
  listing the workings of miracles as gift of the Spirit, 85
  on Macedonia and Achaia sharing their resources with the poor, 154
  making contact through handkerchiefs and aprons, x
  mentioning love first when describing the Spirit's fruit, 95
  on new creation as everything, 52
  noting the joint role of the Son and the Spirit, 32–33
  performed extraordinary miracles as sacraments, 86
  provided tangible expression to the Spirit's empowering presence, 92
  on the purpose of ministry gifts, 91
  relating God's indwelling presence to believers as temples of the Spirit, xiii
  relating Water Baptism to the circumcision of the heart, 51
  on the role believers play in spreading the Gospel of Christ, 24
  as a sacrament, 88, 92, 97, 164
  sacramental imagination in his writings, x
  saying that he died with Christ, 48
  on the second coming of Christ, 176
  self-identifying as an ambassador in chains, 181
  on sending of the Spirit as the dawn of the Messianic Age, 175
  sought counsel from apostles and elders in Jerusalem, 121
  speaking prophetically about danger ahead for a ship, 88
  on the Spirit bestowing gifts, 162
  stressing the joint work of the Spirit and the Son, 13
  stressing the role of corporate worship in the spiritual formation of believers, 120
  suffered as he preached the gospel to Gentiles, 159
  on there is no longer Greek and Jew, circumcised and uncircumcised, barbarian, Scythian, slave and free, 164
  using the gift of discernment to detect a spirit of divination in a slave girl, 89
  working extraordinary miracles, 86
Paul and Barnabas, 79
Paul and Silas, 96, 132
peaceful believers, 96
Pentecost event
  accenting believers as participants in redemption, xi
  attracted representatives from various parts of the known world, 158–59
  demonstrating the sacramental worldview, xii
  disciples manifesting the reality of God's presence, 15
  fulfilled Joel's prophecy, 20, 168
  inaugurated sacramentality of all believers, xvi
  inaugurated the 120 disciples as sacraments of God's presence, xiii
  of Jesus at the Jordan river, xi
  Jesus sending the Spirit to indwell all the disciples and subsequent believers, 13
  of John contrasting with Luke's Pentecost, 181
  manifesting God's presence, xvi
  Spirit engendering the disciples, 12
  Spirit resting upon the 120 disciples and manifesting his presence, xv

symbolizing unjust suffering that believers experience on this side of life, 147
tangible signs of the Spirit's presence, 20
Pentecostal churches, special-needs-accessible facilities and, 152
Pentecostal experience, extending to all believers, xv
Pentecostals
  accenting Spirit encounters or experiences, xiii
  conducting healing campaigns, 80
  continuing the ministry of Jesus and the early church, 135
  early modern stressed the healing presence of God, 78
  as egalitarian and culturally flexible, 177–78
  emphasizing encounters with the Spirit, xii, 110
  encouraging active participation in liturgical activities, 116–17
  encouraging public testimonies, 45
  expecting the Spirit of God in Christ to intervene in the believers' real life, xiv
  expecting to encounter God's presence in tangible ways, 79
  finding inspiration in Jesus, xiv
  healing as synonymous with, 80
  healing testimonies familiar in, 134
  historically not giving hospitality pride of place, 109–10
  holding the world as their parish, 178
  interpreting their entire existence as signs of the end, 168
  laying hands on the sick, 81
  linking Spirit baptism to empowerment and bestowal of spiritual gifts, 64
  as low liturgical churches, 116
  on people as saved the moment they repent from sin and turn to Christ, 46
  prayer and intercession as militaristic or aggressive, 125
  publishing periodic magazines featuring testimonies, 79
  relating speaking in tongues to Spirit baptism, 67
  as sacraments reflecting eschatological hope, 178
  taking the early church as a model, 148
  using physical bodies to provide expression to the Spirit, xiv
  on Water Baptism symbolizing but not initiating salvation, 47
people of color, practicing reverse racism toward White people, 164
Perpetua, 157
Perry, Sam C., 82
persecution, 157, 179
Peter
  acting secondarily to God's primary action, 113
  afflicted individuals set free by his shadow, x
  denying Christ, 40
  on disciples as a chosen race, 183
  discovery that God does not show favoritism, 163
  empowered as a visible significant or sacrament, 70
  exemplifying believers as ambassadors and as sacraments, 182
  exemplifying the sacramentality of believers, 75
  expressing wonder at the Spirit's mode of encounter and manifestation, 21
  on God pouring out his Spirit upon all flesh, 14
  healing by, 77, 86, 151, 152, 175
  inspired by James, 156
  interpreting the event of Pentecost, 14
  interpreting tongues-speech as a prophetic fulfillment, 70
  Jesus asking to stay awake with him, 126
  on Joel's prophecy, 175
  ministering to Cornelius, 8

Peter (cont.)
   ministering to Dorcas (Tabitha), 77
   obeying God rather than any human authority, 101
   performing miracles as sacraments, 86
   pointing others to Jesus as the one performing a miracle, 86
   preaching of as a sacrament, 137
   in prison welcoming or hosting an angel who sets him free, 113
   providing tangible expression to the Spirit's empowering presence, 92
   on repentance and Water Baptism, 56
   requiring repentance first and Water Baptism second, from, 50
   on the resurrection of Christ, 173
   as a sacrament, 8, 75, 86, 89, 92, 164
   showing humility and surrendering being a host, 113
   signifying the Spirit's boldness at Pentecost, 69
   Spirit prompting to meet with the Gentile guests via a vision, 21
   stressing the joint work of the Spirit and the Son, 13
   on suffering, 145
   surprised that the Spirit came upon Gentiles in the same way as Jews, 175
   using the gift of discernment with Ananias and Sapphira, 89
Peter and John, ministering healing to a man born with a disability, 151
Peter and the three thousand, as sacraments, 138
phaneroō, or phanerosis, meaning to manifest or reveal, 13
Pharisees, 108, 174
phenomena, signifying concrete expressions of the Spirit, 81
phenomenology, of Heidegger, 17–20
Philip, 138, 160, 161
physical appearance, of Jesus, 11
plan of salvation, *mystērion* referring to, 2
pneumatological approach, as apt for clarifying sacramentality of believers, 6
political ambassadors, 181

Polycarp, 156
poor believers, 153, 154
poor disciples, in the early church, 153
poor widow, gave out of her poverty, 142
postures, during prayer and intercession, 126
poured-out Spirit, empowering believers to perform signs and wonders, 175
power, Spirit baptism unleashing, 65
power from on high, being clothed with, 61, 66
power motif, in a Pentecostal view of Spirit baptism, 67
practical implications, of believers as sacraments of the Spirit, 184–85
praising or singing believers, as sacraments, 133
prayer
   being invited forward for, 40
   as communicating with the Spirit, 125
   over a suffering member, 148
   people invited to the altar for, 28
   primary purpose as fellowship with God, 127–28
prayer of forgiveness, responding to an altar call for, 37–38
prayer posture, of Jesus, 127
preaching, 74, 136–38
priest of Zeus, offering sacrifices to Paul and Barnabas, 79
priesthood of believers, 37, 92
priests, acting in *persona Christi* or on Christ's behalf, 36–37
primordial relation, baptized brought back to God's, 54
primordial sacrament, Christ as, 11–13, 83, 92
Procopius, 156
prodigal son, 35
proleptic act, Johannine instance as, xvi
prophecy
   gift of, 87
   of Joel, 20, 56, 68, 162, 168, 175
prophesying believers, as sacraments, 87
prophet, Jesus as, 91
prophetic utterance, test of, 88

prophets of Baal, Elijah challenging, 87–88

racial discrimination, believers enduring, 158
racial oppression, 163
racial segregation, at baptismal waters, 160
racially-marginalized believers, comforting Spirit and, 158–59
racism, 164
Rahner, Karl, 69
reality-sign dynamic, illustrating Heidegger's, 18
the reborn
   concretely expressing God's mercies in Christ due to Adam's sin, 31
   especially in Pentecostal church settings introducing themselves with phrases, 45–46
   exhibiting a fundamental character of sacraments, 29
   exhibiting different levels or degrees of sacramental intensity, 41
   functioning as means of grace of God's forgiveness, 46
   as a lens for discerning the Spirit's presence, 27
   providing concrete expression to the convicting Spirit, 36
   receiving the gift of the Spirit, 58
   reflecting God's image, 29
   rendering Christ visible or tangible, 31
   rendering tangible the converting and transforming presence of God, 42
   rendering the Spirit's converting presence tangible, 32
   serving as signs of grace, 32
   showing signs of salvific grace beyond worship contexts, 45
   as signs of reconciliation with God, 35
reconciled sinners, as sacraments of the Spirit, 35–40
reconciliation, 36, 39
the redeemed, as sacraments, 29
redemptive grace, signs of God's, 38
the regenerated, 30–31, 33
regenerating Spirit, 27–59
relational Spirit
   Christ's kindness and, 98–99
   faithful believers and, 100–103
   faithful Daniel and, 103
   faithful disciples and, 101
   faithful Stephen and, 101–2
   forgiving believers and, 105–6
   generous believers and, 99–100
   gentle believers and, 104
   guests or hosted believers and, 111–13
   hospitable or hosted believers and, 106–8
   humble believers and, 105
   joyful believers and, 95–96
   kind believers and, 98
   kind Stephen and, 99
   loving believers and, 95
   manifesting, 93–113
   patient believers and, 97
   patient Paul and, 97
   peaceful believers and, 96
   self-controlled believers and, 104
renewal of the mind, transformation manifesting, 42
repairs, not guaranteeing no other problems, 39
repentance, 27, 30
response, to altar call, 27–28
resurrection, 170, 172, 173
Revelation, using the term "martyr," 155
reverse racists, 164
rich young ruler, comparing Zacchaeus to, 58
rites, as reductionist or minimalist, 22
rites in the Spirit, 116–17, 119
river of the Spirit, believers immersed in, 65
Roman Catholic Church, 2, 36–37, 38, 84
Romanus, as a sacrament, 156

sacrament(s)
   as acts enacted by the Spirit or the biblical text, 165
   believers as, x, xiii, 21–24
   broad meaning of, 6–10
   broad view of, 1–2

sacrament(s) (cont.)
   characteristics of, 68, 96
   defining, 4–5
   as dynamic, 8
   early history of, 1–3
   factors determining, 4
   God working in and through, 80
   individual believers as, 6
   as inferior to reality, 9
   linking to *mystērion*, 2
   making the reality of God tangible by the Spirit, 18–19
   manifesting or disclosing the divine, 48
   participating in the reality they represent, 79
   pointing to the reality of the Trinity, 14
   as promises of grace to come in eternal life, 3
   reductionist view of, x–xi
   rendering visible the reality they symbolize or signify, 11
   as a rite or ritual mediating God's presence, 83
   Samaritans functioning as, 71
   sharing their origin in Christ, 4
   as signs that point to the reality of God, 46
   as speaking of their way of being, xiv
   as a term not defined primarily by any rites, 183
   theology of, 21
   viewing as a person mediating God's presence, 83
   Water Baptism and the Lord's Supper as, 183
Sacrament of Reconciliation, 37
sacrament of the reality of God, Moses as, 18
sacramental and non-sacramental churches, rethinking the chasm between, 186
sacramental characteristics, believers exhibiting, 8
sacramental church traditions, versus non-sacramental, 38
sacramental churches, xii, 47
sacramental events, sides of, 24
sacramental imagination, driven by the incarnation of Christ, xi
sacramental ontology, 33
sacramental outlook, 81
sacramental principle, of Roman Catholic Church tradition, 84
sacramental view, of believers, 182
sacramental worldview, in Pentecostalism, xiv, 82
sacramentality
   of all believers, xiii, 5, 180, 185–86
   of anti-racists, 160
   of believers, 21, 57, 59, 79, 80, 136, 147
   bringing together the creation and the Creator, xii
   of Christ and of believers intersecting on pneumatological ground, 3
   of the empowered, 61
   of fruit-manifesting believers, 94
   of giving believers, 142
   of hospitable believers, 110
   hospitality and, 108–11
   of Jesus, 22
   of Jonah, 10
   multifaceted nature of, xvii
   in a preaching event, 138
   of prophesying believers, 87
   of the reborn, 32, 45
   of the reconciled, 40
   of Spirit-baptized believers, 66
   of Spirit-baptized individuals, 69
   of suffering believers, 146–47
sacrament-reality dynamic, in Peter, 8
sacraments of the Spirit
   believers as, ix–xvii
   converts as, 30–33
   disciples as, 43–44
   the incorporated as, 54–59
   justified as, 34
   reconciled as, 35–40
   transformed as, 40–43
sacramentum Dei, Christ as, 12
sacred (church) space, believers as sacraments of the Spirit for, 7
Sadducees, 108, 174

Subject Index

salt, resonating with sacramental characterization, xii–xiii
salvation, 45, 47, 58
Samaritan woman, 38, 108, 115
Samaritans, 16, 71
Samson, x, 11
sanctification, 47, 53, 54
Sarah, 112
Satan, 144
Saul of Tarsus. *See also* Paul
    conversion of, 29, 34, 120
    exemplifying sacramentality, 31
    reconciled with God without confessing his sins, 37
    Spirit of God's presence encountering, 184
Schatzmann, Siegfried S., 74, 75
Schillebeeckx, Edward, 12, 62
Scribes, 108, 174
Scripture, on Water Baptism and the Lord's Supper as sacraments, 3
Second Vatican Council, 3
secular spaces (market space), believers as sacraments of the Spirit for, 7
self-control, of Christ, 104
self-controlled believers, as sacraments, 104
self-serving purposes, sacraments and, 11
seminary or Bible teachers, drawing students to encounter the Spirit, 138
service, rendering the Spirit tangible, 91
severity, of the sufferings of Jesus, 150–51
Seymour, William, Jr., 158
Shadrach, 102
shining face, of Moses, 20
"sign," Latin word for, 2
sign
    of grace, 11, 25–26
    of martydom, 48
    signifying an encounter with God's salvific grace, 46
    as something impersonal or a person, 10
significant-signifier relation, clarifying the believers' sacramentality, 7–8
Simeon, 150
sin
    being cleansed from, 169
    confessing, 36, 37
    converts not invincible to, 39
    conviction of, 35
    dying to through conversion, 45
    of humanity taken away by Jesus, 57
singing, 129, 131, 132
sinners, 28, 46, 54
slave masters, 159
slave owners, 160
slaves, 159, 162
socioeconomically marginalized believers, 154–55
Solomon, 4
Son of God, xi, 12
soteriological encounter, of Saul of Tarsus, 31
South Africa, past struggles with racism, 166
speaking in tongues, 66, 69
Spirit. *See also* Holy Spirit
    acting in and through empowered believers, 64
    anticipating experiences of suffering, 145
    appearing tangible to the Israelites in and through Moses' shining face, 18
    being denied the gift of due to skin color, 162
    believers responding to actions of, 8
    as the bond between the Father and the Son, 23
    as Christ, 20
    comforting and enabling Christ to see joy ahead, 149
    comforting suffering believers, 146
    constituting believers as concrete signs and means of God's grace, 10
    continuing to manifest in and through believers, xii
    convicting sinners, 28, 32, 57
    delighting in corporate worshipers, 117
    descent of at Pentecost, 66

Spirit (cont.)
    distinguishing from a demonic spirit, 88
    empowered Christ to exercise self-control, 104
    enabling speaking in tongues at Pentecost, xv
    encountering and manifesting in and through believers, 6
    encounters with, 38
    engendering believers as temples of God's presence, 140
    facilitating the conversion of sinners to *imago Dei*, 31
    filling martyrs with hope, 179
    finding expression in and through believers' experiences, 150
    giving the repentant new life in Christ, 29
    as God in us, 13
    imparting depth-understanding to a truth of the gospel, 74
    imparting new life into the believer, 58
    incorporating believers into new communities, 121
    as incorporeal by nature, 13
    indwelling the justified as a guarantee, 34
    inspired Peter's preaching, 138
    interceding on behalf of believers, 129
    leading toward other believers, 120
    manifestating in and through multicultural, multiracial, or multi-ethnic churches, 164–65
    manifested at Pentecost, xii
    manifested in and through the Old and New Testaments, xiv
    manifesting in and through any members seated in pews, 184
    mediating Christ's presence as believers undertake ecclesial rites, 3
    motivating believers to anticipate Christ's return, 175
    not necessarily resolving economic conditions, 153
    Peter as a means of grace of, 8
    as a polemic against racism, tribalism, and nationalism, 162
    as the prime guest and host of believers, 107
    prompting people to confess Christ as Lord and Savior, 32
    as a seal, 181
    signified to the disciples that Christ was seated at the right hand of God, 168
    as the Spirit of Jesus, Spirit of God, and the Spirit of Christ, 13
    spiritual empowerment of, 62
    as superior to believers, 9
    transforming the unregenerate as God's children, 27
    using Paul to manifest his therapeutic presence, 17
Spirit baptism
    Christ shaping, 66
    clothed with power from on high, 61
    as a direct and intense encounter with God's empowering presence, 67
    as distinct and subsequent to the new birth experience, 64
    empowering the believers to witness effectively to God's salvific mission in Christ, xiii
    as encountering the Trinity, 63–64
    enhancing the sacramental intensity of believers, 184
    experience of, 68
    intensifying the Spirit's manifestation, 69
    as a manifestation of the Spirit, 65
    as normative for all believers, 64–65
    pointed to the descent of the Spirit at Pentecost, 64
    as a post-conversion experience, 72
    purpose of, 65–66
Spirit Comforter, 148, 149–50, 151
Spirit empowerment, 61, 62, 66, 101
Spirit infilling, as continuous, 65
Spirit manifestations, 9, 13–15, 21, 184–85
Spirit of Christ, xi, xvi, 23, 33, 145

Spirit of God, xii, 12, 16–17, 163
Spirit-baptized, as themselves
    sacraments, 69
Spirit-baptized Ephesians, 72
Spirit-empowered believers, 60, 79
Spirit-indwelled believers, 96
Spirit-inspired preachers, 137
spiritual disciplines, 39, 84
spiritual gifts, 72–73
spiritual incorporation, Water Baptism
    symbolizing, 54–55
spiritual presence, of the indwelling
    Spirit, 6
"spiritual strongholds" of demonic
    powers, prayer sessions for
    deliverance from, 82
spiritual warfare, 125, 126, 159
spirituality of slaves, linking to modern
    Pentecostalism, 160
sprinkling, Water Baptism through, 49
Stephen
    demonstrated his faithfulness to
        Christ, 102
    forgiving those who stoned him to
        death, 99, 102, 106, 149
    hope peaked at his martyrdom, 179
    killed as he confesses Christ, x
    manifested the fruit of faithfulness,
        101
    martyred due to his confession of
        Christ, 155
    not renouncing his faith in God as
        he is stoned to death, 101
    the relational Spirit and the kind, 99
    as a sacrament, 101, 102, 149
    seeing beyond the immediate realm
        of life, 156
strangers, at the center of God's heart,
    108
strangers (guests), hosts and, 112, 113
subsequence, justifying the doctrine
    of, 71
suffering
    disciples endured, 166
    experiencing by professing faith in
        Christ, 148
    of Job, 144–45
    sharing stories of, 143
    of slaves, 159
    types of, 148
    as unjust when believers are not a
        direct cause, 146
suffering believers
    drawing inspiration from Christ,
        146
    pointing to the reality of God's
        comforting presence, 148
    rendering the comforting Spirit
        tangible, 145, 149
    as sacraments, 145, 146
suffering Blacks, as sacraments, 162
suffering Christ, 149, 150–51
suffering disciples, as sacraments, 151,
    166
suffering preachers, comforting Spirit
    and, 159
symbolic ontology, considering, 7
symptom-disease analogy, clarifying the
    sign-reality dynamic, 18
symptoms, manifesting a disorder, 19–20

tabernacle, cloud over, xv
tangible phenomena, at Pentecost, 66,
    182
teacher, Jesus as, 91–92
teachers, drawing students to encounter
    the Spirit, 138
temperance, as fruit of self-control, 104
temple, 4, 5
temple of the Spirit, Christ as, 16
temples
    believers as, xv, 16, 180
    described, xv
    as physical expressions of
        metaphysical realities, 16
Tertullian, 2
testifying believers, communing Spirit
    and, 133–36
testifying converts, serving as signs of
    God's salvific grace, 45
testimonies, of healing, 79–80
theological implications, of believers as
    sacraments of the Spirit, 183–84
theological traditions, practicing
    liturgical praise or singing in
    diverse ways, 133

theological triad, sacrament integrating, xvii
Thessalonian believers, influenced by belief in Jesus' imminent return, 176
thief, on the cross with Jesus, 28–29, 55
three thousand baptized at Pentecost, 43, 48, 55
tolerance, Christian life requiring, 97
tongues, gift of, 89–90
tongues of fire, sat on each of the disciples, 66
tongues-speaking believers, empowering Spirit and, 68–70
tongues-speech, 14, 68, 70
tragic experiences, 135–36
Transfiguration, Jesus spoke with Moses and Elijah at the mountain of, 12
transformed, as sacraments of the Spirit, 40–43
tribal discrimination, 158
tribalism, 166
Trinitarian community, 116
Trinity
    communal worship reflecting the life and the unity of, 119
    recognizing the role of, 33
    sacraments pointing to the reality of, 14
    Spirit Baptism encountering, 63–64
    Spirit manifestation and, 15–16
triumphs, 16, 148
truth, preachers as conduits of, 137
Turner, Max, 15, 63, 90

unbelievers, 34, 120, 130–31, 172
undeserved sufferings, rendering the Spirit Comforter visible, 149
unity, in church communities, 121
unjust sufferings
    believers enduring as sacraments, 149
    different forms of, 159
    enduring, 148
    Jesus experienced, 150
    relation of Pentecost to, 147
unjustly suffering believers, as sacraments, 146, 148
unjustly suffering preachers, 159
unregenerate, 27, 28
unseen forces, 125, 126
utterance of wisdom, 73, 74

vehicle, analogy of a repaired, 38–39
vertical fellowship, shaping and informing horizontal fellowship, 114
victims, of socioeconomic injustice, 154
victory, emphasizing over suffering, 149

washing others' feet, as a sacrament, 141
Water Baptism
    allowing converts to make a public commitment, 44
    alowing baptized believers to identify with Christ, 48
    believers encountering God's presence indirectly via elements of, 21
    believers making visible their prior encounter with the Spirit, 184
    as central to a community's life, 2
    of Christ, 4, 48, 49, 160
    confirming but not causing one's faith in God, 52
    confirming one's cleansing encounter with God, 57
    described, 65
    experiences of, 22
    facilitating salvation, 56
    by immersion, 50
    implications for the future, 169
    manifesting the washing away of one's sin, 52
    as an ordinance or sacrament, x
    as an outward sign of an inward and spiritual grace, 47
    as a post-conversion or post-regeneration experience, 51, 170
    presupposing regeneration or conversion of heart, 52
    as a public event, 48–49
    reborn individuals identifying themselves with Jesus, 44
    revealing those who have died to the old life of sin, 49

rooted in unambiguous teaching of Scripture, 55
of Saul of Tarsus, 37
signifying a believer's death, burial, and resurrection with Jesus, 169
Spirit baptism analogous to, 64–65
Spirit descended upon Jesus bodily, 22
submission to presupposing a relation to God, 140
symbolizing a person's bonding with Christ by the Spirit, 47
Tertullian on, 2
water-baptized believers, as sacraments, 49, 55, 56–57, 169
wealthy members, sold their properties in the early church, 142
White believers, 158
white brothers and sisters championing the cause against racism, as sacraments, 164
White members of clergy, depriving Black people of Water Baptism and the Lord's Supper, 162
wife, of Job wondering why he does not curse God, 144
will of God, determining if one is healed or not, 135
Williams, J. Rodman, 67

wind, characterizing God's presence in the Upper Room, 14
wisdom, relating to Christ as the very wisdom of God, 73
witnesses of Jesus, 186
witnessing believers, as sacraments, 178
witnessing mission of the church, tied to Christ's return, 178
woman with the issue of blood, 83
women, Spirit poured out upon, 159
the Word
    significance of proclaiming, 3
    Spirit also engendering, 56
words and deeds
    of believers shaped and informed by the life of Christ, 182
    inspiring flow from the Spirit within believers, 19
worship, 117–18, 129, 130
worship leaders, saying "the Spirit is here," 131
worship services, 117, 118, 185
worshipers, 117, 119, 130
worshiping believers, sacramentality of, 115, 118
worshiping community, Spirit's role in, 120

Zacchaeus, 46, 58, 99, 108, 112, 151–52

Author Index

Albrecht, Daniel E., 117n2
Alexander, Kimberly Ervin, 80n55, 82n65, 134n9, 135n13
Anderson, Allan, 81nn56–57, 82n63, 82n66, 82n67, 134n10, 177n3, 178n6, 178n7
Arrington, French L., 86n72, 87n76, 88n84
Asamoah-Gyadu, J.Kwabena, xiiin7, 82n61, 82n62, 82n64, 178n4
Atkinson, William, 67n26
Augustine, 8
Aune, David Edward, 87n77

Bergunder, Michael, 177n3
Boddy, Alex A., 83, 83n69
Boersma, Hans, 6n7, 94n3
Boff, Leonardo, 95, 95n6
Brand, Chad, 61n2
Bruner, Frederick Dale, 71n36
Burgess, Stanley M., 65n16, 67n25, 67n28, 135n12

Cairns, Earle E., 157nn13–14
Cartledge, Mark J., 68n31, 116n1
Clarke, Clifton, xivn10, 150, 150nn5–6
Coffey, David, 9n14
Courey, David, 16n26
Cross, Terry L., 23n30

de Lubac, Henri, 6n8, 12, 12n19
Depoortere, Kristiaan, 7n12
du Plessis, David, 65n17, 67, 67n29

Dunn, James D. G., 62, 62n5, 73nn37–39, 75, 75nn45–47, 76, 76nn51–52, 87n74, 88n81, 90n87

Eusebius, 156, 156n9, 157n11, 157n15

Fee, Gordon D., 23, 23n29, 73, 73n41, 76n49, 76n53, 88n80, 90n86, 90nn88–89, 94n1, 95n4, 96n8, 98n11, 101n13
Ferguson, Everett, 157n16, 179n8

Gause, R. H., 8n13
Green, Chris W., 14n23

Heidegger, Martin, 17, 17n28, 18, 76, 76n50
Hemphill, Ken, 62, 62nn7–8
Hicks, John Mark, 6n9
Hocken, Peter, 73, 73n40
Hollenweber, Walter J., xiv, xivn9
Horton, Harold, 74, 74n44
Horton, Stanley M., 65n14, 67, 67n24, 68n32
Hughes, Graham, 29n2
Hunter, Harold D., 67n26, 178n7

Ingalls, Monique Marie, 131n4
Irenaeus, xi

Jacobsen, Douglas G., 134n6
Josephus, 160n18

Kaatz, Kevin W., 157n12
Kalu, Ogbu, 82n61

Kärkkäinen, Veli-Matti, 82n64
Kay, William K., 65n12, 65n20, 178n3
Keener, Craig S., xiin3, 62n3, 95, 95n5, 96n7, 97n9, 98, 98n10, 98n12, 103, 103n14, 146, 146n2
Kleist, James A., 156n10
Koenig, John, 106n15
Kwiyani, Harvey C., 178n4

Land, Steven Jack, 168n2
Larson-Miller, Lizette, 6, 6n6, 13n22
Litfin, Bryan M., 155n8
Lombard, Peter, 2n4
Lösel, Steffen, 29n2
Ludwig, Frieder, 178n4

Ma, Wonsuk, 137n16, 147n3
Macchia, Frank D., 61, 61n1, 64n11, 66, 66n21, 67n22, 67n26, 68, 68n33, 81n60
Macquarie, John, 18
Martin, David, 45n3, 178n5
McPherson, Aimee Semple, 168n1
Menzies, Robert P., xiiin8, 62n3, 65n15, 65n18, 67, 67n23, 67n27, 67n30, 68, 68n34, 71n36, 87n79
Menzies, William W., xiiin8, 62n3, 65n15, 65n18, 67n27, 67n30
Mittelstadt, Martin William, 65n19, 146, 146n1
Moltmann, Jürgen, 6n8, 150, 150n4

Neumann, Peter D., xiiin5

Onyinah, Opoku, 125n3
Osborne, Kenan B., xvii, 3, 3n5, 11n17

Perry, Sam C., 82, 82n68

Rahner, Karl, 6n8, 11nn16–17, 69, 69n35
Richie, Tony, 134n8

Robeck, Cecil M., 178n7
Robinson, Edward, 18
Ruthven, Jon, 134n11

Saliers, Don E., 15n25
Schatzmann, Siegfried, 74, 74n42, 75, 75n48, 86, 86n73, 88n82
Schillebeeckx, Edward, 6n10, 9n15, 11n18, 12, 12n20, 62, 62n5
Semmelroth, Otto, 6n8
Seymour, W. J., 81n59
Sisso, Elizabeth, 168n1
Smail, Thomas, 81n58, 94n2
Smith, James K. A., 134n7
Stronstad, 62, 62n4
Sullivan, Francis A., 71n36

Tertullian, 2nn1–3
Thomas, John Christopher, 141n17
Tillich, Paul, 6n11
Tomberlin, Daniel, xivn10, 28n1
Torr, Stephen C., 16n27, 136n15
Turner, Edith L. B., 136n14
Turner, Max, 15, 15n24, 63, 63n10, 76n53, 87n78, 90, 90n91

van der Maas, Ed M., 65n16, 67n25, 67n28, 135n12
Vondey, Wolfgang, 63n10, 65n13, 160n17, 168n1
Vorgrimler, Herbert, 6n8, 11n18, 12n21

Wacker, Grant, 133n5
Warrington, Keith, xiiin4
Williams, 67
Williams, J. Rodman, 74n43, 76n54, 85nn70–71, 87n75, 87n79, 88n83, 89n85, 90n90
Wolfgang, Vondey, 14n23

Yong, Amos, xiiin6, 76n53, 131n4, 152n7

Ancient Document Index

OLD TESTAMENT

Genesis

1:2	13, 33, 107
1:22, 28	106
1:26–27	31
1:27	13
1:28	106
2:5, 8	107
2:8	106, 107
2:8–14	106
2:23	106
3	31
3:7–8	54
3:8	106
3:21	54, 107
3:23	35, 107
3:24	35
12	51
12:7	28
15:18	107
17	51
17:7	51
17:10–11	51
17:12, 23–27	51
17:19, 21	122
17:21	122
17:23–27	51
18:1	112
18:2	112
18:4–8	112
18:10	112
18:14	112
18:23–32	104
22:1–14	122
26:25	28
41:14–38	74

Exodus

2:24	122
3	7
3:7–8	122
5:1	115
7:16	115
8:1, 20	115
8:20	115
8:23	122
9:1, 13	115
9:4	122
9:13	115
10:3	115
11:5	122
11:7	53, 122
12	22, 172
12:11	121
12:13–14	122
12:14	123
12:17	123
12:21	121
12:24	123
12:27	121
12:43	121
12:48	121
14	22
14:13	25
14:15	24, 25
14:16	24, 25
14:19, 20	174

Exodus (*cont.*)

14:20	174
14:21	x, 25
14:21–31	53
15:1–21	132
15:20–21	132
17:11	126
17:15	28
22:21	163
27:21	123
28:43	123
29:9, 28	123
30:21	123
34:29–30	18
34:35	12, 18
40:34	5
40:34–38	xv

Leviticus

14:14, 17	64
14:17	64
21:20	161
23:5	121

Numbers

9:1–14	122
9:2–6	121
9:15–22	xv
12:3	105
27:11	123
35:29	123

Deuteronomy

6:4	120
7:9	100
10:16	52
10:18	154
16:1–2	121
16:5–6	121
18:15–19	91
23:1	161
24:17	154
27:19	154
30:6	52
32:4	154

Joshua

5:10–11	121
7	89

Judges

14	xiv
16:3	x
16:17	11

Ruth

2:20	98

1 Samuel

16:7	52
17:50	x
24:4	100
24:6	100
30:25	123

2 Samuel

6:16	132
9:3	99
12:13	40
12:14–31	136
24:10	32

1 Kings

3:6	98
17	xiv, 85
17:1	38
18	85
18:17	174
18:24	87
18:30	88
18:38	76
18:38–39	88
18:39	76

2 Kings

2:1	174
2:7	x
2:8	x
2:9–15	174
2:11	174

2:14	x, 77
2:15	77
6	xiv
23:21–23	121

1 Chronicles

15:29	132

2 Chronicles

1:8	98
5:14	5
7:1–3	4
7:14	4
7:15	4
7:16	4
30:1–2	121
30:4	121
30:15	121
32:31	181
35:6–19	121

Ezra

6:19–20	121

Nehemiah

8:10	95, 131

Job

1	136
1:1	144
1:14–17	144
1:15–17	144
1:18–19	144
1:21	144
1:21–22	144
2:7	144
2:9–10	144
3	144
4	144
5	144
6	144
8	144
9	144
10	144
11	144
13	144
14	144
15	144
15:11	104
18	144
19	144
20	144
23	144
26	144
41:11	142

Psalms

5:11	95–96
8:4	10
8:5	22
9:14	96
13:5	96
22	136
22:3	118, 132
22:22	133
47:1	132
51	40
51:3	32
95:2	130
98:4	131
98:8	131
100:2	118, 130
119:11	32
143:6	16
144:3	10
146–50	132
147:6	105
147:7	16
149:1–3	132
150:6	130

Proverbs

3:34	105
13:17	181
20:9	32
24:16	36
29:23	105

Ecclesiastes

4:1	148

Isaiah

5:7	154
6:3	118
29:13	130
32:14–16	174
44:3	53
52:9	148
53:3–4	134
53:7	122
56:4–5	161
60:3–16	177
61	108
61:1	137
61:1–2	16
61:1–8	154
62:5	130
66:1–2	5

Jeremiah

4:2	154
4:4	52
7:5–6	154
8:18	148
9:25–26	52
10:24	104
22:3–4	154
49:14	181

Lamentations

19, 16 ?	148

Ezekiel

2:7	xii
17:15	181
18:5–9	154
21:26	105
34:11–16	91
36:25	51
37	xii
44:7, 9	52
44:9	52
45:21	121

Daniel

3:7–10	102
3:11	102
3:12	102
3:17–18	102
3:25	102
3:29	102
6:4	103
6:7	103
6:10–11	127
6:11	103
6:22	103
6:26	103
6:26–27	127
7:13	176

Hosea

11:4	104
11:12	100

Joel

2:13	98
2:28	20
2:28–29	5, 15, 23, 56, 68, 137, 162, 175
2:29–29	70

Amos

2:6–7	154
3:1–2	154
4:1	154
5:24	154

Jonah

1:2	10
1:3	11
3:10	10

Micah

3:9–12	154
6:8	154

Zephaniah

3:17	118, 130

Zechariah

7:9–10	154
14:8–9	174
14:16–19	177

NEW TESTAMENT

Matthew

1:20	158
1:23	13
3:2, 6	50
3:6	50
3:7	50, 170
3:8	42
3:11	23
3:13	57
3:15	48, 169
3:16	xi, 4, 12, 13, 15, 33, 50, 61, 63, 64, 66, 181
3:17	107, 169
4:1	150
4:1–11	146
4:2	128
4:10	132
5:4	148
5:10	179
5:13	xii
5:13, 14	183
5:14	xii, 183
5:14–16	31
5:24	40
5:43–48	110
5:45	99, 110
5:48	110
6:16–18	128
7:16	93, 182
7:20	182
7:21	94
7:29	137
8:1–4	98–99
8:3	xiv, 83
8:3–4	155
8:8	100
8:20	107
9:9–17	108
9:21	83
9:33	12
9:36	99
10:8	10, 20, 78, 108
10:24–25	43
10:28	72
10:32	155
10:33	44
10:39	48
10:44–48	162
11:19	108
11:21	59
11:21–23	61
11:23–23	66
11:29	104
12:10	108
12:19–20	104
12:23	12, 33
12:24	97
12:28	13, 33
12:40	10
13:21	149
13:54	91
13:54–55	12, 33
13:57	91
13:57–58	59
14:5	91
14:14	99
14:16	111
14:21	108
14:36	xiv, 80, 83
15:8	130
15:32	99
16:4	10
16:21	173
16:24	146
16:25	48
17:1–5	12
17:2	119
17:22–23	150
18:11	91
18:16–20	181
18:20	13, 16, 114, 115, 118
19:12	161
19:16–22	58
19:27	43
20:19	173

Matthew (cont.)

20:29–34	72
20:34	83, 99
21:5	104
21:10–11	91
21:11	ix
21:20–22	87
22:8	107
22:38	93
22:39	93, 154
23:1–39	174
24:30	176
24:36	169
25:6–7	176
25:40	154
25:40, 45	112
25:43	106, 107
25:44–45	142
25:45	107, 112
26:2, 17–19	123
26:5	151
26:14–39	118
26:15	124
26:17–19	123
26:17–30	119
26:21	124
26:23	124
26:26	123, 139
26:26, 28	4
26:26–28	22
26:26–29	125
26:28	4, 139
26:29	171
26:38, 40	128
26:39	100
26:40	126, 128
26:41	39
26:51	104
26:53	104
26:56	158
26:60–75	40
26:61	33
26:64	176
27:46	145
28:17	59
28:18–10	61
28:18–20	60, 61, 66, 178
28:19	4, 44, 48, 160, 162, 186
28:19–20	160

Mark

1:8	12, 16, 23, 64
1:9	57
1:10	xi, 4, 12, 15, 49, 50, 61, 63, 64, 66, 181
1:11	107, 169
1:12–13	146
1:13	150
1:14–15	91
1:15–22	108
1:21–28	118, 119
1:22	91
1:35	128
1:41	xiv, 80, 83, 99
1:44	155
3:1–6	118
3:2	108
3:2–22	97
3:10	xiv
3:15	20
4:17	149
5:19	99
5:27	xiv
5:30–31	xiv
6:2, 14	61, 66
6:3	12
6:4–6	59
6:13	20, 84
6:14	61, 66
6:34	99
6:44	108
6:56	xiv, 80, 83
7:6	130
7:33	xiv, 83
8:2	99
8:22	xiv
8:31	173
8:34	146
8:35	48
9:2	128
9:2–7	12
9:22	99
10:13	xiv

10:17–22	58	3:21, 22	22
10:28	43	3:22	xi, 12, 15, 22, 61, 63, 64, 66, 107, 169, 181
10:34–35	173		
10:39	146		
10:45	72	3:23	150
11:15–16	104	4:1, 18–19	16
11:20–24	87	4:1–13	146
11:24	127	4:2	128, 150
12:29	120	4:15–21	118
12:35–40	174	4:16–21	119, 154
12:39	108	4:18	108, 137
12:42–44	142	4:18–19	xiii, xv, 16
13:11	174	4:18–21	xvi, 12, 33
13:32	169	4:22–32	137
14:1; 12, 6 ?	123	4:31–37	118, 119
14:12–26	119	4:32	12, 33
14:20	124	5:13	xiv, 83
14:22	123, 139	5:14	155
14:22, 24	4	5:16	128
14:22–25	22, 125	5:17	137
14:24	4, 139	5:27–32	43
14:25	171	5:29–39	108
14:32–34	128	6:12	125
14:36	100	6:19	xiv
14:38	39	6:22–23	95
14:62	176	6:27–36	110
14:66–72	40	6:35	98
15:13–14	150	6:35–36	110
15:34	145	6:40	43
16:9–20	56	7:11–17	119
16:16	4, 56	7:13	99
16:17	20	7:14	xiv, 83
16:18	81, 83	7:34	108
16:19–20	168	8:1–3	95
16:20	ix	8:3	91
		8:42–43	33
Luke		8:45, 47	xiv
1:35	11, 12, 13, 33, 111	8:47	xiv, 80
2:25–35	150	8:48	99
2:40, 46, 47, 52	22	8:49–56	119
2:41	123	9:6	45
2:46	22	9:14	108
2:47	22	9:23	146
2:52	22	9:24	48
3:7	50, 170	9:28	128
3:16	23, 64	9:42–43	12
3:21	4, 57, 127	9:58	107
		10:13	59, 61, 66

Luke (cont.)

10:21	95, 128
11:13	162
11:15	97
11:29	10
11:37–54	174
12:9	44
13:10–17	118
13:16	154
13:33	91
14:7	108
15:10	35
15:11–32	35
15:17	36
15:20	35
15:22–23	35
16:8	31
17:33	48
18:1	125, 128
18:1–8	128
18:15	xiv
18:18–23	58
18:28	43
18:33	173
19:3	151
19:5	99
19:7	108
19:8	46
19:8–9	58
19:8–10	152
19:10	91
19–27	118
20:4	4
20:45–47	174
20:46	108
21:1–4	142
22:5	123
22:7–23	118
22:7–39	119
22:8, 11, 13	123
22:11	123
22:11, 5	123
22:13	123
22:16	171
22:16–18	171
22:19	4, 22, 123, 125, 139, 140
22:20	123, 139
22:40, 46	39
22:42	100, 127
22:43	125, 127
22:44	127
22:46	39
22:50	98
22:51	xiv, 80, 83
23:21	150
23:31	146
23:34	36, 99, 106, 149
23:39–43	44
23:40	29
23:42	28, 29
23:43	28
23:46	155
24:7	173
24:19	17, 61, 66, 91
24:49	xii, 20, 23, 61, 64, 66, 119, 175, 178
24:49–51	60, 66
24:50–53	168

John

1:1	155
1:5	94
1:9	31
1:12	55, 57, 58, 181
1:12–13	27
1:14	ix, 105, 107
1:27, 33	107
1:29	22, 57, 123
1:29, 36	122
1:29–34	57
1:32	xi, 12, 15, 61, 63, 64, 66, 182
1:32, 33	63
1:33	4, 63, 107
1:36	122
1:38	91–92
2	143
2:13, 23	123
2:19	172
2:19–22	33
2:21	5
3:1–2	92
3:1–8	49, 58

3:3, 5–6	29	8:41	158
3:4, 9	56	8:46	27
3:5	51, 170	8:58	10
3:5–6	29	9:5	xii, 31
3:5–7	57, 58	9:14–16	108
3:5–8	31	9:24	135
3:5–10	32	9:25	77, 134
3:6	27, 28, 56	10:11, 4	91
3:6, 8	58, 164	10:14	91
3:8	3, 58, 164	10:21	12
3:9	56	10:28	182
3:16	12, 100	11:3	173
3:23	49	11:6	173
4:1–2	22	11:19	173
4:2	4	11:21	173
4:6	115	11:21, 32	173
4:10	33	11:23	173
4:14	53	11:25	173
4:21	16	11:32	173
4:21, 23	115	11:38–44	119
4:23	16, 115	11:39	173
4:23–24	118, 140	11:41–42	127
4:24	16, 115	11:41–44	173
4:27	108	12:25	48
4:29, 30	115	12:27	100, 172
4:30	115	13:1–17	118
4:31–32	128	13:14	141
4:39–42	38	13:17	141
4:42	28, 115	13:21	124
5:15	xii	13:35	43
5:19	19	14:1–4	173
5:29	173	14:3	15, 176
6:10–13	108	14:6	28, 118
6:14	109	14:9	19
6:26	108	14:12	174
6:27	182	14:16	14, 23, 120
6:32	139	14:16, 26	146–47, 148
6:54	4	14:16–17, 20, 21	5
6:54–56	125	14:17	xiv, xvi, 1, 6, 15, 41, 57, 58, 184
7:37–39	23, 53	14:17, 23	12
7:38	xiii	14:19–31	13
7:46	12, 137	14:20	5, 23, 37, 112
8:8–11	59	14:21	5
8:12	xii, 31	14:23	12
8:28	19	14:26	63, 140, 146–47, 148, 149
8:29	100		
8:31	43		
8:39	51	15:4	112

John (cont.)

15:8	43
15:11	95
15:20	146, 159
15:26	14, 134, 147, 148, 149
16:7	147, 148, 149, 174
16:7–13	140
16:8	58, 138, 140
16:8–9	32
16:14	15, 63
16:33	149
17:1–25	127
17:11, 22	121
17:16–19	53
17:19	54
17:21	112
17:22	121
17:23	23
17:26	94
18:4–8	12
18:8	104
18:15–27	40
19:5	112
19:6, 10, 15	150
19:9	104
19:10	150
19:15	150
20:19–23	181, 186
20:21	185
20:21–23	xvi
20:22	xii, 181, 182
20:23	37
20:29	173
21:15–17	40
21:23	xv

Acts

1:4	5
1:4, 5, 8	14
1:4, 8	64
1:4–14	181
1:5	12, 14, 16, 23, 62
1:5, 8	23
1:8	xii, xv, 4, 7, 14, 15, 20, 23, 60, 61, 62, 64, 66, 68, 72, 155, 162, 175, 178, 186
1:9	173
1:9–10	168
1:9–11	173, 174
1:10	174
1:11	xv, 168, 176, 180
1:14	125
1:22	57
2	13, 20, 61
2:1	116, 118, 120
2:1–4	xi, xii, xv, xvi, 23, 61, 65, 66, 68, 168, 181, 182
2:2	14
2:2, 3	70
2:2–4	70
2:3	14, 66, 70
2:4	5, 14, 62, 66, 70
2:4–7	159
2:5–12	xv
2:6–13	69
2:8	30
2:8–11	69
2:9–11	159
2:12	120
2:15–17	14
2:16	68
2:16, 33	5
2:16–17	20, 137
2:16–18	15, 175
2:16–20	56
2:17	62
2:18	62
2:33	5, 62, 70, 168
2:37	14, 27, 30, 35
2:37–41	50
2:38	9, 14, 29, 33, 43, 44, 47, 48, 49, 52, 56, 57, 58, 62, 140, 142, 162, 186
2:39	xi, 52
2:41	30, 49, 55, 56, 58, 137, 170
2:42	43, 120, 121, 125, 127, 136, 143
2:42, 46	121
2:42–46	171

Ancient Document Index

2:46	121, 140	7:57–60	101
3	152	7:59	x, 155
3:1	86	7:59–60	106
3:1–10	78	7:60	99, 102, 149
3:1–12	151	8	160
3:2	86	8:1	149
3:6	xiv	8:4	45
3:6, 12	182	8:5	71
3:6, 16	86	8:8, 12	47
3:12	182	8:12	47, 50, 55
3:15	142	8:12–17	64
3:16	8, 86	8:15, 17, 19	62
3:22	91	8:15–16	71
4	159	8:16	62
4–7	166	8:17	5, 62, 71
4:12	28	8:18	62
4:13	xvi, 182	8:19	62
4:27	12, 33	8:26	160
4:29	127	8:26–27	160
4:31	64, 65, 127	8:27	161
4:33	66	8:27–28	161
4:34–37	142, 153	8:28	138
4:36	91	8:29	177
4:42	182	8:29–35	138
5:3	75	8:36	57
5:3, 9	89	8:38	55
5–7	157	8:39	138
5:8	75	9:1	31
5:9	89	9:1–2	31
5:12	78	9:1–10	120
5:14	70, 166	9:4	29
5:15	x, 79, 86, 175, 184	9:4–6	37, 120
5:16	70	9:4–9	31
5:25, 40, 42	182	9:5	29, 32, 34, 37, 159, 184
5:29	101		
5:40	101, 143, 149, 182	9:9–15	37
6	91, 158, 159	9:13	41
6:1	163	9:13–14	34
6:1–3	155	9:18	37, 49, 55, 58
6:2–6	91	9:34	77
6:3	163	9:35	77
6:8	xiv, 78, 101	9:36	77
7	159	9:39	91
7:48	5, 16	9:40	77
7:54–59	102	9:42	77
7:54–60	156	10	153
7:55–56	155, 168	10:4	21
7:55–60	179	10:15	8

Acts (*cont.*)

10:19–20	177
10:20	21
10:28	163
10:34–35	159, 163, 165
10:35	71
10:38	xiii, xv, 12, 33, 61, 66, 83, 92, 184
10:44	5, 8, 21, 62, 177
10:44, 46	71
10:44–46	64
10:44–48	49, 58, 162, 163
10:45	62, 142, 175
10:45, 47	68
10:45–47	68
10:46	21, 71
10:47	62, 68, 71
10:47–48	55
10:48	21
11:12–18	177
11:13–14	170
11:14–16	64
11:15	62
11:16	16, 23, 62
11:17	62
11:19	8, 149
11:24, 25	43
11:26	27, 43, 44
12:1–2	156
12:1–5	166
12:3	156
12:7–11	113
12:11	113
13:2	38, 118, 128, 137
13:9	43
13:50	149
14:8	79
14:8–20	17
14:23	128
14:27	175
15:1–2	121
15:3	175
15:5	xiv
15:7–9	64
15:36–38	40
15:39–40	40
16:7	13, 23, 33
16:15	55, 106, 170
16:16	89
16:17	89
16:19–24	89
16:23	101, 143, 149
16:23, 25	182
16:23–30	96
16:25	132, 182
16:31	47
16:33	55, 170
17:5	106
17:24	5, 16
17:28	10, 107, 109, 128
18:2–3, 7	106
18:7	106
18:8	50, 55, 170
19:1–7	50
19:2	62
19:4–5	72
19:5	55
19:6	5, 62, 68
19:6–7	72
19:8–10	72
19:11	86
19:11–12	81
19:12	x, xiv, 86, 184
20:32	54
21:10–13	172
21:16	106
22:8	32, 159
22:24	101, 143, 149
25:30–34	132
26:15	32, 159
26:18	53
26:20	42
26:28	54
27:9–10	88
27:11, 37	88
27:21–25	88
27:33–36	88
27:37	88
28:8	83

Romans

1:20	22
2:4	97
2:28–29	124

2:29	51, 52
3:12	98
3:23	31, 35, 36
3:24	27, 31, 34, 118
3:25	124
4:1—5:21	34
4:11	52
4:12	51
4:13–18	52
4:16	107
5:1	35
5:1, 9	33
5:2	118
5:5	95, 168
5:5–10	168
5:7–8	95
5:9	33
5:10	35, 39
5:12	35
5:17	31
6:1–4	51
6:1–11	2
6:3	55
6:3–5	50
6:4	29, 44, 49, 58
6:8	48
6:11	44
6:23	142
7:6	29
7:18–20	32
8:1	27, 32, 34, 41, 48
8:1–2, 6	29
8:3–4	33
8:6	29
8:9	13, 23, 33, 34
8:9, 11	xiii, 1, 6, 13, 15, 33, 140
8:9, 14	13, 33
8:9–11	xiv, 12
8:10	13, 23
8:11	xiii, 1, 6, 13, 15, 33, 140, 169
8:14	13, 33
8:15–17	33, 49, 58
8:17	52
8:18	145, 158
8:23	173, 175
8:24	169
8:26	32
8:26, 27, 34	125
8:26–27, 34	125
8:27	125
8:34	125
8:35	149
9:22	97
10:9	27, 44
10:9–13	58
10:14	24
11:13	31
11:22	98
11:35–36	142
12:1	38, 94
12:2	42
12:5	20, 120
12:16	105
14:17	96, 131
15:13	96, 131, 167, 168, 173
15:16	32, 53, 54
15:19	13, 33
15:25–26	154
15:27	154
15:33	96
16:20	96
16:25–26	2

1 Corinthians

1–3	74
1:4–7	33
1:7	xv, 176
1:9	16, 100
1:16	55, 170
1:17	74
1:24	73
2:4	74, 138
2:4–5, 12	33
2:6–16	34
2:7	2
2:11	13, 33
2:12	23, 33
3:1	x
3:16	xiii, xiv, xv, 1, 12, 13, 33, 140
3:16, 17	15
3:16–17	xvi, 6, 12, 16, 116

1 Corinthians (*cont.*)

3:17	15
4:7	108
4:12	159
4:21	104
5:7	124
5:7 NKJV	123
6:11	32, 34, 47, 54
6:11, 19–20	33
6:15	20
6:19	xiii, xiv, xv, xvi, 1, 6, 12, 13, 15, 16, 33, 41, 107, 116, 118, 140
6:19–20	33
7:5	128
7:11	40
7:40	13, 33
8:6	120
9:6	40
10:1	53
10:2–4	164
10:13	100
10:17	120
11:1	32, 48
11:23	171
11:24	22, 123, 139
11:24–25	123, 125, 140
11:25	123, 139
11:25, 26	4
11:26	2, 4, 171
11:28	124, 140
11:33	140
12:1–31	64
12:3	13, 29–30, 32, 33, 34, 55
12:4	142
12:7	xiv, 1, 72, 73, 184
12:8	73, 74
12:8–10	73
12:9	75, 76
12:10	85, 87, 88, 89, 90
12:11	162, 184
12:12	20
12:12–27	120
12:13	49, 53, 54, 58
12:22–23	20
13:4–7	93
13:12	19
13:13	21
14:2	90
14:14	90
14:16	90
14:33	96
15:14	172
15:23	50
15:45	35

2 Corinthians

1:3–5	148
1:5	146
1:18	100
1:21	64
1:21–22	33, 175
1:22	12, 33, 34, 35, 139, 149–50, 168
3:6	28, 29
3:7–18	174
3:18	40, 145
4:9	159
4:14	169
4:17–18	145
5:5	12, 33, 34, 35, 139, 150, 168, 172, 175, 180, 181
5:17	27, 29, 32, 41, 42, 43, 54, 181
5:18	35, 36, 39
5:18–19	40
5:20	39, 180, 181
5:21	54, 57
6:4	97
6:5	128
6:16	xv, xvi, 6, 12, 15, 16, 33
6:16—7:1	12
7:6	148
7:10	36, 42
8:14–15	106
10:1	104
10:4	126
11:23	101, 143, 149
11:27	128
12:7	152

12:11–12	92	2:7	99
13:3, 5	xiv	2:12	168
13:5	xiv, 12	2:13–17	96
13:11	96, 148	2:16	36, 39
13:14	120, 143	2:18	33
15:20, 23 ?	175	2:20–22	33
		2:21–22	12

Galatians

		3:3–5	2
		3:12	5, 118
1:1	169	3:17	xiv
1:15–16	xiv	3:17–19	13, 23
1:23	42	4:2	104
2:8	8, 34, 92	4:10	91
2:19–20	172	4:10–11	91
2:20	xiv, 13, 23, 48, 55	4:11	92
3:1–5	33	4:12–13	91
3:6–9, 14, 29	107	4:13, 15	32
3:13–18	52	4:15	32
3:14	107	4:18	172
3:20	120	4:22–24	49, 58
3:26	55	4:25	20
3:27	55	4:30	13, 33, 175
3:28	124, 155	4:32	99
3:29	107	5:9	94
4:4	107	5:23	28
4:6	23	5:30	20
4:13	151	6:12	126
4:19	xiv	6:20	181
4:28	122		
5:5	167, 168		
5:13	34	## Philippians	
5:22	93, 131	1:19	13, 23, 33
5:22–23	94–95, 95	1:23	172
5:23	104	1:29	145
5:24	29	2:1	120, 143
5:25	29	2:6–8	105
6:1	x, 104	2:8	9, 104
6:10	110	2:11	27
6:15	52	2:13	8, 73
		3:3	13, 33
## Ephesians		3:9	27
		3:20	xv
1:5	40	4:4	96
1:13	175	4:4–7	96
1:13–14	34	4:9	96
1:17	33	4:10	146
2:5	118		

Colossians

1:11	97
1:13	31
1:15	xvi, 31
1:18	31
1:20	36, 39
1:21	172
1:27	xiv, 2, 13, 23, 168
2:2	148
2:9	4, 12, 19, 22, 63, 69, 182
2:11–12	51, 52
2:12	44, 49, 58
2:20	48
2:29	31
3:1	29
3:3	48
3:11	124, 164
3:12	99, 104
3:12–13	95, 97
3:16	33, 132
4:10	40

1 Thessalonians

1:6	131
1:9–10	176
2:7	104
3:7	149
4:13	173
4:14	169
5:14	97
5:16–18	96
5:17	125
5:23	96, 118

2 Thessalonians

2:13	32
3:16	96

1 Timothy

1:1	168
1:15	91
2:4–5	27
2:5	28, 105
3:3	104
3:16	33
6:11	104
6:14	176

2 Timothy

1:7	104
1:11	31
1:14	xiv, 6, 15
2:3	148
2:19	181
2:24	104
2:25	104
3:16	132
4:1, 8	176
4:8	176

Titus

1:12–13	176
2:11–12	104
2:12–13	168
2:13	176
3:2	104
3:4	98
3:5	49, 58

Hebrews

1:3	xvi
2:4	142
2:9	10, 22
2:17	42
3:1	91
3:1–2	103
4:16	5, 36, 37, 118
6:1–2	42
6:1–18	52
6:4	26
8:6, 8	123
8:8	123
8:13	123
9:10	53
9:15	123
9:22	64, 124
10:10	53
10:18	124
10:25	140
10:29	53
10:33	149

12:2	100, 149, 155
12:3	103
12:22	124
12:22–25	129
12:23	31
12:24	123

James

1:27	154
2:9	58
3:17	104
4:5	xiv, 6, 15
4:6, 10	105
4:10	105
5:10–11	97
5:13	96
5:14	83, 85
5:16	37, 39, 140
5:17	85

1 Peter

1:3–6	173
1:11	13, 23, 33
1:18–19	122
2:5–9	37
2:9	30, 183
2:18	104
2:21	56
2:22, 24	57
2:24	57, 134
2:25	91
3:4	104
3:4, 16	104
3:8	99
3:14	146
3:16	104
3:17	146
4:10	72, 91, 185
4:12	146
4:13	145, 146
4:14	13, 33
4:15	146
4:16	146
5:3	94
5:4	91
5:5–6	105

5:8	39

2 Peter

1:4	xiv, 16
1:6	104
1:21	132
2:7	99
3:11	176
3:18	32

1 John

1:1	155
1:3, 7	127
1:9	36, 39, 100
2:1	36, 39
2:8	31
2:20	64
3:2	180
3:2–3	41
3:3	176
3:5	57
3:8	100
3:17	99
3:24	13, 23
4:2	13, 33
4:3	27
4:8, 16	93
4:16	13, 93
4:17	11, 41

3 John

1:11	33

Jude

1:22	99
1:24	15

Revelation

1:10	171
2:10	149
3:20	13, 123
4:2	171
4:8	118
5:9	175
6:11	23

Revelation (*cont.*)

7:9	23, 177
7:13	23
7:14	23
13:8	122
15:3	129
17:3	171
17:6	155
19:7, 9	170
19:9	170

ANCIENT JEWISH WRITERS

Josephus

Against Apion 2.270–271	160n18

EARLY CHRISTIAN WRITINGS

Eusebius

Ecclesial History, Book 5	157n11
History, 8.6	157n15
The Martyrs of Palestine, 1–48	156, 156n9

Irenaeus

Against Heresies	xin2

Tertullian

De spectaculis, 3:10	2n1
Five Books against Marcion	2
On Water Baptism	2
Writings, 12:133–34	2n2
Writings, ch.9	2n3

www.ingramcontent.com/pod-product-compliance
Lightning Source LLC
Chambersburg PA
CBHW070246230426
43664CB00014B/2422